AQA GCSE

ENGLISH AND ENGLISH LANGUAGE

Aim for an A*

Peter Buckroyd (Chapters 1–12 & 14)

Adrian Beard (Chapter 13)

www.pearsonschools.co.uk
✓ Free online support
✓ Useful weblinks
✓ 24 hour online ordering

0845 630 22 22

Part of Pearson

Heinemann is an imprint of Pearson Education Limited, a company incorporated in England and Wales, having its registered office at Edinburgh Gate, Harlow, Essex, CM20 2JE. Registered company number: 872828

www.pearsonschools.co.uk

Heinemann is the registered trademark of Pearson Education Limited

First published 2010

14
10 9 8 7

British Library Cataloguing in Publication Data
A catalogue record for this book is available from the British Library on request.

ISBN 978 0 435118 12 9

Websites
The websites used in this book were correct and up-to-date at the time of publication. It is essential for tutors to preview each website before using it in class so as to ensure that the URL is still accurate, relevant and appropriate.

Designed and produced by Kamae Design, Oxford
Cover design by Wooden Ark Studios, Leeds
Original illustrations © Pearson Education Limited 2010
Illustrated by Kathryn Baker and Rory Walker
Picture research by Virginia Stroud-Lewis
Cover photo © David Hoare/Alamy
Printed and bound in Malaysia, CTP-PJB

Acknowledgements
The author and publisher would like to thank the following individuals and organisations for permission to reproduce photographs:

ppiv-v Getty Images News; pp2-3 ©Alamy/vario images GmbH & Co. KG/Bernhard Classen; p4 (timetable) Alamy/Alex Segre, (girls pointing at timetable) ©Alamy/Bubbles Photolibrary/Chris Rout; p5 Wayne HUTCHINSON/Alamy; p6 ©Science Photo Library/Henny Allis; p7 ©Alamy/Brotch Images; p8 Corbis/Nik Wheeler; p9 Alamy/Colin Palmer Photography; p12 Courtesy of The Advertising Archives; p13 ©Getty Images/Stu Forster; p14, 32 ©Corbis/Jonathan Blair; p17 ©Getty Images/Martin Gray; p20 ©Getty Images/Odd Andersen; p21 Pearson Education Ltd. Jules Selmes; p23 ©Getty Images/AFP/Carl Souza; p27, 64-65 ©Getty Images/Jeff J Mitchell; p30 NASA; p31 Pictorial Press Ltd/Alamy; p33 ©South West News Agency; pp34-35 ©Corbis/Benjamin Rondel; p39 Shutterstock/Ivonne Wierink; p41 ©Nicholas Hendrickx/Barcroft Media; p43 (shop) Rex Features/Sipa Press, (jewellery) Corbis/Frank Trapper; p44 (Germaine Greer) Alamy/Guillem Lopez, (Carol Ann Duffy) ©Rex Features/Kippa Matthews; pp48-49 Solent News and Photo Agency; pp52-53 (globe) ©Shutterstock/Edyta Pawlowska, (flag) Shutterstock/R. Gino Santa Maria, (girl) Panos Pictures/Carolyn Drake; p58 Ian Francis/Alamy; p59 Ragdoll BBC Worldwide; p61 ©Getty Images/Photographer's Choice/Bob Handelman; p63 (Queen) 2009 The Press Association/Anwar Hussein/EMPICS Entertainment, (town hall) ©Wikimedia Commons; p67 Shutterstock/matt; p71 Yellowj. Shutterstock; p73 Brendan Howard.Shutterstock; pp74-75 ©Corbis/Paul Souders; p79 Stefanie Mohr Photography. Shutterstock; p82 Shutterstock/Saponjic; p83 ©Alamy/Gary Roebuck; pp84-85 Alamy/National Trust Photolibrary/Jerry Harpur; pp86-87 ©Alamy/Mark J. Barrett; p88 (top) Rex Features/Ciaran McCrickard, (bottom) Rex Features/Daniela Lanini; pp88-89 (main photo) Corbis/Drew Gardner; p89 (left) ©Soeren Stache/dpa/Corbis, (right) Rex Features/Ciaran McCrickard; pp90-91 Alamy/Marc Hill; p95 Geoff Delderfield.Shutterstock; p96 Photodisc.Keith Brofsky; p98 ©Caters News Agency; p100 ©Alamy/Mike Booth; p101 Alamy/Sarah & Richard Greenhill;pp104-105, 114-115 ©Shutterstock/Thomas M Perkins; pp106-107 Xavier MARCHANT. Shutterstock; p108 Joe Gough. Shutterstock; p109 Shutterstock/c.; p113 ©Cartoonstock.com; p121 Woodfall/Photoshot/Erlend Haarberg; p122 Andrew Milligan/PA Archive/Press Association Images; p126 Corbis/Reuters/National Geographic Society/Peter Schouten; p127 Rex Features/Stephen Barker; pp130-131 Getty Images/Digital Vision.

Every effort has been made to contact copyright holders of material reproduced in this book. Any omissions will be rectified in subsequent printings if notice is given to the publishers.

'Make your money grow further' by Matt James, *News of the World* 8 March 2009, used with permission of NI Syndication; 'Reiki' by Jim Gow, GM8 Issue 2, copyright © Gay Men's Health Limited, 2008; 'Christmas lunch-lite' by Amanda Ursell, *The Times* 8 December 2008, used with permission of NI Syndication; 'A stroll around 1066 and all that ...' by John Nichol, *The Mail on Sunday* 14 December 2009, used with permission of John Nichol; 'New toe job a woe job, Paula' by Vicki Orvice, *The Sun* 6 March 2009, used with permission of NI Syndication; '4* Cyprus' advertisement used with kind permission of Mercury Direct; 'It's a bit lacking in dognity' by Fred Attewill, *Metro* 26 August 2009, text used with permission of Solo Syndication, photos by Ren Netherland used with permission of Barcroft Media; 'The full, festive genius of Vanbrugh' by Marcus Binney, *The Times* 12 December 2008, text used with permission of NI Syndication, drawing from the V&A for a house, unbuilt, designed by Sir John Vanbrugh reproduced by permission of V&A Images, Victoria and Albert Museum; 'Eccentric Britain – quirky days out. Cerne Abbas Giant' © Orange.co.uk/travel /Lee Ward; 'Let schools decide how to teach' *The Independent* 9 December 2008, used with permission of Solo Syndication; 'Cherish your foxes as status symbols' by Simon Barnes, *The Times* 9 May 2009, used with permission of NI Syndication; Extracts from *Green View* Spring Issue 2009, used with kind permission of North West Green Party; 'This exposes Labour's poverty of ambition' by Sean O'Grady, *The Independent* 8 May 2009, used with permission of Solo Syndication; 'Ve are not amused' by Robert Jobson, *News of the World* 15 March 2009, used with permission of NI Syndication; 'How a frail 97-year-old beat the wheelie bin police' by Andy Dolan, *Daily Mail* 11 March 2009 used with permission of Solo Syndication; 'So who says the EU is boring?' by Margot Wallstrom, *The Independent* 8 May 2009, used with permission of Solo Syndication; 'A writer who endures an embarrassment of talent' by William Langley, *The Sunday Telegraph* 10 May 2009, © Telegraph Media Group Limited 2009; 'The fantastic Mr Fly' by Ross McGuinness *Metro* 4 November 2007, used with permission of Solo Syndication; 'Spelling' by Philip Howard, *The Times* 23 March 2009, used with permission of NI Syndication; 'Smash and Drag' by Peter Allen, *Daily Mirror* 6 December 2008, used with permission of Mirrorpix; 'I'd be happy if the new laureate blew all her money on the horses or invested in fetish gear' by Germaine Greer, *The Guardian*, 11 May 2009, copyright © Germaine Greer; 'The above-par birdie' by Ross McGuinness, *Metro* 18 March 2009, used with permission of Solo Syndication; 'Plan of the Ground Floor and general information' from *Sir John Soane's Museum leaflet*. Reproduced by kind permission of the Trustees of Sir John Soane's Museum, London; 'World factfiles: Pakistan' *The Guardian* 23 April 2009, copyright Guardian News and Media Ltd 2009; 'A wild kind of fish' by Bart Johnson, *Sunday Telegraph Stella magazine* 10 May 2009, © Telegraph Media Group Limited 2009 <photo acknowledgement to come>; 'Kids TV gets touchy-feely' by Victoria Richards, *Daily Star* 19 May 2009, used by permission of Northern & Shell Media Publications; 'The new laureate shows how far we have come' by Jeanette Winterson, *The Times* 2 May 2009, used with permission of NI Syndication; 'Pssst! Heard the news?' *Daily Mail* 9 May 2009, used by permission of Solo Syndication; 'Sport of Queens' *The Times* 14 March 2009, used with permission of NI Syndication; 'Union Jackasses' by Jerry Lawton. *Daily Star* 19 May 2009 used with permission of Northern & Shell Media Publications; 'Gravy train is arriving for MPs' by Fred Attewill, *Metro* 22 April 2009, used with permission of Solo Syndication; 'The gravy train must stop - PM orders expenses shakeup' by Patrick Wintour, *The Guardian* 22 April 2009, copyright Guardian News and Media Ltd 2009; 'Lanhydrock' from *Enjoy a great day out in Cornwall. Beautiful and inspiring places to visit in 2008, National Trust leaflet*, used with kind permission of Liz Luck/National Trust; 'We're worth every penny' by Jay Curson, *The Guardian* 19 October 2002, copyright Guardian News and Media 2002; 'Grabbing a bite to eat' by Miles Irwin, *Metro* 30 April 2009, used with permission of Solo Syndication; 'Rhine Valley by Eurostar' advert, *The Guardian* 27 August 2009, used by permission of Guardian News and Media Limited 2009; 'Letters Pray' *The Times* 23 June 2009 used with permission of NI Syndication; 'Bring back the beaver - he will save money and clean our rivers' by Valerie Elliott, *The Times* 18 March 2009, used with permission of NI Syndication; 'Seasonal stray-dog crisis comes early' by Fiona Hamilton, *The Times* 16 December 2008, used with permission of NI Syndication; Extract from *The Source*, Copyright © Gillian Clarke 2008, reprinted by permission of Carcanet Press Limited; 'Hobbit feet provide clue to ancient race' by Mark Henderon, *The Times* 7 May 2009, used with permission of NI Syndication; 'The small patch of earth that may reveal big secrets of Stonehenge' by Simon Bruxelles, *The Times* 1 April 2008 used with permission of NI Syndication; 'Latest discoveries' by Rachel Firth reproduced from *Usborne Discovery: Dinosaurs* by permission of Usborne Publishing, 83-85 Saffron Hill, London EC1N 8RT, UK. www.usborne.com Copyright © 2009 Usborne Publishing Ltd., bambiraptor skeleton image reproduced by permission of David Burnham.

Contents

Introduction

From Peter Buckroyd

This book is designed to help students to improve their responses and exam skills.

The book breaks down the Assessment Objectives into their component parts. It then provides students with:

- guidance and teaching on the key skills that they need to develop
- examples of students' work with teacher comments
- activities that allow students to reflect and improve on their learning.

The approach that this book uses comes out of many years of experience and out of workshops, training sessions and revision courses with teachers and students. It can be used with confidence by all students.

The book also includes a section on the Spoken Language Study that provides you with activities and possible approaches to this new requirement of the English Language specification.

I hope you enjoy using it and wish you every success!

Peter Buckroyd

Peter Buckroyd

How is the book structured?

The book is broken down into four sections: ▶ Reading ▶ Writing ▶ Spoken Language Study ▶ Exam practice.

The Reading and Writing sections are divided into chapters. These chapters relate either to complete Assessment Objectives, elements of Assessment Objectives or helpful deconstruction of the Assessment Objectives.

Each chapter is then broken down into lessons, each of which opens with its own learning objectives ('My learning'). These introduce the skills, and then through stepped activities lead to a final activity that allows students to tackle an exam-style question.

Most chapters conclude with Grade Studio, which provides an opportunity to read sample student answers and comments on the final activity in the chapter. These can be read by students before or after they assess their work in the 'Peer/Self-assessment' activity.

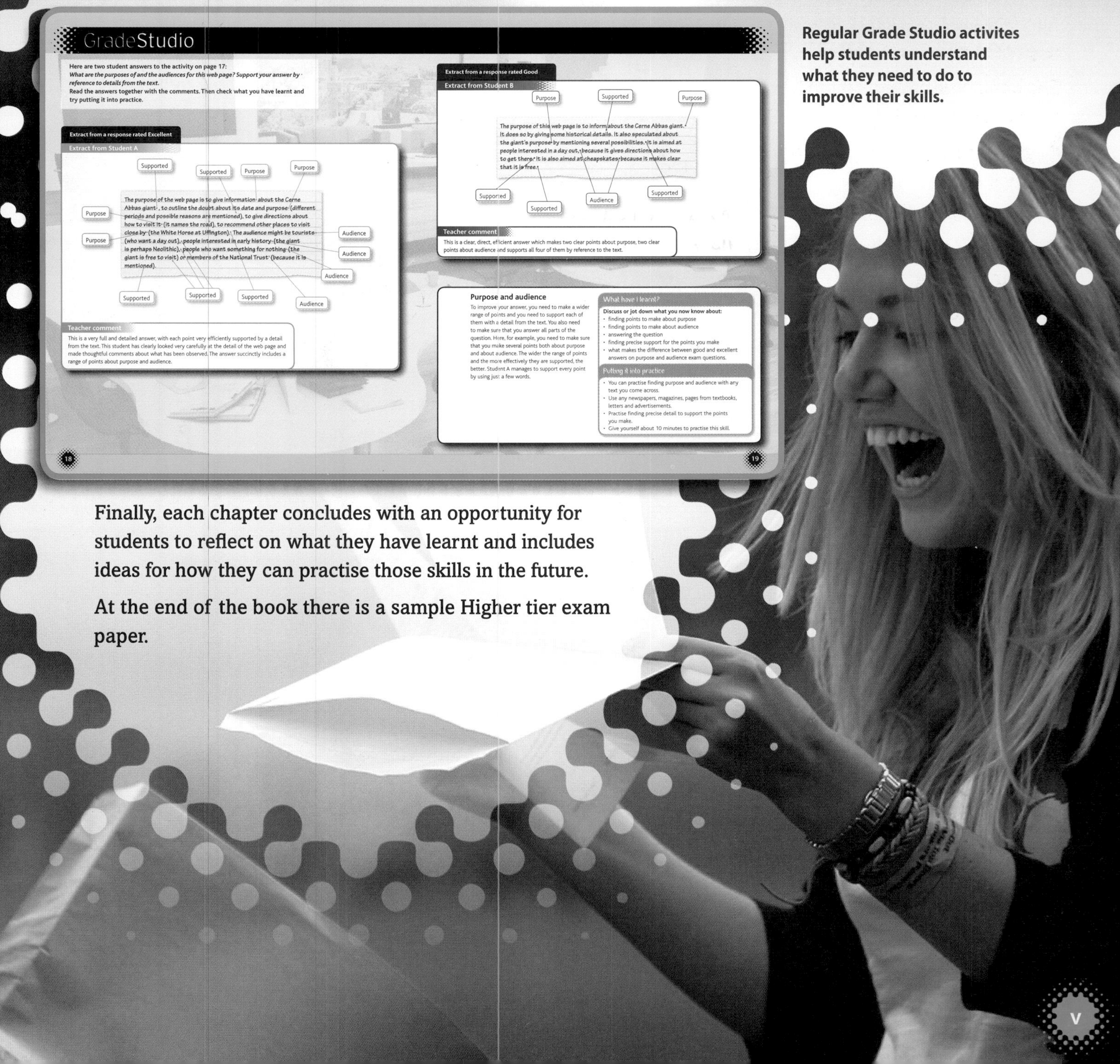

GradeStudio

Here are two student answers to the activity on page 17:
What are the purposes of and the audiences for this web page? Support your answer by reference to details from the text.
Read the answers together with the comments. Then check what you have learnt and try putting it into practice.

Extract from a response rated Excellent

Extract from Student A

The purpose of the web page is to give information about the Cerne Abbas giant, to outline the doubt about its date and purpose (different periods and possible reasons are mentioned), to give directions about how to visit it (it names the road), to recommend other places to visit close by (the White Horse at Uffington). The audience might be tourists (who want a day out), people interested in early history (the giant is perhaps Neolithic), people who want something for nothing (the giant is free to visit) or members of the National Trust (because it is mentioned).

Teacher comment

This is a very full and detailed answer, with each point very efficiently supported by a detail from the text. This student has clearly looked very carefully at the detail of the web page and made thoughtful comments about what has been observed. The answer succinctly includes a range of points about purpose and audience.

Extract from a response rated Good

Extract from Student B

The purpose of this web page is to inform about the Cerne Abbas giant. It does so by giving some historical details. It also speculated about the giant's purpose by mentioning several possibilities. It is aimed at people interested in a day out, because it gives directions about how to get there. It is also aimed at cheapskates because it makes clear that it is free.

Teacher comment

This is a clear, direct, efficient answer which makes two clear points about purpose, two clear points about audience and supports all four of them by reference to the text.

Purpose and audience

To improve your answer, you need to make a wider range of points and you need to support each of them with a detail from the text. You also need to make sure that you answer all parts of the question. Here, for example, you need to make sure that you make several points both about purpose and about audience. The wider the range of points and the more effectively they are supported, the better. Student A manages to support every point by using just a few words.

What have I learnt?

Discuss or jot down what you now know about:
- finding points to make about purpose
- finding points to make about audience
- answering the question
- finding precise support for the points you make
- what makes the difference between good and excellent answers on purpose and audience exam questions.

Putting it into practice

- You can practise finding purpose and audience with any text you come across.
- Use any newspapers, magazines, pages from textbooks, letters and advertisements.
- Practise finding precise detail to support the points you make.
- Give yourself about 10 minutes to practise this skill.

18 19

Regular Grade Studio activites help students understand what they need to do to improve their skills.

Finally, each chapter concludes with an opportunity for students to reflect on what they have learnt and includes ideas for how they can practise those skills in the future.

At the end of the book there is a sample Higher tier exam paper.

The AQA GCSE English and English Language specifications

This book is predominantly for students taking the AQA GCSE English and English Language Unit 1 exam. Chapters 1 to 12 provide activities and assessment practice for the exam, while chapter 14 includes a sample exam paper. The book is also useful for those students tackling the new Spoken Language Study – chapter 13 explains the requirements of this new area of study as well as providing a wealth of activities to get students started.

An overview of the specifications for both GCSE English and GCSE English Language can be found below and on the following pages.

GCSE English and GCSE English Language Unit 1

Here is an overview of the Unit 1 exam, which is common to both GCSE English and GCSE English Language.

What is this unit worth?	40% of the total marks
How long is this exam?	2 hours
What is Section A of the exam?	Reading responses to non-fiction texts
What is Section A worth?	20% of the total marks
How long should you spend on Section A?	1 hour
What is Section B of the exam?	Two Writing responses
What is Section B worth?	20% of the total marks
How long should you spend on Section B?	1 hour

For full details, see the corresponding Heinemann Teacher Guide and AQA specifications.

HEINEMANN
AQA
GCSE
English and
English Language
Aim for an A*
Teacher Guide
Lesson Plans: Esther Menon
Controlled Assessment: Adrian Beard, Peter Thomas
EAL guidance: Dianne Excell, Simon Murison-Bowie
naldic
ALWAYS LEARNING
PEARSON

Unit 1: Resources from Heinemann

- Student Books – as well as this book, further student books are available from Heinemann to support the teaching of Unit 1. We have developed the *Aim for a C* and *Basic Skills* student books so that you can pitch the learning at the appropriate level for your students.
- Teacher Guide – full colour lesson plans can be found in the corresponding Heinemann Teacher Guide, written by experienced author and LA Adviser, Esther Menon. These lesson plans make use of and reference the BBC footage and other resources in the ActiveTeach CD-ROM as well as providing support for EAL students written by NALDIC (professional body of EAL teachers and advisors).

  Each Teacher Guide is accompanied by a CD-ROM which contains the lesson plans as Word files, so they are fully customisable. If you have purchased both components these lesson plans can be uploaded into ActiveTeach.

Explains which assessment objectives are being covered.

Advice from NALDIC on how to help EAL students access the content for each lesson.

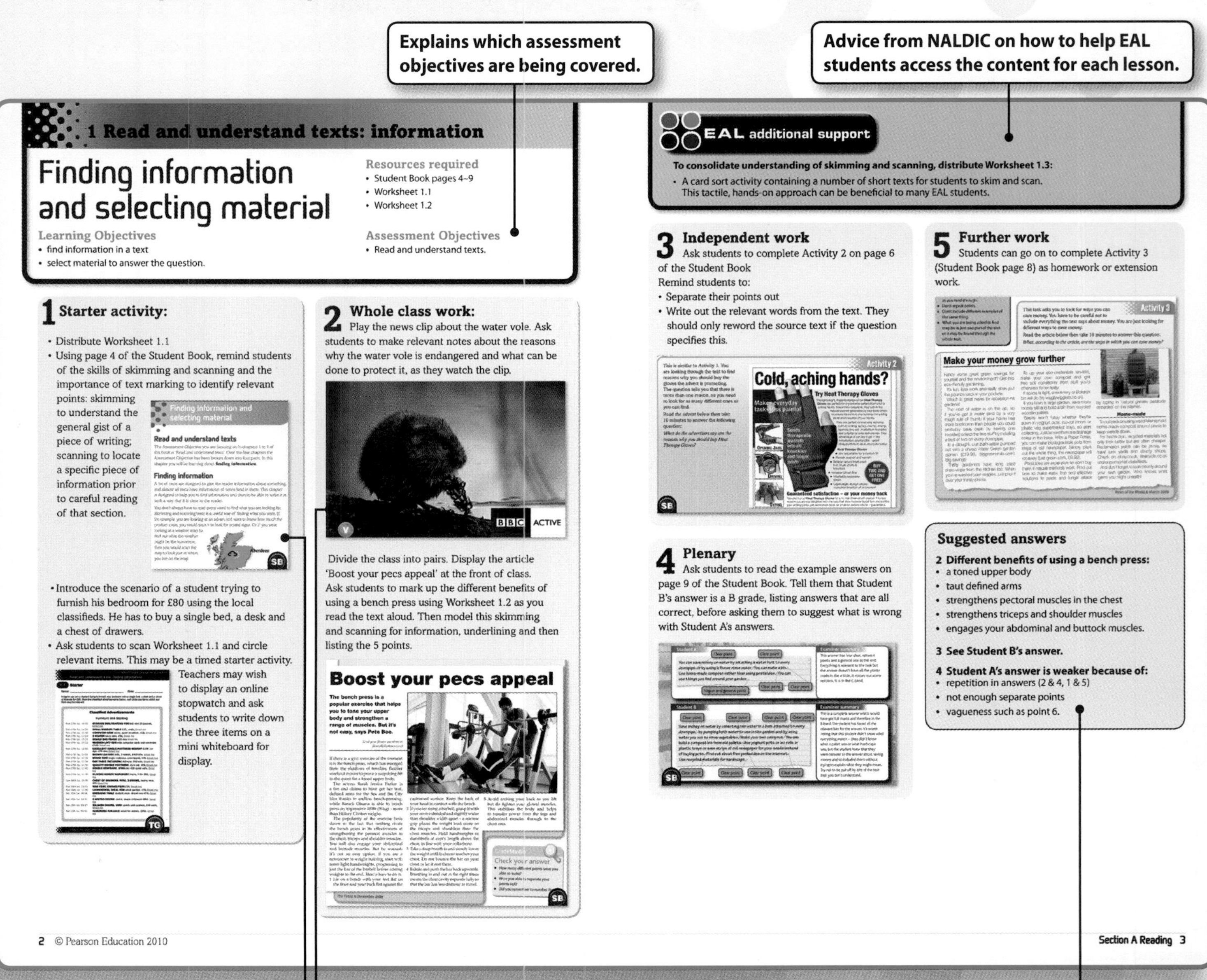

1 Read and understand texts: information

Finding information and selecting material

Learning Objectives
- find information in a text
- select material to answer the question.

Resources required
- Student Book pages 4–9
- Worksheet 1.1
- Worksheet 1.2

Assessment Objectives
- Read and understand texts.

1 Starter activity:
- Distribute Worksheet 1.1
- Using page 4 of the Student Book, remind students of the skills of skimming and scanning and the importance of text marking to identify relevant points: skimming to understand the general gist of a piece of writing; scanning to locate a specific piece of information prior to careful reading of that section.
- Introduce the scenario of a student trying to furnish his bedroom for £80 using the local classifieds. He has to buy a single bed, a desk and a chest of drawers.
- Ask students to scan Worksheet 1.1 and circle relevant items. This may be a timed starter activity.

Teachers may wish to display an online stopwatch and ask students to write down the three items on a mini whiteboard for display.

2 Whole class work:
Play the news clip about the water vole. Ask students to make relevant notes about the reasons why the water vole is endangered and what can be done to protect it, as they watch the clip.

Divide the class into pairs. Display the article 'Boost your pecs appeal' at the front of class. Ask students to mark up the different benefits of using a bench press using Worksheet 1.2 as you read the text aloud. Then model this skimming and scanning for information, underlining and then listing the 5 points.

Boost your pecs appeal

EAL additional support

To consolidate understanding of skimming and scanning, distribute Worksheet 1.3:
- A card sort activity containing a number of short texts for students to skim and scan. This tactile, hands-on approach can be beneficial to many EAL students.

3 Independent work
Ask students to complete Activity 2 on page 6 of the Student Book
Remind students to:
- Separate their points out
- Write out the relevant words from the text. They should only reword the source text if the question specifies this.

Cold, aching hands?

4 Plenary
Ask students to read the example answers on page 9 of the Student Book. Tell them that Student B's answer is a B grade, listing answers that are all correct, before asking them to suggest what is wrong with Student A's answers.

5 Further work
Students can go on to complete Activity 3 (Student Book page 8) as homework or extension work.

Make your money grow further

Suggested answers

2 Different benefits of using a bench press:
- a toned upper body
- taut defined arms
- strengthens pectoral muscles in the chest
- strengthens triceps and shoulder muscles
- engages your abdominal and buttock muscles.

3 See Student B's answer.

4 Student A's answer is weaker because of:
- repetition in answers (2 & 4, 1 & 5)
- not enough separate points
- vagueness such as point 6.

2 © Pearson Education 2010 Section A Reading 3

Full colour lesson plans show exactly where resources from the student book and ActiveTeach could be used.

Answers to student book activities are provided throughout.

- ActiveTeach CD-ROM – onscreen version of the student book together with BBC footage and other assets including: Grade Studio activities; additional video footage and worksheets. ActiveTeach allows you to play and customise lessons and import your own resources.

A wealth of digital resources, including exclusive BBC footage.

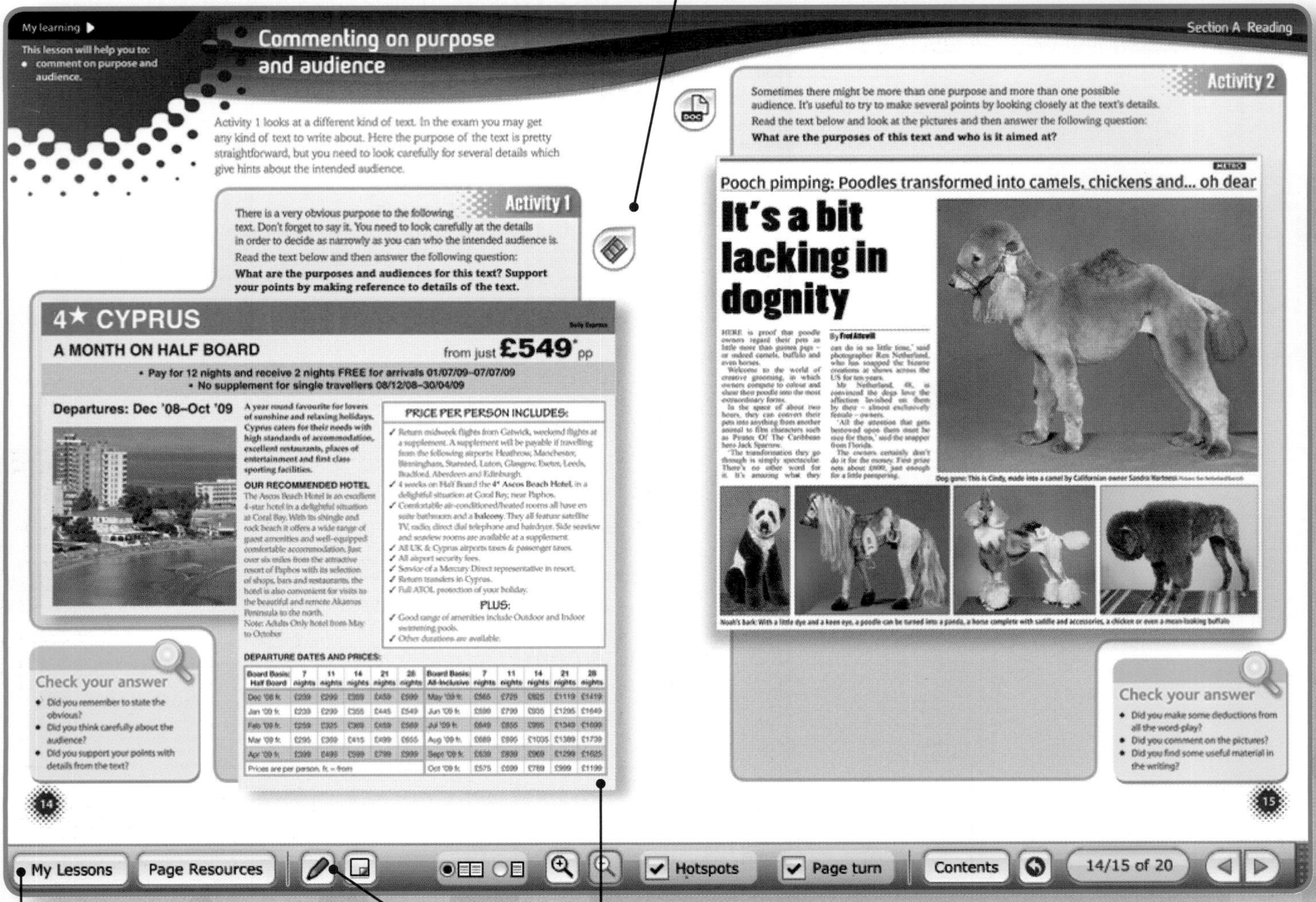

My learning
This lesson will help you to:
- comment on purpose and audience.

Commenting on purpose and audience

Section A Reading

Activity 1 looks at a different kind of text. In the exam you may get any kind of text to write about. Here the purpose of the text is pretty straightforward, but you need to look carefully for several details which give hints about the intended audience.

Activity 1

There is a very obvious purpose to the following text. Don't forget to say it. You need to look carefully at the details in order to decide as narrowly as you can who the intended audience is.

Read the text below and then answer the following question:

What are the purposes and audiences for this text? Support your points by making reference to details of the text.

4★ CYPRUS

A MONTH ON HALF BOARD from just £549* pp

Departures: Dec '08–Oct '09

PRICE PER PERSON INCLUDES:

Check your answer
- Did you remember to state the obvious?
- Did you think carefully about the audience?
- Did you support your points with details from the text?

Activity 2

Sometimes there might be more than one purpose and more than one possible audience. It's useful to try to make several points by looking closely at the text's details.

Read the text below and look at the pictures and then answer the following question:

What are the purposes of this text and who is it aimed at?

Pooch pimping: Poodles transformed into camels, chickens and... oh dear

It's a bit lacking in dognity

Check your answer
- Did you make some deductions from all the word-play?
- Did you comment on the pictures?
- Did you find some useful material in the writing?

My Lessons | Page Resources | Hotspots | Page turn | Contents | 14/15 of 20

Personalise the resources by adding your own annotations and save them for future use.

Makes customisation easy by allowing you to play and re-order lessons and incorporate your own tried-and-tested resources.

GCSE English and GCSE English Language Unit 2

This is the Speaking and Listening Unit and is the same for GCSE English and GCSE English Language. It is worth 20% of the total marks and is assessed through Controlled Assessment. For full details, see the AQA specifications.

GCSE English and GCSE English Language Unit 3

There is commonality here between GCSE English and GCSE English Language, but for clarity they have been set out separately below. Unit 3 is assessed through Controlled Assessment and is worth 40% of the total marks.

GCSE English: Understanding and producing creative texts

This comprises:

- Understanding creative texts (literary reading) – worth 20% of the total marks
- Producing creative texts (creative writing) – worth 20% of the total marks.

GCSE English Language: Understanding spoken and written texts and writing creatively

This comprises:

- Extended reading – worth 15% of the total marks
- Creative writing – worth 15% of the total marks
- Spoken Language Study – worth 10% of the total marks.

Controlled Assessment resources from Heinemann

This student book includes a section on the new Spoken Language Study. The Teacher Guides include comprehensive support for each of the three areas of Controlled Assessment. Each Controlled Assessment section includes:

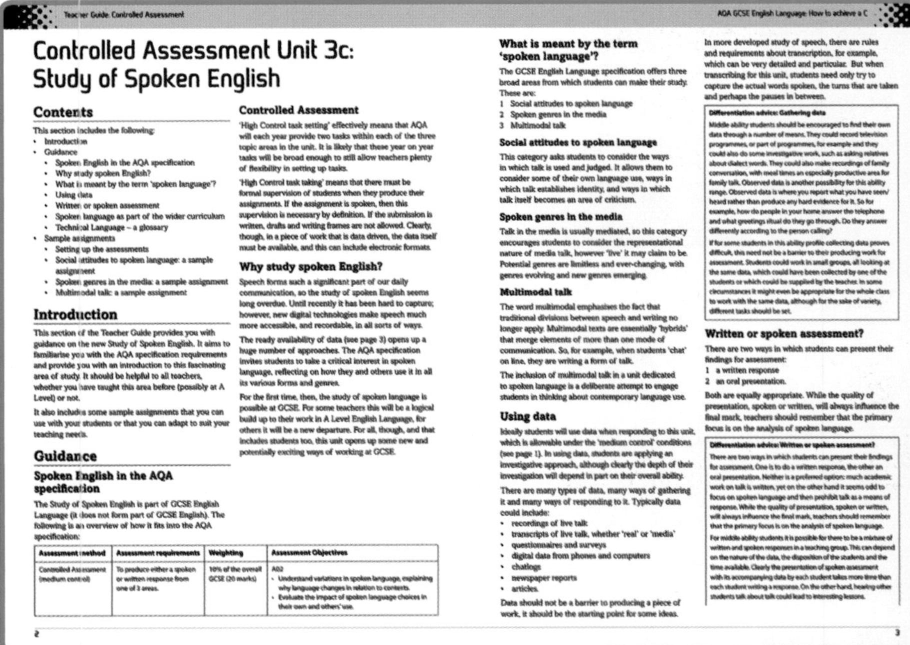
Teacher Guide: Controlled Assessment

Controlled Assessment Unit 3c: Study of Spoken English

Contents

This section includes the following:

- Introduction
- Guidance
  - Spoken English in the AQA specification
  - Why study spoken English?
  - What is meant by the term 'spoken language'?
  - Using data
  - Written or spoken assessment
  - Spoken language as part of the wider curriculum
  - Technical Language – a glossary
- Sample assignments
  - Setting up the assessments
  - Social attitudes to spoken language: a sample assignment
  - Spoken genres in the media: a sample assignment
  - Multimodal talk: a sample assignment

Introduction

This section of the Teacher Guide provides you with guidance on the new Study of Spoken English. It aims to familiarise you with the AQA specification requirements and provide you with an introduction to this fascinating area of study. It should be helpful to all teachers, whether you have taught this area before (possibly at A Level) or not.

It also includes some sample assignments that you can use with your students or that you can adapt to suit your teaching needs.

Guidance

Spoken English in the AQA specification

The Study of Spoken English is part of GCSE English Language (it does not form part of GCSE English). The following is an overview of how it fits into the AQA specification:

Assessment method	Assessment requirements	Weighting	Assessment Objectives
Controlled Assessment (medium control)	To produce either a spoken or written response from one of 3 areas.	10% of the overall GCSE (20 marks)	AO2 • Understand variations in spoken language, explaining why language changes in relation to contexts. • Evaluate the impact of spoken language choices in their own and others' use.

Controlled Assessment

'High Control task setting' effectively means that AQA will each year provide two tasks within each of the three topic areas in the unit. It is likely that these year on year tasks will be broad enough to still allow teachers plenty of flexibility in setting up tasks.

'High Control task taking' means that there must be formal supervision of students when they produce their assignments. If the assignment is spoken, then this supervision is necessary by definition. If the submission is written, drafts and writing frames are not allowed. Clearly, though, in a piece of work that is data driven, the data itself must be available, and this can include electronic formats.

Why study spoken English?

Speech forms such a significant part of our daily communication, so the study of spoken English seems long overdue. Until recently it has been hard to capture; however, new digital technologies make speech much more accessible, and recordable, in all sorts of ways.

The ready availability of data (see page 3) opens up a huge number of approaches. The AQA specification invites students to take a critical interest in spoken language, reflecting on how they and others use it in all its various forms and genres.

For the first time, then, the study of spoken language is possible at GCSE. For some teachers this will be a logical build up to their work in A Level English Language, for others it will be a new departure. For all, though, and that includes students too, this unit opens up some new and potentially exciting ways of working at GCSE.

2

AQA GCSE English Language: How to achieve a C

What is meant by the term 'spoken language'?

The GCSE English Language specification offers three broad areas from which students can make their study. These are:

1 Social attitudes to spoken language
2 Spoken genres in the media
3 Multimodal talk

Social attitudes to spoken language

This category asks students to consider the ways in which talk is used and judged. It allows them to consider some of their own language use, ways in which talk establishes identity, and ways in which talk itself becomes an area of criticism.

Spoken genres in the media

Talk in the media is usually mediated, so this category encourages students to consider the representational nature of media talk, however 'live' it may claim to be. Potential genres are limitless and ever-changing, with genres evolving and new genres emerging.

Multimodal talk

The word multimodal emphasises the fact that traditional divisions between speech and writing no longer apply. Multimodal texts are essentially 'hybrids' that merge elements of more than one mode of communication. So, for example, when students 'chat' on line, they are writing a form of talk.

The inclusion of multimodal talk in a unit dedicated to spoken language is a deliberate attempt to engage students in thinking about contemporary language use.

Using data

Ideally students will use data when responding to this unit, which is allowable under the 'medium control' conditions (see page 1). In using data, students are applying an investigative approach, although clearly the depth of their investigation will depend in part on their overall ability.

There are many types of data, many ways of gathering it and many ways of responding to it. Typically data could include:

- recordings of live talk
- transcripts of live talk, whether 'real' or 'media'
- questionnaires and surveys
- digital data from phones and computers
- chatlogs
- newspaper reports
- articles.

Data should not be a barrier to producing a piece of work, it should be the starting point for some ideas.

In more developed study of speech, there are rules and requirements about transcription, for example, which can be very detailed and particular. But when transcribing for this unit, students need only try to capture the actual words spoken, the turns that are taken and perhaps the pauses in between.

Differentiation advice: Gathering data

Middle ability students should be encouraged to find their own data through a number of means. They could record television programmes, or part of programmes, for example and they could also do some investigative work, such as asking relatives about dialect words. They could also make recordings of family conversation, with meal times an especially productive area for family talk. Observed data is another possibility for this ability range. Observed data is where you report what you have seen/heard rather than produce any hard evidence for it. So for example, how do people in your home answer the telephone and what greetings ritual do they go through. Do they answer differently according to the person calling?

If for some students in this ability profile collecting data proves difficult, this need not be a barrier to their producing work for assessment. Students could work in small groups, all looking at the same data, which could have been collected by one of the students or which could be supplied by the teacher. In some circumstances it might even be appropriate for the whole class to work with the same data, although for the sake of variety, different tasks should be set.

Written or spoken assessment?

There are two ways in which students can present their findings for assessment:

1 a written response
2 an oral presentation.

Both are equally appropriate. While the quality of presentation, spoken or written, will always influence the final mark, teachers should remember that the primary focus is on the analysis of spoken language.

Differentiation advice: Written or spoken assessment?

There are two ways in which students can present their findings for assessment. One is to do a written response, the other an oral presentation. Neither is a preferred option: much academic work on talk is written, yet on the other hand it seems odd to focus on spoken language and then prohibit talk as a means of response. While the quality of presentation, spoken or written, will always influence the final mark, teachers should remember that the primary focus is on the analysis of spoken language.

For middle ability students it is possible for there to be a mixture of written and spoken responses in a teaching group. This can depend on the nature of the data, the disposition of the students and the time available. Clearly the presentation of spoken assessment with its accompanying data by each student takes more time than each student writing a response. On the other hand, hearing other students talk about talk could lead to interesting lessons.

3

- advice on the impact of the shift from coursework to Controlled Assessment
- specific guidance on all of the task types in the AQA Controlled Assessment Task Bank
- exemplar answers showing what kinds of responses you might expect to see
- suggestions for how you might approach, timetable and differentiate the Controlled Assessments.

For full details, see the corresponding Heinemann Teacher Guide or AQA specifications.

Section A

Reading

Introduction

This section aims to encourage you to develop your reading skills in response to a range of texts. The teaching, texts, activities and tips are all focused on helping you to achieve the best grade you can in your exam.

This part of your course encourages you to look at the range and use of media and non-fiction texts. These texts appear everywhere in daily life and the selection in this book should help you to see and appreciate how the English language is presented and used. The texts chosen in this book also aim to improve your reading skills.

Reading media and non-fiction texts is something you do every day without necessarily realising it. This book will help contribute to your understanding, enjoyment and analyses of texts.

The skills that you will work on in this book can be applied to any texts that you read, whether these are in print form or onscreen. You don't just have to rely on English lessons to practise these skills.

This book focuses on the skills that you need to be successful in the exam. You will find a wide range of different kinds of texts and activities based around the kinds of questions that you might get in the exam.

Assessment Objectives

The Assessment Objectives underpin everything you will learn about and be tested upon. It is vital that you understand what these are asking of you. So, here are the Assessment Objectives that relate to your Reading exam together with comments to help you understand what they are.

- Read and understand texts, selecting material appropriate to purpose, collating from different sources and making comparisons and cross-references as appropriate.
- Explain and evaluate how writers use linguistic, grammatical, structural and presentational features to achieve effects and engage and influence the reader.

This Assessment Objective is asking you to show that you can:
- understand what you read
- answer the question by selecting appropriate material from the text to support the points that you make
- select texts, when asked, from which to answer the question
- make comparisons between texts.

This Assessment Objective is asking you to show that you can identify each of the following and then explain what effect they have on the reader:
- a range of features of language
- features of grammar
- structural devices
- presentational devices.

Examiner and student concerns

To help you improve your responses it is helpful to know what concerns examiners and students most about the Reading section of the exam. Below is a list of some of the concerns that they have.

What concerns examiners?

- **Failure to focus on the task.**
- **Giving several examples of the same thing rather than looking for a range of things.**
- **Spending more time on questions with few marks than on questions with more marks.**
- **Missing questions out altogether.**

What concerns students?

- **I haven't got time to think before I write.**
- **How many points should I make?**
- **How much should I write?**
- **I'd rather do one question properly than spend my time equally between the questions.**

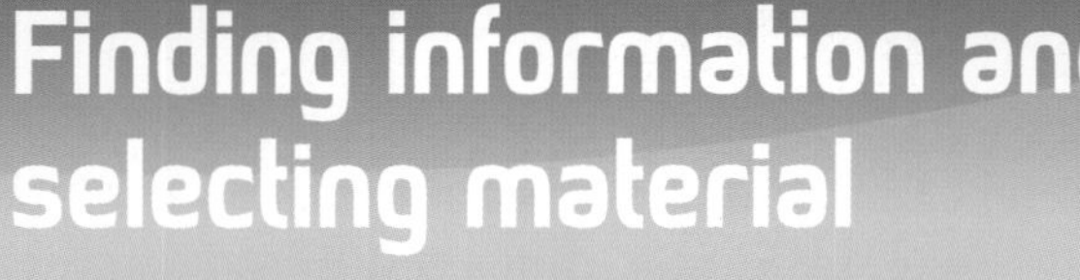

Finding information and selecting material

My learning

This lesson will help you to:

- find information in a text
- select material to answer the question.

A lot of texts are designed to give the reader information about something, and almost all texts have information of some kind in them. This chapter is designed to help you find information and then to be able to write it in such a way that it is clear to the reader.

Skimming and scanning

You don't always have to read every word to find what you are looking for. **Skimming** and **scanning** texts is a useful way of finding what you want. If, for example, you are looking at a holiday brochure and want to know how much the holiday costs, you would scan it to look for pound signs.

Look at the train timetable below. Scan it to find what time the next train for East Grinstead is.

Top tips

In the exam you are likely to be asked to:

- find specific points in a text
- put the specific points together
- put the specific points in your own words
- explain the specific points.

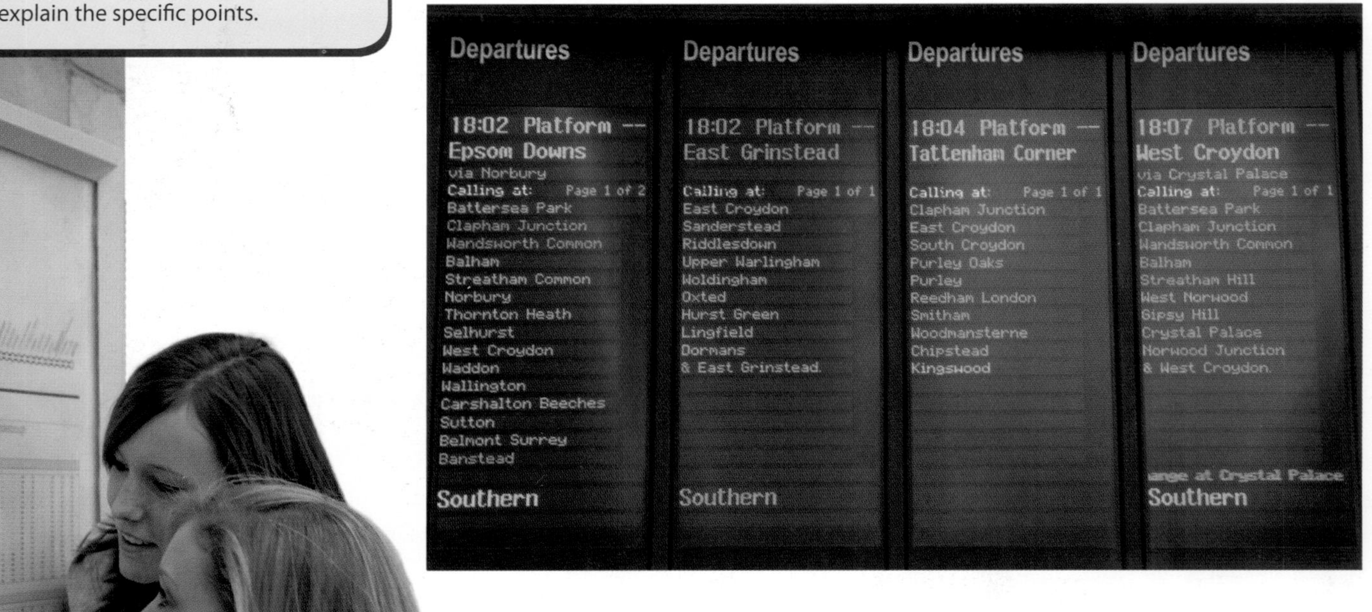

Departures
18:02 Platform --
Epsom Downs
via Norbury
Calling at: Page 1 of 2
Battersea Park
Clapham Junction
Wandsworth Common
Balham
Streatham Common
Norbury
Thornton Heath
Selhurst
West Croydon
Waddon
Wallington
Carshalton Beeches
Sutton
Belmont Surrey
Banstead
Southern
Departures
18:02 Platform --
East Grinstead
Calling at: Page 1 of 1
East Croydon
Sanderstead
Riddlesdown
Upper Warlingham
Woldingham
Oxted
Hurst Green
Lingfield
Dormans
& East Grinstead.
Southern
Departures
18:04 Platform --
Tattenham Corner
Calling at: Page 1 of 1
Clapham Junction
East Croydon
South Croydon
Purley Oaks
Purley
Reedham London
Smitham
Woodmansterne
Chipstead
Kingswood
Departures
18:07 Platform --
West Croydon
via Crystal Palace
Calling at: Page 1 of 1
Battersea Park
Clapham Junction
Wandsworth Common
Balham
Streatham Hill
West Norwood
Gipsy Hill
Crystal Palace
Norwood Junction
& West Croydon.
Southern

Activity 1

This activity gets you to go through the text to find the relevant main points that are being made about saving money.

Read the 'Make your money grow further' article below and then answer this question:

What, according to the article, are the ways in which you can save money?

Make your money grow further

Fancy some great green savings for yourself and the environment? Get into eco-friendly gardening.

It's fun, less work and really does put the pounds back in your pockets.

Which is great news for recession-hit gardens!

The cost of water is on the up, so if you've got a meter (and by a very rough rule of thumb if your home has more bedrooms than people you could probably save cash by having one installed) collect the free stuff by installing a butt or two on every downpipe.

In a drought, use bath-water pumped out with a cheap Water Green garden siphon (£19.99, biggreensmile.com). Big savings!

Thrifty gardeners have long used rinse-water from the kitchen too. When you've washed your veggies, just pour it over your thirsty plants.

To up your eco-credentials ten-fold, make your own compost and get free soil conditioner from stuff you'd otherwise throw away.

If space is tight, a wormery or Bokashi bin will do (try wigglywigglers.co.uk).

If you have a large garden, save more money still and build a bin from recycled wooden pallets.

Seeds aren't fussy whether they're sown in yoghurt pots, loo-roll inners or plastic veg supermarket trays, so start collecting. Just be sure there are drainage holes in the base. With a Paper Potter, you can make biodegradable pots from strips of old newspaper. Simply plant out the whole thing, the newspaper will rot away (just-green.com, £8.99).

Pesticides are expensive so don't buy them if natural methods work. Find out how to make easy, free and effective solutions to pests and fungal attack by typing in 'natural garden pesticide remedies' on the internet.

Home-made

To cut back on using weed killer spread home-made compost around plants to keep weeds down.

For hardscape, recycled materials not only look better but are often cheaper. Reclamation yards can be pricey, so trawl junk yards and charity shops. Check on ebay.co.uk, freecycle.co.uk and supermarket classifieds.

And don't forget to look closely around your own garden. Who knows what gems you might unearth!

NEWS OF THE WORLD

Check your answer

- Did you include all the different points you could find?
- Have you avoided repetition and examples of the same thing?
- Is your answer clear and detailed?

Activity 2

This activity is more demanding because it asks you to find two specific kinds of information – information about what Reiki is and information about how it works. When you are answering, it would be useful to organise your material under these two headings.

Read the article below and then answer this question:

What is Reiki and how does it work?

REIKI

Reiki (pronounced Ray-Key) is a Japanese word meaning 'Universal Life Energy'. This life force energy is that energy which resides and acts in all created matter – animal, vegetable or mineral. This vital life energy which flows can be activated for the purpose of healing and dates back to 1000 BC. It was rediscovered in the 19th century by Dr. Mikao Usui during a three week meditation on Mount Koriyama in Japan. Dr. Usui named the healing energy Reiki.

How Does Reiki Work?

Reiki encourages the body's natural ability to heal itself and is channelled through the practitioner's hands. The Reiki energy will then go as deeply into the body as it needs, gently helping it to restore itself.

What happens during a treatment?

A Reiki treatment is gentle, safe and non-intrusive. You remain fully clothed throughout and lie down comfortably on a treatment table. The practitioner will place their hands gently on your body in a series of hand positions. Each position is held for a few minutes as required – starting with the head and face, followed by the body; covering the main energy points (Chakras) and finally your legs and feet. The Reiki energy will go direct to the source of any imbalance and not simply to the manifesting symptoms, gently and peacefully restoring harmony and balance.

What are Chakras?

Chakras are energy points in the body that govern emotions, glands and areas of the body. Each Chakra has a different colour and vibration. Blockages or imbalances in our Chakras can affect our feelings, emotions, cause illness and even lead to disease.

What will I experience during a treatment?

You will notice a feeling of warmth from the practitioner's hands (occasionally some people experience a cool sensation). Stress and tension are released as the energy brings balance to your body and you will feel a deep sense of relaxation: it's been known for patients to fall asleep during a treatment.

How many treatments will I need?

The number of treatments required will depend on levels of health and why you choose Reiki. For a quick boost of energy, one session may be all that's required; however, the longer you have had a health imbalance the longer it will take to release it.

Each person's experience of Reiki will be different and unique, because each of us is special and individual. Reiki works in the priority best suited to each individual personally and this could be on a body, mind, emotional, or spiritual level.

Check your answer

- Did you answer both parts of the question clearly and in detail?
- Did you read the whole article to find all of the relevant points?

Activity 3

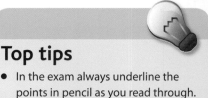

This activity makes you read a bit more carefully and in more detail in order to find the relevant information.

Read the article below and then answer this question:

According to this article, what can be done to create a low-fat Christmas lunch?

Top tips

- In the exam always underline the points in pencil as you read through.
- Don't repeat points.
- Don't include different examples of the same thing.
- What you are being asked to find may be in just one part of the text or it may be found through the whole text.

THE TIMES

nutrition

Christmas lunch-lite

Q&A

Times nutritionist **Amanda Ursell** answers your questions

My dad has just been put on a fat-free diet until he can have his gall bladder removed in January. What would be a healthy alternative to the indulgent Christmas Day lunch?

Gosh, this is rather bad timing for your dad because traditional things such as big tins of chocolates and brandy butter are off the agenda. But, looking on the bright side, most people with gallstones can tolerate some fat, and the condition often involves sufferers adjusting intakes according to individual tolerance levels. It is therefore more a case of going 'low fat' rather than 'fat free'.

There are lots of things that your dad can still tuck into that have a real seasonal feel, and he may well find that, overall, he is in a healthier state come January. He may shed a few pounds (if he needs to) and his cholesterol and blood pressure levels may benefit as well.

Anyway, let's concentrate on Christmas lunch. I'd advise him to buy a free-range or organic bird with about 2g of fat per 100g once roasted, compared with a self-basted bird with 10g of fat per 100g, and serve it without the skin. Have this with carrots puréed with a little stock along with sprouts and chestnuts, broccoli and a baked sweet potato, as these tend to be more moist than standard ones.

> *He may shed a few pounds and his blood pressure level may benefit*

You can make a low-fat gravy by 'frying' half a finely chopped onion in a little water or Fry Light cooking spray until soft and golden, then using powdered Bisto and making it up according to the pack instructions, adding vegetable stock. The whole main course supplies only 5g of fat and 375 calories.

For dessert, there is a great low-fat Christmas pudding recipe on www.weightlossresources.co.uk that has only 1.6g of fat (and 219 calories) per serving, compared with 11g per serving for the traditional version. It can be served with custard made with skimmed milk.

Alternatively, you could bake or grill some bananas and serve them with Grand Marnier, which you flambé at the table, or a beautiful fresh-fruit salad garnished with redcurrants and pomegranate seeds to give a seasonal feel.

Check your answer

- Did you find all the recommendations?
- Did you express them clearly?
- Did you scan the whole article for relevant material?

My learning ▶

This lesson will help you to:

- practise an exam-style question
- assess your answer by looking at other responses.

Assessment practice

Now you are going to have a go at an exam-style question. Attempt the activity in the time suggested and then complete the Peer/Self-assessment activity that follows.

Activity 1

Read the article below and then take 10 minutes to answer the following question:

According to the author, John Nichol, what are the pleasures of a visit to Battle?

DATE WITH DESTINY: Bayeux Tapestry battle scene

A stroll round 1066 and all that...

By **John Nichol**

The date 1066 must be one of the most famous in our glorious history. Every schoolchild knows the significance. King Edward the Confessor had shuffled off this mortal coil and the throne passed to his brother-in-law Harold. But Edward's cousin William, Duke of Normandy, believed the crown (and ergo England) was rightfully his. Suffice to say that William won the argument and was henceforth known as William the Conqueror, and Harold's last words were something along the lines of: 'You really should be careful with that bow and arrow; you'll have someone's eye out!'

I'm a few letters along the alphabet from being an A-grade student of history. I'd always marvelled at the truly amazing coincidence that Wills and Harry had decided to fight right in the middle of a hamlet called Battle. The fact that this monumental event is known as the Battle of Hastings, not the Battle of Battle, had always mystified me. Obviously, a trip was required to fill the gaps in my knowledge.

My base was The Powder Mills hotel about a mile south of Battle, where I was greeted by two welcome sights on a cold, damp, winter morning: a roaring fire permeating the ground floor with the sweet aroma of burning logs, and three beautiful spaniels snoring contentedly on the flagstones.

They were so dangerously close to the burning logs that steam was rising gently from their damp coats. As far as I'm concerned, any hotel that welcomes pets is a place worth staying. And I wasn't wrong. The hotel stands in a thickly wooded valley with a meandering stream, a large pond and countless species of wildlife. Its origins as a country house are obvious as you wander the grandeur of the public rooms, and the bedrooms are a mix of modern and 'olde-world'.

It even has its own organic farm. So, after a hearty breakfast of local produce, I set off to discover history.

Present-day Battle is a picture-postcard English market town. The High Street is full of individual shops selling everything from cakes to cockatoos. Restaurants and tiny cafes abound in listed buildings, many medieval.

A small farmers' market was in full swing on the day I visited and it was a pleasure to sample everything from local game pie to some rather decent ham, cheese and even a local wine.

The Mail on Sunday

TURF WAR: The battlefield at Battle, with a sign explaining details of the historic action

Towering above the market place is Battle Abbey, built by William the Conqueror as a monument to the thousands of soldiers who were slaughtered. The 1066 exhibition uses hands-on displays and video to paint the complex picture of the years that led up to the battle.

Well worth a few moments of your time is the short film, narrated by the eminent historian David Starkey, which dramatically, yet simply, explains the events of the time. But for me, the best way to understand death and conflict is to walk the battlefield. There is an excellent audio tour that recreates the sounds of the battle and a family tour using 'interviews' with soldiers, monks and key figures. You can stand on the ridge where the Saxon army's 'shield wall' watched the Normans advancing towards them, or sit at the spot where Harold fell.

It takes a good few hours to cover the entire site, by which time I was totally immersed in the past. After ten hours of brutal fighting, Harold lay dead with an arrow in his eye, his army was vanquished and 'the fields were covered in corpses and all around the only colour to meet the gaze was blood-red'.

It was an excellent way to improve my education.

Peer/Self-assessment activity

1 Check your answer to Activity 1.
- Did you find a range of points?
- Did you make sure that everything was about the pleasures?
- Did you support your points by making reference to the details of the text?

2 Now assess your answer to Activity 1 using the criteria below. You will need to be careful and precise in your marking. Before you do this, you might like to read some sample answers to this activity on pages 10 and 11.

Good
- clear and effective attempt to engage with activity
- range of relevant points
- material chosen to focus on the pleasures of a visit.

Very strong
- full and detailed response
- material absorbed and shaped for purpose
- good understanding of material.

Excellent
- full, detailed, conceptualised response
- material fully absorbed and shaped for purpose
- full understanding of material.

GradeStudio

Here are two student answers to the activity on page 8:
According to the author, John Nichol, what are the pleasures of a visit to Battle?
Read the answers together with the comments. Then check what you have learnt and try putting it into practice.

Extract from a response rated 'Excellent'

Extract from Student A

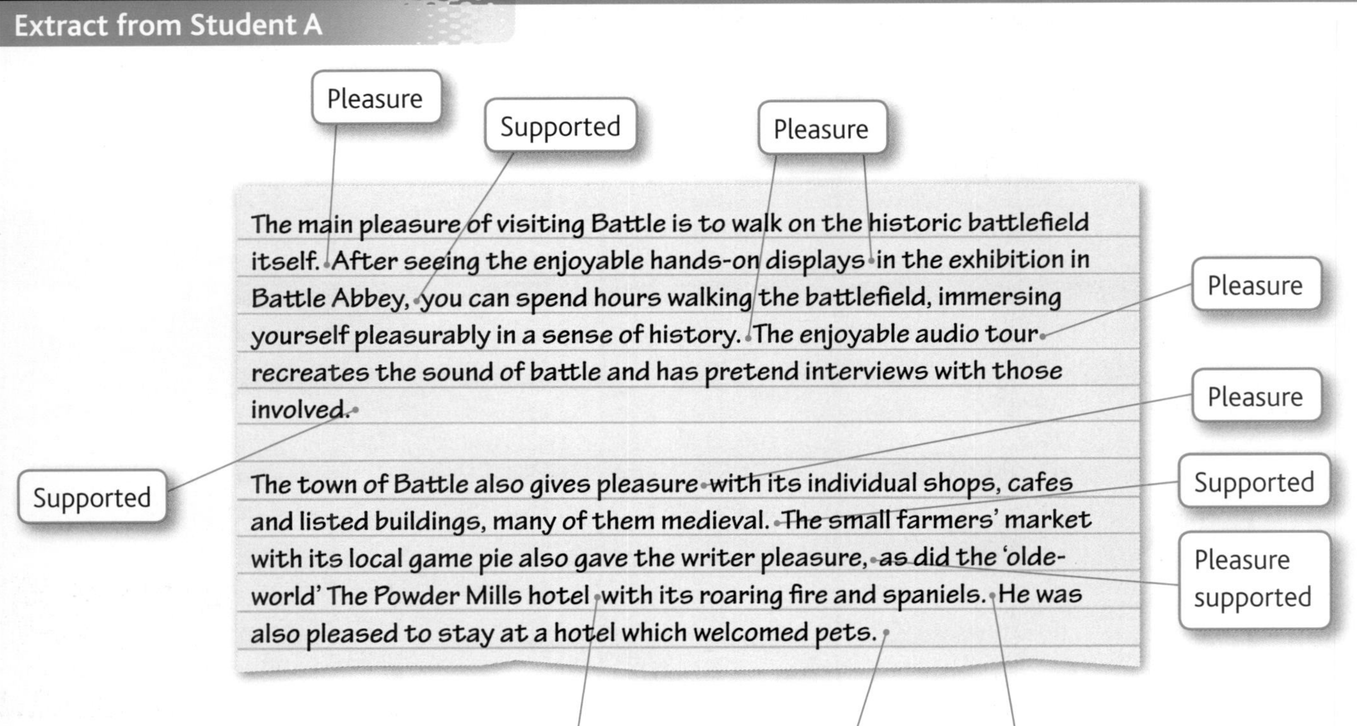

Pleasure
Supported
Pleasure
Pleasure
Pleasure
Supported
Supported
Pleasure supported
Pleasure
Pleasure
Supported
The main pleasure of visiting Battle is to walk on the historic battlefield itself. After seeing the enjoyable hands-on displays in the exhibition in Battle Abbey, you can spend hours walking the battlefield, immersing yourself pleasurably in a sense of history. The enjoyable audio tour recreates the sound of battle and has pretend interviews with those involved.
The town of Battle also gives pleasure with its individual shops, cafes and listed buildings, many of them medieval. The small farmers' market with its local game pie also gave the writer pleasure, as did the 'olde-world' The Powder Mills hotel with its roaring fire and spaniels. He was also pleased to stay at a hotel which welcomed pets.

Teacher comment

This is a complete answer which would have got full marks. The student has found all the relevant bits for the answer and has re-sequenced them in order to present what he thought gave the most pleasure first. It is a full and detailed answer, showing that the material in the article has been fully absorbed and shaped for the purpose of answering the question.

Extract from a response rated 'Good'

Extract from Student B

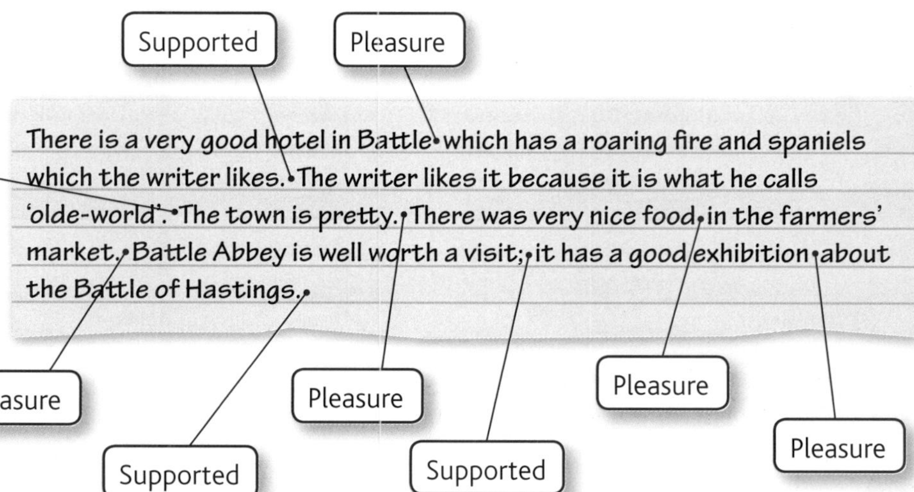
There is a very good hotel in Battle which has a roaring fire and spaniels which the writer likes. The writer likes it because it is what he calls 'olde-world'. The town is pretty. There was very nice food in the farmers' market. Battle Abbey is well worth a visit; it has a good exhibition about the Battle of Hastings.

Teacher comment

This answer has several clear, relevant points. Everything is relevant to the activity but the answer doesn't have all the points made in the article. It misses out some sections. Typical of students capable of doing better, it hasn't included material at the end of the article – about the battlefield itself.

Finding information

To improve your answer, you need to make a wider range of points and to be exact and specific in the points you make. You need to ensure that you have found all the sections of the text which give you information for the question. Then you need to make sure that you include it all. Don't pad out your answer with material which doesn't answer the question: find all the points and make them clearly. If you can organise and present them interestingly, all the better.

What have I learnt?

Discuss or jot down what you now know about:

- finding information in texts
- separating the points out
- answering the question
- what makes the difference between good and excellent answers on understanding texts exam questions.

Putting it into practice

- You can practise this exercise with any information text you come across.
- Use any newspapers, magazines, pages from textbooks, letters and advertisements.
- Give yourself about 10 minutes to practise.

My learning

This lesson will help you to:
- identify the purpose and audience of a text.

Identifying purpose and audience

What is purpose?

The **purpose** is the main reason for the text. The purpose of an advert is to sell the product to the kinds of people who would buy it, so it's important to make sure that it is as persuasive as possible.

What is audience?

The **audience** is who the text is aimed at – who the reader is. For instance, an advert for a car showing businessmen tells us who it's aimed at. You can pick up clues from the illustrations, the writing, the tone and the language about who the intended audience is.

There may, of course, be several different purposes and several different audiences for any text. Look at the advert below. What is its purpose and who do you think it is aimed at?

Top tips

In the exam you might be asked:
- about the purpose of a text
- about the audience of a text
- to compare texts in terms of purpose and audience
- to comment on the choices the writer has made because of the text's purpose and audience.

Top tips

- A detail means something short from the text which supports the point that you are making. For instance, if you made the point that a text is trying to sell you something, then 'Reader Offers' could be the detail of that text which supported your point.
- The examiner wants to know what bits of text you are looking at when you make a point, so you should always include one detail from the text to support the point that you are making.

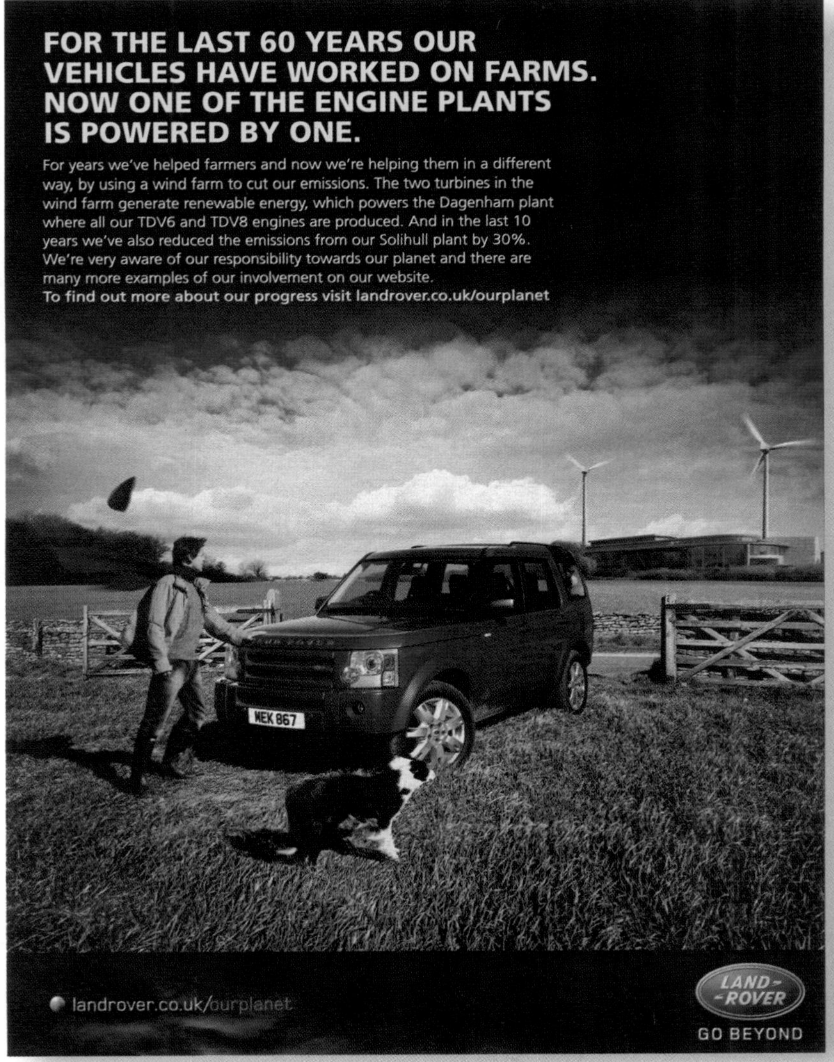

FOR THE LAST 60 YEARS OUR VEHICLES HAVE WORKED ON FARMS. NOW ONE OF THE ENGINE PLANTS IS POWERED BY ONE.
For years we've helped farmers and now we're helping them in a different way, by using a wind farm to cut our emissions. The two turbines in the wind farm generate renewable energy, which powers the Dagenham plant where all our TDV6 and TDV8 engines are produced. And in the last 10 years we've also reduced the emissions from our Solihull plant by 30%. We're very aware of our responsibility towards our planet and there are many more examples of our involvement on our website.
To find out more about our progress visit landrover.co.uk/ourplanet
MEK 867
landrover.co.uk/ourplanet
LAND-ROVER
GO BEYOND

This activity asks you to identify the purposes of, and audiences for, a text. You need to look for several different points to make about purpose and several about audience. Each point should be supported by reference to a detail from the text.

Activity 1

Read the text below and then answer the following question:

What are the purposes of, and audiences for, this text? Support your points by making reference to the details of the text.

Sun

New toe job a woe job, Paula

By VIKKI ORVICE

PAULA RADCLIFFE has been forced to pull out of this year's London Marathon because of a broken toe.

The world record holder was aiming to win her fourth London title on April 26 but suffered the injury on Tuesday while altitude training in New Mexico.

It comes exactly a year after she withdrew from last year's event with another toe problem.

That was the start of an injury-plagued year which resulted in her finishing only 23rd at the Beijing Olympics.

Radcliffe (*right*), who came back after Beijing to win the New York Marathon in style, intended to use London as a warm-up ahead of this summer's World Championships.

Her appearance on the start-line in Berlin could now be in jeopardy if she fails to recover in time.

Radcliffe, 35, set her world record in London in 2003 but has not competed there for four years.

She said: 'I am desperately disappointed that I have to pull out of this year's race.

'I was looking forward to running in front of the amazing crowds.

'I am considering surgery to get myself totally healthy as soon as physically possible and ultimately prevent any future problems.'

London Marathon race director Dave Bedford said: 'This is a major blow for Paula. I know how much she wanted to run here this year but luck just does not seem to be on her side.

'Paula's priority must now be to get fully fit for the World Championships and we wish her all the best for a speedy recovery.'

Meanwhile coach Charles Van Commenee, who took charge of British athletics last month, has targeted at least **FIVE** medals from the European Indoors in Turin starting today.

He said: 'We have a good history in this event, especially two years ago – when we won 10 medals with the home advantage in Birmingham.

'It would really be a disappointment if we end up with less.'

Check your answer

- Did you find more than one purpose?
- Did you find more than one audience?
- Did you support each point you made?

This lesson will help you to:

- comment on purpose and audience.

Commenting on purpose and audience

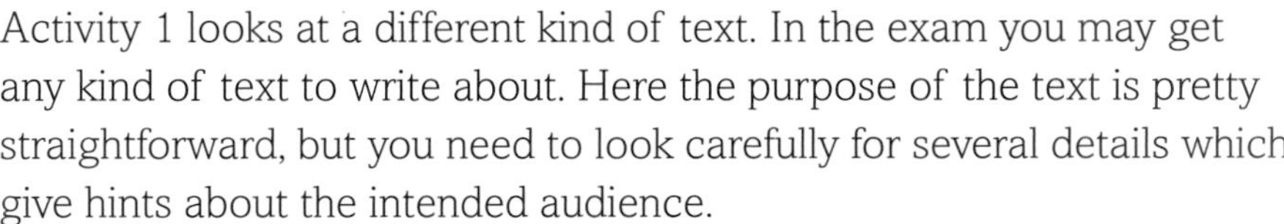

Activity 1 looks at a different kind of text. In the exam you may get any kind of text to write about. Here the purpose of the text is pretty straightforward, but you need to look carefully for several details which give hints about the intended audience.

Activity 1

There is a very obvious purpose to the following text. Don't forget to say it. You need to look carefully at the details in order to decide as narrowly as you can who the intended audience is.

Read the text below and then answer the following question:

What are the purposes and audiences for this text? Support your points by making reference to details of the text.

4★ CYPRUS

Daily Express

A MONTH ON HALF BOARD

from just **£549*** pp

- **Pay for 12 nights and receive 2 nights FREE for arrivals 01/07/09–07/07/09**
- **No supplement for single travellers 08/12/08–30/04/09**

Departures: Dec '08–Oct '09

A year round favourite for lovers of sunshine and relaxing holidays. Cyprus caters for their needs with high standards of accommodation, excellent restaurants, places of entertainment and first class sporting facilities.

OUR RECOMMENDED HOTEL

The Ascos Beach Hotel is an excellent 4-star hotel in a delightful situation at Coral Bay. With its shingle and rock beach it offers a wide range of guest amenities and well-equipped comfortable accommodation. Just over six miles from the attractive resort of Paphos with its selection of shops, bars and restaurants, the hotel is also convenient for visits to the beautiful and remote Akamus Peninsula to the north.

Note: Adults Only hotel from May to October

PRICE PER PERSON INCLUDES:

- ✓ Return midweek flights from Gatwick, weekend flights at a supplement. A supplement will be payable if travelling from the following airports: Heathrow, Manchester, Birmingham, Stansted, Luton, Glasgow, Exeter, Leeds, Bradford, Aberdeen and Edinburgh.
- ✓ 4 weeks on Half Board the **4* Ascos Beach Hotel**, in a delightful situation at Coral Bay, near Paphos.
- ✓ Comfortable air-conditioned/heated rooms all have en suite bathroom and a **balcony**. They all feature satellite TV, radio, direct dial telephone and hairdryer. Side seaview and seaview rooms are available at a supplement.
- ✓ All UK & Cyprus airports taxes & passenger taxes.
- ✓ All airport security fees.
- ✓ Service of a Mercury Direct representative in resort.
- ✓ Return transfers in Cyprus.
- ✓ Full ATOL protection of your holiday.

PLUS:

- ✓ Good range of amenities include Outdoor and Indoor swimming pools.
- ✓ Other durations are available.

DEPARTURE DATES AND PRICES:

Board Basis: Half Board	7 nights	11 nights	14 nights	21 nights	28 nights
Dec '08 fr.	£239	£299	£359	£459	£599
Jan '09 fr.	£239	£299	£355	£445	£549
Feb '09 fr.	£259	£325	£369	£459	£569
Mar '09 fr.	£295	£369	£415	£499	£655
Apr '09 fr.	£399	£499	£599	£799	£999
Prices are per person. fr. = from					

Board Basis: All-Inclusive	7 nights	11 nights	14 nights	21 nights	28 nights
May '09 fr.	£565	£725	£825	£1119	£1419
Jun '09 fr.	£599	£799	£935	£1295	£1649
Jul '09 fr.	£649	£855	£995	£1349	£1699
Aug '09 fr.	£689	£895	£1035	£1389	£1739
Sept '09 fr.	£639	£839	£969	£1299	£1625
Oct '09 fr.	£575	£699	£789	£999	£1199

Check your answer

- Did you remember to state the obvious?
- Did you think carefully about the audience?
- Did you support your points with details from the text?

Activity 2

Sometimes there might be more than one purpose and more than one possible audience. It's useful to try to make several points by looking closely at the text's details.

Read the text below and look at the pictures and then answer the following question:

What are the purposes of this text and who is it aimed at?

METRO

Pooch pimping: Poodles transformed into camels, chickens and... oh dear

It's a bit lacking in dognity

By Fred Attewill

HERE is proof that poodle owners regard their pets as little more than guinea pigs – or indeed camels, buffalo and even horses.

Welcome to the world of creative grooming, in which owners compete to colour and shear their poodle into the most extraordinary forms.

In the space of about two hours, they can convert their pets into anything from another animal to film characters such as Pirates Of The Caribbean hero Jack Sparrow.

'The transformation they go through is simply spectacular. There's no other word for it. It's amazing what they can do in so little time,' said photographer Ren Netherland, who has snapped the bizarre creations at shows across the US for ten years.

Mr Netherland, 48, is convinced the dogs love the affection lavished on them by their – almost exclusively female – owners.

'All the attention that gets bestowed upon them must be nice for them,' said the snapper from Florida.

The owners certainly don't do it for the money. First prize nets about £600, just enough for a little pampering.

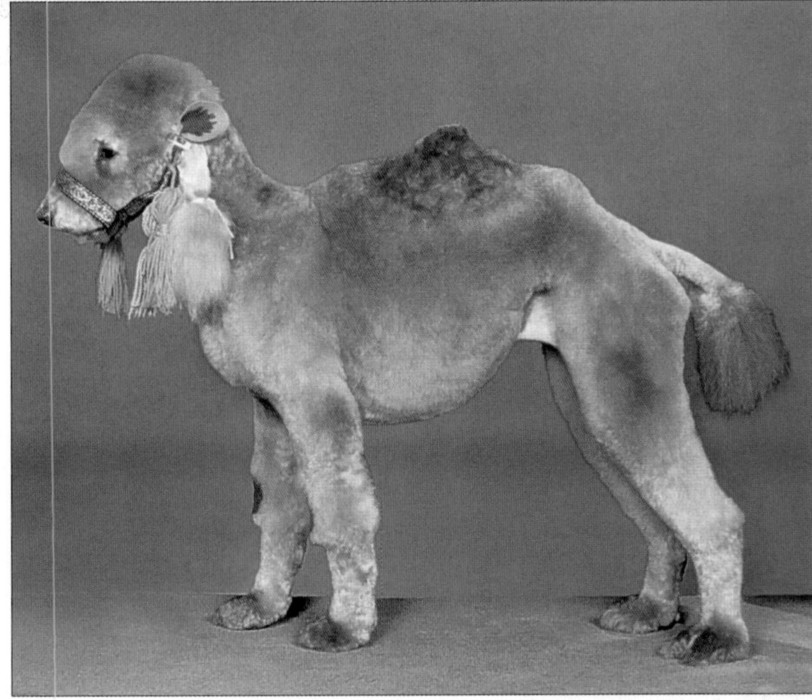

Dog gone: This is Cindy, made into a camel by Californian owner Sandra Hartness Pictures: Ren Netherland/Barcroft

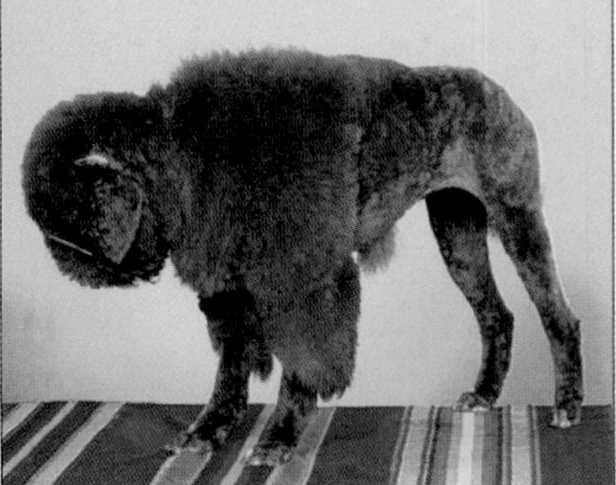

Noah's bark: With a little dye and a keen eye, a poodle can be turned into a panda, a horse complete with saddle and accessories, a chicken or even a mean-looking buffalo

Check your answer

- Did you make some deductions from all the word-play?
- Did you comment on the pictures?
- Did you find some useful material in the writing?

Activity 3

This is a more dense and complex text. Read it and then answer the following question:

How do the language and layout of this text reveal what its possible purposes and audiences are? Support your answer by using details from the text.

The full, festive genius of Vanbrugh

Marcus Binney
Architecture Correspondent

If ever an architect understood princely magnificence it was Sir John Vanbrugh. Indeed, the Duke of Marlborough ranked as a prince of the Holy Roman Empire and was expected to dine in public – hence the painted figures peering down from the walls of Blenheim's saloon.

The magazine *Country Life* began taking large-format glass negatives of Vanbrugh's work more than 100 years ago. Reproduced almost full-size in this handsome volume, these images allow one to absorb the full, festive richness of Vanbrugh's detail, the gorgeous urns, busts and statues on the roof of Castle Howard as well as the friezes carved with merhorses and roman shields. More than any recent book these illustrations show how Vanbrugh could alternate between an elemental simplicity and an explosion of ornament.

Vanbrugh's genius lay in his astonishingly bold handling of the raw materials of architecture – mass, space and light – as well as an original and highly theatrical handling of the classical vocabulary.

Vanbrugh was a master of what the Adam brothers called movement in architecture, the rise and fall in silhouette, the advance and recession in façades, and the added modelling and depth given by arcades, colonnades and deep-set windows.

Musson's text is constantly enlivened by quotations from Vanbrugh's extensive correspondence, and the descriptions of the houses are full of illuminating observation, for example of the amusing sculptures of British lions clasping French cockerels on either side of the gateways to Blenheim's kitchen and stable courts.

Vanbrugh's architecture grew from a wider range of experience than any British architect before him. As Musson says: 'Here was a man who had been travelling to India, been imprisoned in France as a suspected spy, been a successful playwright in London of Pope and Walpole, played a role in introducing Italian opera to London, who walked tall with the Whig nobility and was ridiculed by Dean Jonathan Swift.' Changing opinions of Vanbrugh down the centuries are sharp and perceptive even when critical. To the admiring Adams 'his taste kept no pace with his genius' and his works were 'crowded with barbarisms and absurdities and borne down by their own preposterous weight'. To Sir John Soane, Vanbrugh 'had all the fire and power of Michael Angelo and Bernini, without any of the elegant softness and classical delicacy of Palladio'.

Vanbrugh himself had the best phrase of all, that his buildings should 'slap you in the face'. In this book, King's Weston, Lumley Castle, Seaton Delaval Hall and Grimsthorpe Castle do just that and, even more, the sumptuous pictorial essays of Castle Howard and Blenheim.

The Country Houses of Sir John Vanbrugh by Jeremy Musson (Aurum Press, £40)

Drawing from the V&A for a house, unbuilt, designed by Sir John Vanbrugh.

THE TIMES

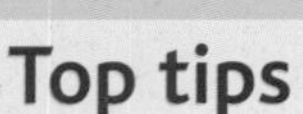

Top tips

- If you are asked about purpose be as specific as you can.
- Look for more than one possible purpose.
- If you are asked about audience be as specific as you can.
- Look for more than one possible audience.
- Find a precise detail to support every point that you make.

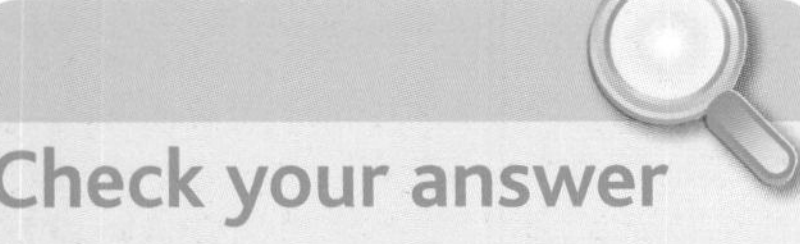

Check your answer

- Did you include the genre of the text?
- Did you think about different specific audiences?
- Did you support your points by reference to the text's language?
- Did you support your points by reference to the text's layout?

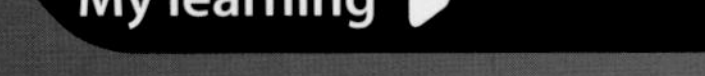

Assessment practice

This lesson will help you to:
- practise an exam-style question
- assess your answer by looking at other responses.

Now you are going to have a go at an exam-style question. Attempt the activity in the time suggested and then complete the Peer/Self-assessment activity that follows.

Activity 1

Read the text below and then spend 10 minutes answering this question:

What are the purposes of and the audiences for this web page? Support your answer by reference to details from the text.

Eccentric Britain – quirky days out

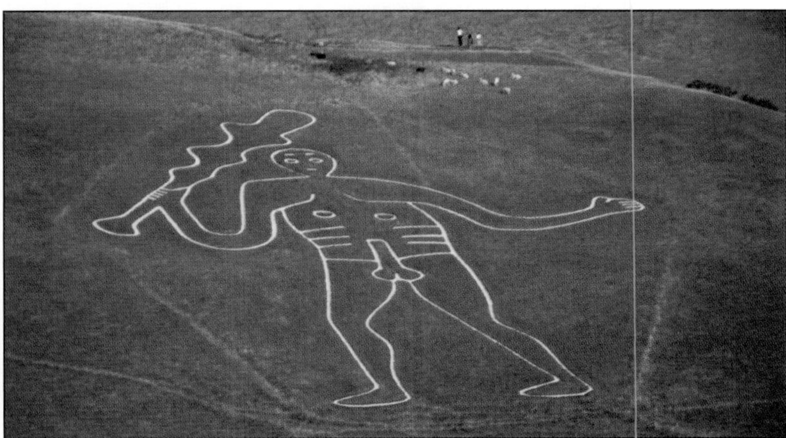

Cerne Abbas Giant

Proof that the British have been eccentric for a considerable period of time, the Cerne Abbas giant, overlooking the valley of the river Cerne like a Neolithic advert for Viagra, has long been a source of puzzlement.

No one is quite sure when the giant was created, since there's no written record of the area before the late 17th century. So either he was cut into the valley during the English Civil War by the servants of the lord of the manor, as a satirical depiction of Oliver Cromwell (who was sometimes called the English Hercules), or he represents the place where, according to local legend, a giant was slain, with locals cutting around the outline in chalk. Take your pick.

Where is it? The village of Cerne Abbas is eight miles north of Dorchester on the A352 Sherbourne road. Get driving directions.

When can you go? You can visit any time of year.

How much? There's no charge. Don't forget to visit the nearby White Horse at Uffington.

Find out more on the National Trust website.

From Orange website

Peer/Self-assessment activity

1 Check your answer to Activity 1.
- Did you find an overall purpose?
- Did you find some other purposes?
- Did you find some different audiences?
- Did you support each point by reference to the text's details?

2 Now assess your answer to Activity 1 using the criteria below. You will need to be careful and precise in your marking. Before you do this, you might like to read some sample answers to this activity on pages 18 and 19.

Good
- clear response to activity
- more than one point about purpose supported
- more than one point about audience supported.

Very strong
- full and detailed response
- material absorbed and shaped for purpose
- good understanding of material.

Excellent
- full, detailed and conceptualised response
- material fully absorbed and shaped for purpose
- full understanding of material.

GradeStudio

Here are two student answers to the activity on page 17:
What are the purposes of and the audiences for this web page? Support your answer by reference to details from the text.
Read the answers together with the comments. Then check what you have learnt and try putting it into practice.

Extract from a response rated 'Excellent'

Extract from Student A

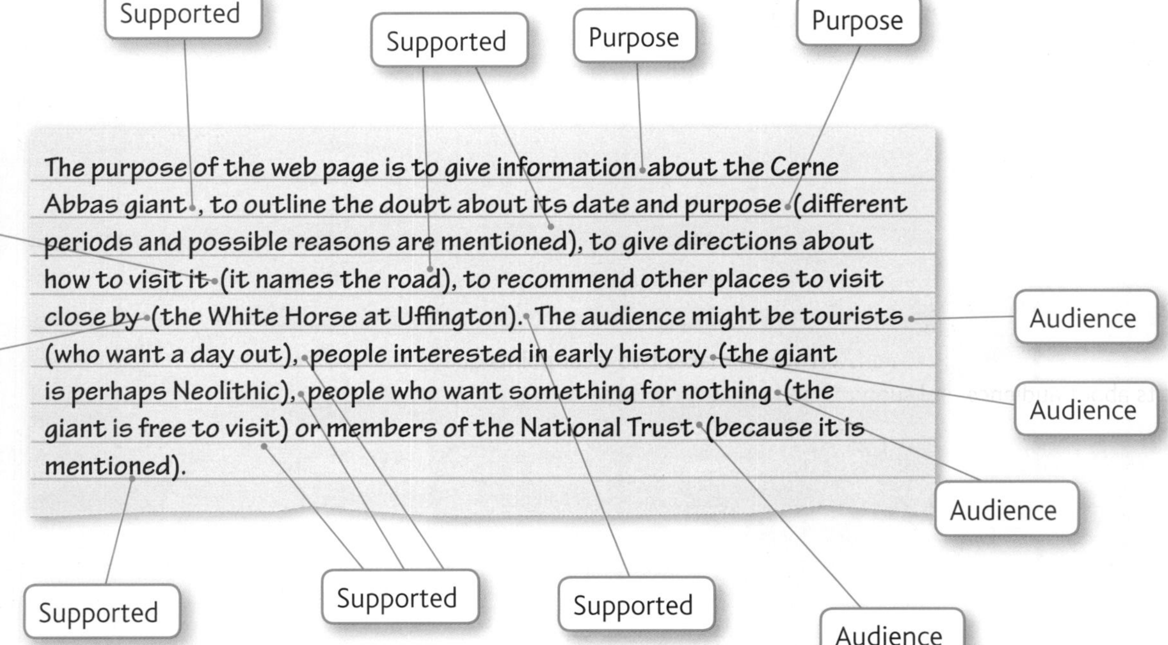

The purpose of the web page is to give information about the Cerne Abbas giant, to outline the doubt about its date and purpose (different periods and possible reasons are mentioned), to give directions about how to visit it (it names the road), to recommend other places to visit close by (the White Horse at Uffington). The audience might be tourists (who want a day out), people interested in early history (the giant is perhaps Neolithic), people who want something for nothing (the giant is free to visit) or members of the National Trust (because it is mentioned).

Teacher comment

This is a very full and detailed answer, with each point very efficiently supported by a detail from the text. This student has clearly looked very carefully at the detail of the web page and made thoughtful comments about what has been observed. The answer succinctly includes a range of points about purpose and audience.

Extract from a response rated 'Good'

Extract from Student B

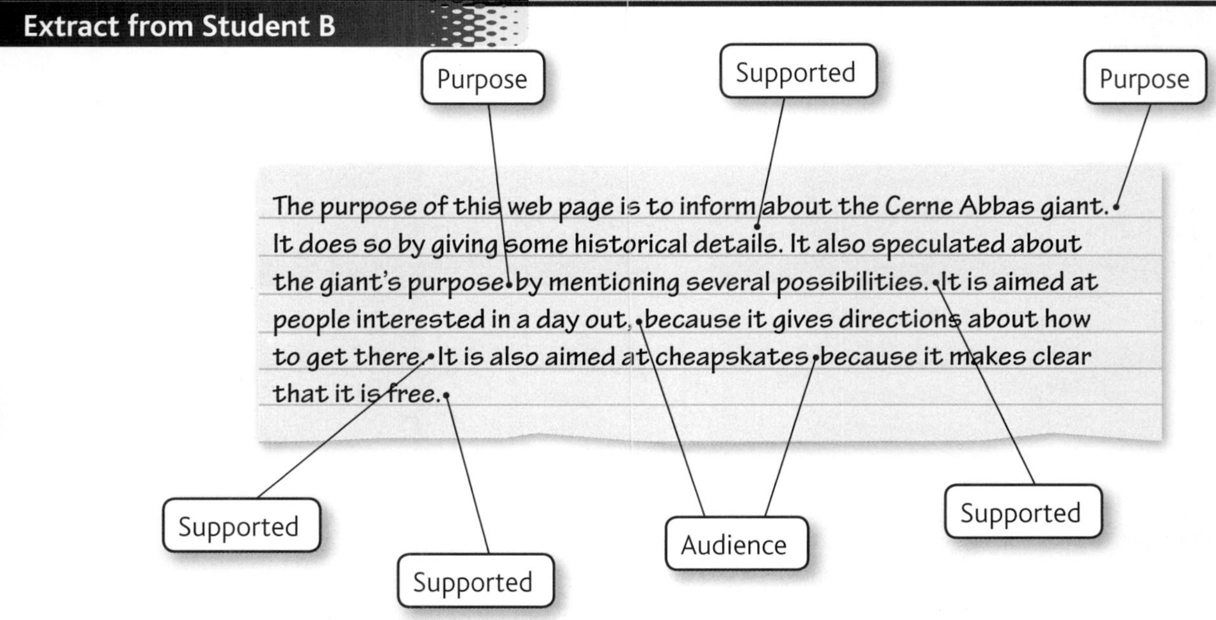

Teacher comment

This is a clear, direct, efficient answer which makes two clear points about purpose, two clear points about audience and supports all four of them by reference to the text.

Purpose and audience

To improve your answer, you need to make a wider range of points and you need to support each of them with a detail from the text. You also need to make sure that you answer all parts of the question. Here, for example, you need to make sure that you make several points both about purpose and about audience. The wider the range of points and the more effectively they are supported, the better. Student A manages to support every point by using just a few words.

What have I learnt?

Discuss or jot down what you now know about:

- finding points to make about purpose
- finding points to make about audience
- answering the question
- finding precise support for the points you make
- what makes the difference between good and excellent answers on purpose and audience exam questions.

Putting it into practice

- You can practise finding purpose and audience with any text you come across.
- Use any newspapers, magazines, pages from textbooks, letters and advertisements.
- Practise finding precise detail to support the points you make.
- Give yourself about 10 minutes to practise this skill.

My learning

This lesson will help you to:
- find the main points in an argument
- select material to answer the question.

Introducing arguments, facts and opinions

The use of facts and opinions is one of a writer's main tools in developing an argument.

What are arguments?

An **argument** is what the text has to say. There may be one or more main points.

When you are looking for arguments:

- always look at the headline first – there may be a clue
- try to work out the main point of the article
- recognise different stages in the argument as you read through.

Top tips

In the exam you might be asked to:
- find the main points in an argument
- show the stages in an argument
- find facts and say how they are used to support the argument
- find opinions and say how they are used to support the argument.

What are facts?

A **fact** is something that can be proved. The most obvious facts are names and places and dates and figures because these can be looked up and checked. For example, the following statements are both facts.

- Paris is the capital of France.
- England won the Rugby World Cup in 2003.

When you are trying to find facts:

- don't read the whole article first – skim it
- look for names of places or people (with upper case letters) first
- then look for numbers or dates.

What are opinions?

An **opinion** is something that someone thinks, but that is not necessarily true. For example, it is an opinion to claim that rugby is better than football.

When you are trying to find opinions:

- don't read the whole article first – skim it
- look for quotations (in quotation marks) first
- then when you read the article you can find other opinions – especially those of the writer.

The text in Activity 1 below is a 'leader' from a newspaper. A leader gives the view of the newspaper on a topical issue. This one discusses the Rose Report on primary school education.

This activity is asking you to distinguish between the Rose Report and what the newspaper says about the report. The question is about the newspaper's view, so don't include what the report itself says.

Activity 1

1 Read through the text listing the main points so that when you come to answer the question you just have to concentrate on writing them out clearly. In the exam you can underline the main points on the exam paper.

2 Now answer the following question:
What is *The Independent*'s view about the Rose Report?

THE INDEPENDENT

Let schools decide how to teach

SIR JIM Rose's review of primary school teaching, commissioned by the Government, has been touted as a blueprint for the most radical reform of education in two decades. The interim report certainly contains suggestions that will have traditionalists spluttering with indignation.

Sir Jim argues that 'areas of learning' should replace individual 'non-core' subjects such as history, geography and science. He also recommends that 'emotional well-being' and 'social skills' should be a compulsory part of the curriculum. Another suggestion is that computer skills should be taught to primary school children, rather than introducing such tuition at secondary school level as at present. Already, the report has been accused of advocating further dumbing down of our education system. Others have criticised it for asking teachers to do the job of parents by teaching children how to behave and interact with others.

Yet these objections rather miss the point. Many primary schools already blur traditional subject boundaries in class. They have made a choice about the most effective way to impart knowledge and understanding. This is the real issue. The goal of primary education reform should be to let individual schools tailor lessons as they see fit. If schools want to conduct lessons in history, or the vaguer 'human, social and environmental understanding', that should be a matter for them.

As for imparting social skills, again, let individual schools tailor their approach according to their intake. Let them make a judgement on what is likely to produce the best educational results.

The Rose Report suggests that children should be taught to use podcasts or make their own radio programmes. But that might not be appropriate in many schools where the priority will, rightly, be on raising basic literacy levels. The point is to let the individual schools and teachers decide the best way to teach.

At present there are too many tests and the curriculum is over-loaded. Schools need to be given the power to ignore top-down directives. If this report can help set primary schools free, it might well live up to its billing as the most significant shake-up in primary education in 20 years. Otherwise, it will end up as just the latest in a long line of meddling and counter-productive prescriptions from Whitehall.

Check your answer

- Did you manage to find several different points?
- Did you manage to present these clearly?
- Did you manage to make everything you wrote relevant to the question?
- Did you manage to avoid repeating the same point?

Top tips

- Most arguments have a main point and several supporting points
- Most arguments are supported by facts and/or opinions.

There are two things to do in Activity 2: find the main points in the argument and then think about how the writer supports them. In the exam it would be useful to underline the main points as you read through the text and to make a note each time you underline something about what method the writer has used to support his point. Here you could list the main points as you find them.

When you come to write your answer you need to remember that there are two things to be addressed – the how and the what.

Activity 2

Read the text below and then answer the following question:

What is the writer's argument in this text and how does he support it?

Cherish your foxes as status symbols

Simon Barnes

I went for a pee and had a vision of transcendent beauty. I had managed to get my fair share of prosecco at my sister's house in Mortlake and found it necessary, as my grandfather used to say, to 'make a call'. And a moment of glorious revelation from the bathroom window.

The outlook was wonderfully and suburbanly verdant, my sister's garden playing a full part in the landscape of intricately compartmented green. And there, on the roof of the neat little shed that stood hard against the wall – just before it disappeared behind the branches of a stupendous lilac in full purple bloom – a fox.

Not just any fox. A fox of beauty and charm and elegance, apparently freshly groomed, lithe and gleaming red. The white tip of his brush vanished into the lilac and then for a moment I saw him continue his journey along the top of the wall, a creature at home in his world, unstoppably self-confident and positively glowing with health.

It is always a deeply cheering thing to come up against the wild world deep in the haunts of humankind. It is a message that we haven't concreted over every last square inch; that we haven't buggered it all up quite yet; that there is a way in which human beings can live alongside the wild world. Never mind the prosecco, that was a champagne moment.

Urban myths

You are much more likely to a see a fox in Mortlake than around my place in Suffolk. Urban foxes are not only a fact of modern life, they are also, by the nature of their chosen lives, a great deal more visible than country foxes. Now hear a strange fact: just about everything you know about urban foxes is a myth.

They are not 'coming in'. They are not increasing, either. They have an established and stable population in most towns and cities in this country. Foxes started being seen in towns after the First World War, and have been there in substantial numbers ever since the Second. Towns expanded into the countryside and the foxes changed their behaviour and adapted, thrived and made the most of this new opportunity – so much so that foxes have been seen in Downing Street and Buckingham Palace gardens.

Another myth: urban foxes do not represent some pitiful scavenging underclass. What's more, they are not invariably mangy. The talk of mangy foxes mostly comes from sightings of foxes during their annual moult, when they do indeed look deeply unprepossessing. But the point is that a thriving and stable population of any creature cannot be dominated by sick, ill-fed and diseased animals. There are plenty of urban foxes, therefore they must be healthy. If they weren't, they would die out.

Check your answer

- Did you find the main points?
- Did you find different sides of the argument?
- Did you mention facts which supported the argument?
- Did you mention the writer's use of opinions to support his argument?

THE TIMES

At home: the Downing Street fox saunters by No 10.

Yet another myth: they don't survive by raiding dustbins. Quite apart from anything else, there aren't many left. As a species, dustbins are more or less extinct. Towns are more or less dustbin free. And foxes can't open wheelie bins. A study on the feeding of urban foxes carried out by Professor Stephen Harris, of the University of Bristol, showed that more than half the food of urban foxes is deliberately put out for them by human beings. For the rest, foxes take mice, insects and other invertebrates.

One more myth is that all urban foxes are skinny and underfed. True, they are thinner than most of the canids we are used to seeing in towns, but then most domestic dogs are overfed and under-exercised. Foxes, urban or not, are lean, pared-down survival machines.

Yet urban foxes arouse huge hostility from some people. They find it disturbing, rather than the reverse, to have wild things playing an intimate part in human life. Foxes are sometimes shot and generally seen as vermin. Newspapers play up the scary aspects and, besides, the pro-hunt people always cast foxes as anthropomorphic villains. In truth, foxes are just mammals trying to make a living, same as you and me.

There are a few legitimate complaints about urban foxes. They like to leave aromatic reminders of their presence, and they can dig up lawns when looking for worms. Me, I'm inclined to say, so what? But even if you resent this, there really is not a lot you can do about them. Foxes can get through the smallest gaps and exterminating them is difficult, expensive and never successful. If you shoot up your local foxes, you are merely creating a vacancy.

Here's a fact rather than a myth: foxes like a good class of neighbourhood. They prefer leafy suburbs populated by middle-class property owners. Cherish your local foxes. They are not pests but status symbols.

My learning

This lesson will help you to:
- follow an argument
- comment on how facts and opinions are used.

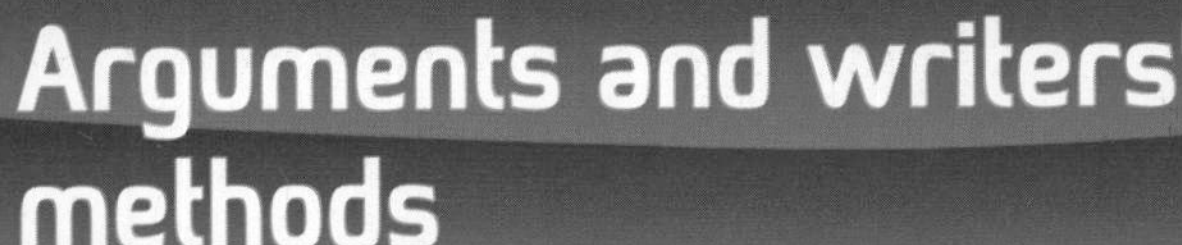

Arguments and writers' methods

Facts and opinions can be used by writers to support their argument. In the activity below you need to identify the argument but then look at how the writer uses facts and opinions to support the argument.

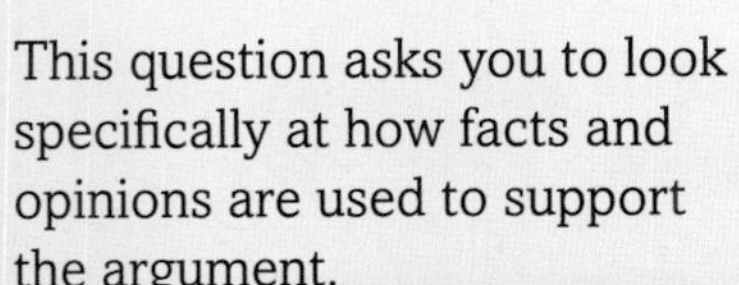

Activity 1

This question asks you to look specifically at how facts and opinions are used to support the argument.

Read the article opposite and then answer the following question:

What is the argument of this political pamphlet and how does it use facts and opinions to support that argument?

Green View

Spring Issue www.northwest.greenparty.org.uk

Jobs Jobs Jobs

The recession will be hard for many of us. But Greens say we have a chance to create many new green jobs.

We all need to work. It's not just about making a living, it's part of wanting to contribute: to our family, our community or society. But somewhere along the line, the Labour Government decided that big banking and speculation was more important to our economy than people are. Greens say this is the wrong way round.

The Green Party says it's time for a 'Green New Deal' for Britain and Europe. We want to take a grip of the recession with a program of laws and public investment, similar to Obama's economic package. In fact, he borrowed the phrase 'Green New Deal' from us. We want to create more jobs in new technologies, create better banking regulation and put Britain on a firm footing for the challenges of the 21st century. In fact according to research by Caroline Lucas and Jean Lambert, who are the two British Green Euro-MPs in the European Parliament, we could create 100,000 jobs now in the North West in green industries. Have a look online and find out more at **www.greenparty.org.uk**

Trust and honesty

They're both key to politics. You can't be expected to vote for people you don't trust. That's why the latest series of scandals involving Labour government expenses and smears is so disappointing. Our promise to you is that if you vote Green, you will get Green. And we have our record to prove it. Our Leader Caroline Lucas was recently voted Ethical Politician of the Year in the *Observer's* awards.

Peter Craine, Green candidate for the North West, with Green party Euro-MP Jean Lambert

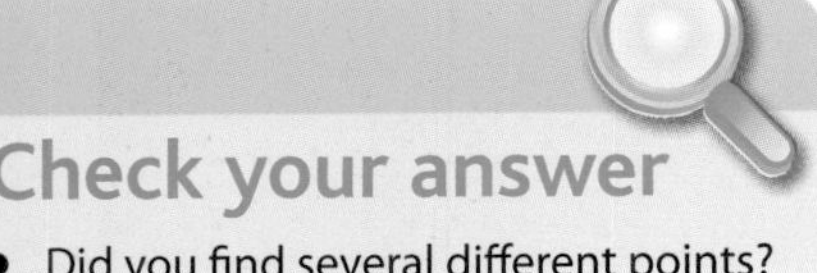

Check your answer

- Did you find several different points?
- Did you mention the facts used?
- Did you mention the opinions used?

Green Party Euro-MPs representing you in the European Parliament

Peter Cranie

An anti-racist Green Euro-MP for the North West of England.

Peter Cranie works for a children's charity and lives with his wife and baby son in Liverpool. He's the Green Party's lead candidate for the European elections in June. **Peter says** 'Because Euro-MPs are elected by proportional representation, every single Green vote counts. This is your chance to get more Greens into positions where we can really make a difference world-wide. If our children are to have a viable future, it's got to be a Green future. The policies for creating new jobs and sustainable industries are the same policies we need to tackle the climate crisis. If 10% of our region's voters make Green their choice, a Green Party Euro-MP will be elected, and we can push for home insulation and lower fuel bills, more jobs, more affordable housing, better public transport, better education, healthy locally-produced food, and generally a better quality of life for us all.'

This lesson will help you to:
- practise an exam-style question
- assess your answer by looking at other responses.

Assessment practice

Now you are going to have a go at an exam-style question. Attempt the activity in the time suggested and then complete the Peer/Self-assessment activity that follows.

The text in Activity 1 has quite a detailed argument and it uses several methods. Notice that the question here doesn't ask you what the argument is; that is given to you in the activity. Instead it is wholly on the methods that the writer uses (for example, the use of facts and opinions).

So this time when you are reading through it, you are identifying methods rather than the different points in the argument. In the exam if you write these in the margin of the text as you are reading, then you will have plenty of material which is focused directly on the question.

Activity 1

1 Read the question and the article below. As you are reading the article, make a quick list of the different methods used by the writer. This will help prepare you to answer the question.

2 Now take 10 minutes to answer the following question:

How does Sean O'Grady support the argument that relative poverty is higher now than it was under Harold Macmillan's government?

This exposes Labour's poverty

Sean O'Grady

Comment

THAT RELATIVE poverty – the gap between rich and poor rather than the absolute availability of basic necessities – should be higher than it was when Harold Macmillan was prime minister is a galling discovery. The Institute for Fiscal Studies, a sort of non-partisan unofficial opposition party equipped with massive brainpower, tells us that the distance between our richest and our least fortunate citizens is as high as it has been since their data starts, in 1961. Which leaves open the possibility that Brown's Britain may be more unequal than we were before the creation of the NHS and the modern welfare state. Supermac's misquoted catchphrase was 'you've never had it so good'; Gordon Brown's might be that 'you've never had it so bad' – if you have the misfortune to be poor.

An extra 200,000 people fell into poverty in Mr Brown's first year in power, bringing the total to 13.5 million. These people are the ones living in homes with incomes below 60 per cent of the typical British household's. They are not starving, but they lack many of the easy luxuries Middle England takes for granted. They are prey for the BNP.

The Government's ambitions to halve child poverty by 2010 and to eradicate it by 2020 looked achievable during the boom. But with the economic downturn the chances of achieving the 2010 goal are nil. And with the mess the public finances are in, the 2020 target also recedes into the realms of 'aspiration'.

Mr Brown is right to highlight all the schemes he has funded to improve the life chances of today's youngsters. Maybe without them things would be worse. However, the fortunes of the 'Blair Generation' are about to take a bad turn.

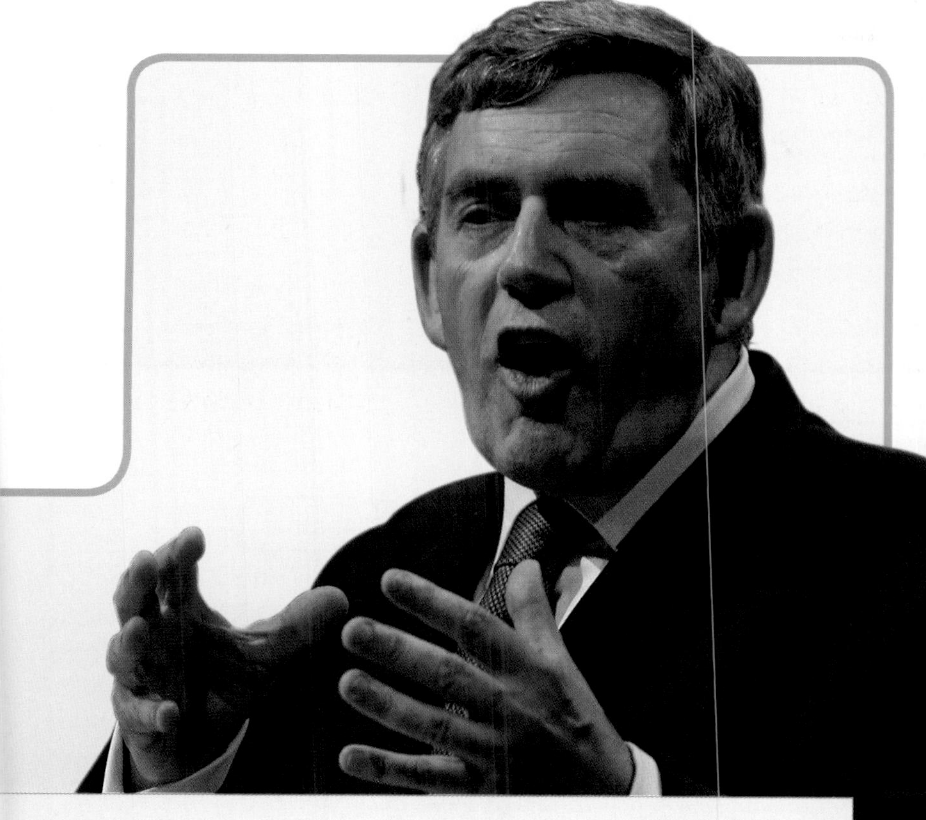

THE INDEPENDENT

# of ambition

Those who started school in 1997 are 16 now and ready to belly-flop on to the worst jobs market in decades. Low-skilled younger workers usually do badly in recessions; they are the easiest to sack. They soon turn into 'Neets' – not in employment, education or training schemes. So it is proving this time round. Youth unemployment is already higher than when John Major left a good luck card on his desk at No 10 for Tony Blair. Given that joblessness is usually the single most important determinant of poverty, the generation who reached adulthood under Blair and Brown will be the people driving the poverty numbers higher over the coming months and years. Mr Brown made his political career passionately railing against the lost generation of unemployed youngsters in the 1980s. Twenty years on, another lost generation – and lost votes – may be his undoing.

Peer/Self-assessment activity

1 Check your answer to Activity 1.
- Did you manage to find several different points?
- Did you manage to present these clearly?
- Did you examine the methods Sean O'Grady uses to support the argument?

2 Now assess your answer to Activity 1 using the criteria below. You will need to be careful and precise in your marking. Before you do this, you might like to read some sample answers to this activity on pages 28 and 29.

Good
- clear and effective attempt to engage with activity
- range of relevant points
- material chosen to focus on methods.

Very strong
- full and detailed grasp of methods
- material absorbed and shaped for purpose
- good understanding of material.

Excellent
- full, detailed and conceptualised grasp of methods
- material fully absorbed and shaped for purpose
- full understanding of material.

GradeStudio

Here are two student answers to the activity on page 26:
How does Sean O'Grady support the argument that relative poverty is higher now than it was under Harold Macmillan's government?
Read the answers together with the comments. Then check what you have learnt and try putting it into practice.

Extract from an answer rated 'Good'

Extract from Student A

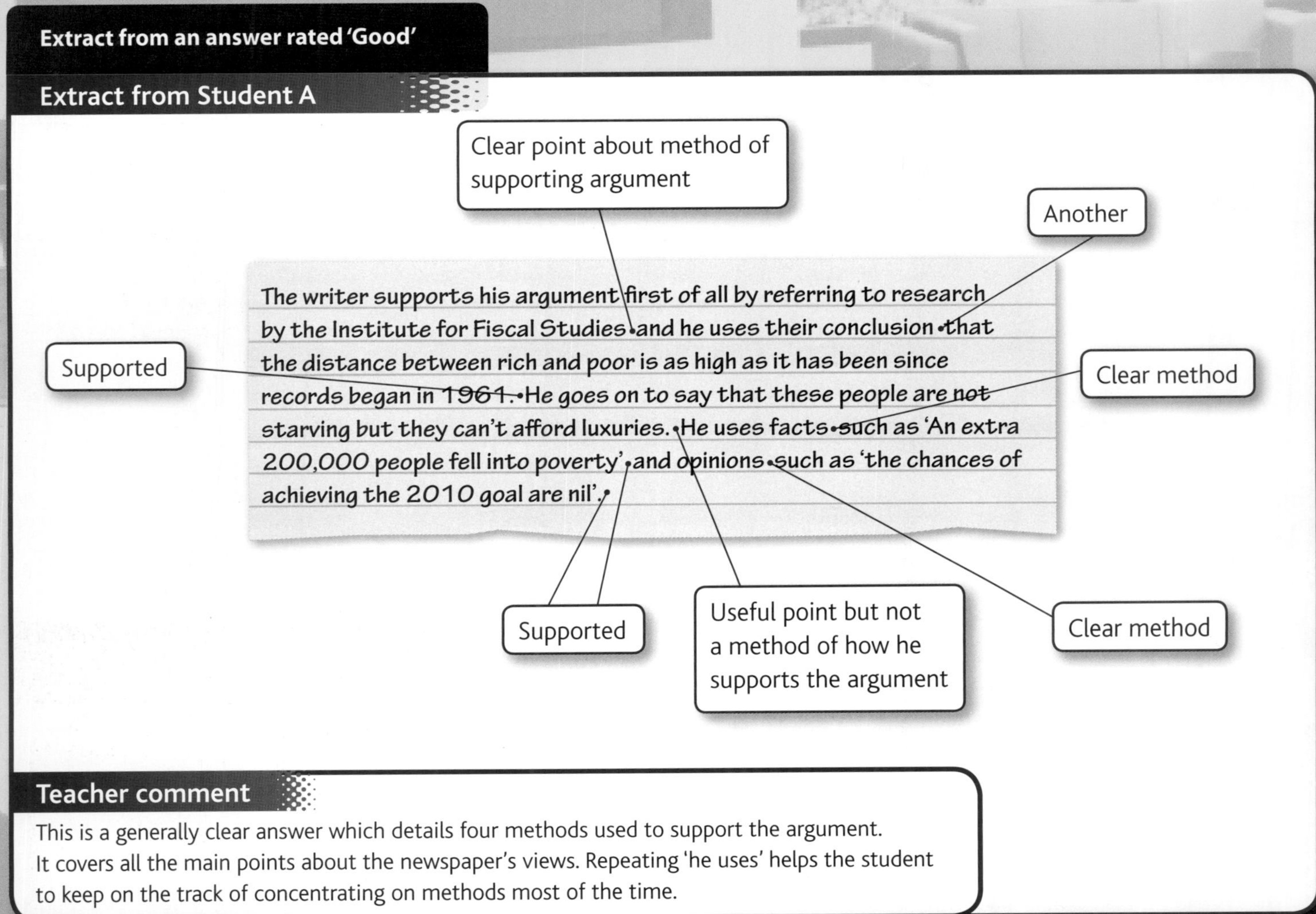

Clear point about method of supporting argument
Another
Supported
Clear method
The writer supports his argument first of all by referring to research by the Institute for Fiscal Studies and he uses their conclusion that the distance between rich and poor is as high as it has been since records began in 1961. He goes on to say that these people are not starving but they can't afford luxuries. He uses facts such as 'An extra 200,000 people fell into poverty', and opinions such as 'the chances of achieving the 2010 goal are nil'.
Supported
Useful point but not a method of how he supports the argument
Clear method

Teacher comment

This is a generally clear answer which details four methods used to support the argument. It covers all the main points about the newspaper's views. Repeating 'he uses' helps the student to keep on the track of concentrating on methods most of the time.

Extract from an answer rated 'Excellent'

Extract from Student B

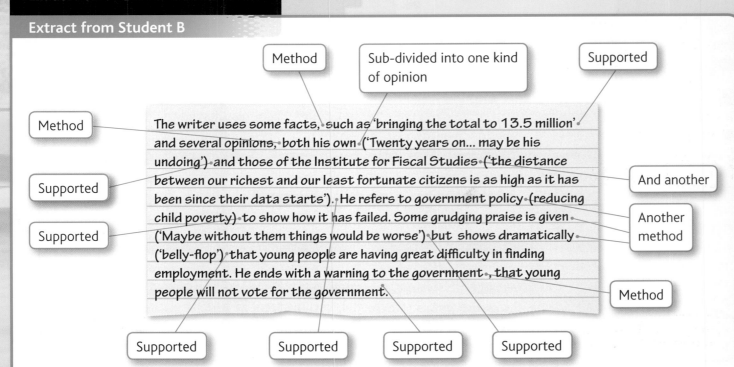

The writer uses some facts, such as 'bringing the total to 13.5 million' and several opinions, both his own ('Twenty years on... may be his undoing') and those of the Institute for Fiscal Studies ('the distance between our richest and our least fortunate citizens is as high as it has been since their data starts'). He refers to government policy (reducing child poverty) to show how it has failed. Some grudging praise is given ('Maybe without them things would be worse') but shows dramatically ('belly-flop') that young people are having great difficulty in finding employment. He ends with a warning to the government, that young people will not vote for the government.

Teacher comment

This answer is very full and detailed and concentrates on looking at methods of supporting the argument all the way through. It finds a wide range of methods and supports its points clearly and succinctly throughout.

Argument, fact and opinion

To improve your answer, read the question you have to answer before you read the passage. When you are reading the text underline the key points so that when you have finished you just have to write the answer out. Don't copy out more than you need to. If you are showing the different points in an argument, make sure that you don't repeat yourself.

What have I learnt?

Discuss or jot down what you now know about:

- following an argument
- finding the main points in an argument
- answering the question
- finding facts which support the argument
- finding opinions which support the argument
- what makes the difference between good and excellent answers on argument exam questions.

Putting it into practice

- You can practise this skill with any text you come across.
- Work out what is the main point being made.
- Find the different points that make up the argument.
- Take a few minutes to find some facts.
- Take a few minutes to find some opinions.

My learning

This lesson will help you to:

- read between the lines
- select material to answer questions about implications and assumptions.

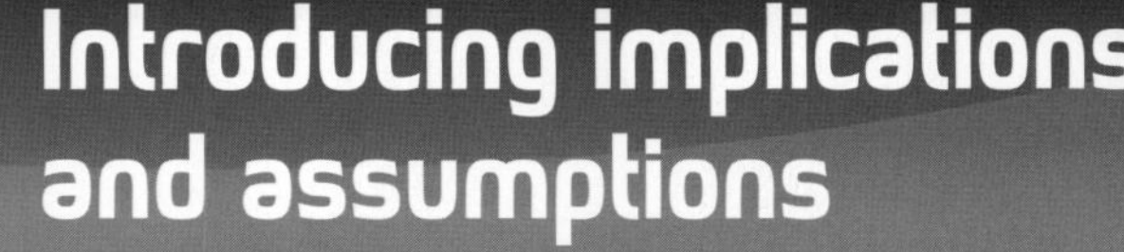

Introducing implications and assumptions

What are implications?

An **implication** is something that is suggested but not directly said. For example, when the astronaut Neil Armstrong referred to his first step on the moon as 'one small step for man, one giant leap for mankind…' he was implying that the human race had made significant technological advances.

What are assumptions?

An **assumption** is something that you are expected to know and as a result it isn't explained. Or it could be something about the reader that the writer has taken for granted.

A writer makes many assumptions about the reader, taking for granted what they expect the reader to know, what attitudes they expect the reader to have or what experiences the reader should be familiar with. Working out these assumptions can be a very useful pointer to the intended audience of a text. For instance, you would not expect an article on hip-hop, using teenage slang, to point to an over 60s audience.

Top tips

In the exam you will be asked to:

- think more deeply than just on the surface
- work out what is being hinted at
- think about what the writer assumes the reader knows
- think about what the writer assumes the reader doesn't know
- answer questions about implications and assumptions.

Activity 1 looks at three distinct things:

- what is assumed about the reader's interests
- what is implied about the Queen
- what is implied about the royal family as a whole.

By asking you to support your points by reference to details in the text this activity asks you for the specific evidence which leads you to your conclusion. The examiner wants to know what bits of text you are looking at when you make a point, so you should try to include one detail from the text to support each point that you are making.

Activity 1

Read the text below and then answer the following questions:

1 **What does the text assume the reader is interested in?**

2 **What is its attitude towards the Queen?**

3 **What does the overall article imply about the royal family?**

Use a detail from the text to support each point you make.

Ve are not amused!

QUEEN: FILM VICTORIA IS TOO GERMAN

By **ROBERT JOBSON,** ROYAL EDITOR

The Queen has seen a special screening of Fergie's film *The Young Victoria* – and complained it was too GERMAN.

Her Majesty (*descended from a long line of Germans*) was shown the movie about her great great gran Queen Victoria (*quite a lot German*) and Prince Albert (*all German*) at Buckingham Palace. While her ex daughter-in-law's production wasn't the wurst she'd seen, she found the German bits heil-y overdone.

A senior source said: 'She thought the film had a lot of good points but she is a stickler for accuracy. She wasn't too impressed they had Albert diving in front of Victoria to take the bullet in an assassination attempt.

'It simply did not happen and Her Majesty questioned the need for such a dramatic inaccuracy. She also thought the uniforms worn by the British officers looked too Germanic.'

Prince Andrew's ex Sarah Ferguson produced *The Young Victoria* after becoming fascinated with the legendary Queen's life.

Her daughter Beatrice has a cameo role in the film, which is currently No 4 in the UK box office chart.

MOVIE GRAN: Victoria.

NEWS OF THE WORLD

Check your answer

- Did you mention the obvious – the film and the royal family?
- Did you find any implications about the Queen and her views?
- Did you put the information about different members of the royal family together to come to any conclusions about what the article suggested about them?

My learning

This lesson will help you to:

- understand what assumptions are being made about audiences
- understand attitudes in a text by looking at the implications.

Assumptions, audiences and attitudes

When you are reading ask yourself some of these questions:

- What am I meant to know?
- If I don't understand it, what is the writer assuming I know?
- What is spelt out for me and what is not?

When you are answering a question, use the key words of the activity all the way through your answer in order to make sure that you keep on track all the time.

Activity 1

This activity asks you to use specific details from the advertisement to work out some assumptions about the target audience. You could start by looking at the prices, the amenities and the length of the stays.

Read the text below and then answer the following question:

What assumptions have been made about the readers of this advertisement?

4★ CYPRUS

Daily Express

A MONTH ON HALF BOARD

from just **£549*** pp

- **Pay for 12 nights and receive 2 nights FREE for arrivals 01/07/09–07/07/09**
- **No supplement for single travellers 08/12/08–30/04/09**

Departures: Dec '08–Oct '09

A year round favourite for lovers of sunshine and relaxing holidays. Cyprus caters for their needs with high standards of accommodation, excellent restaurants, places of entertainment and first class sporting facilities.

OUR RECOMMENDED HOTEL

The Ascos Beach Hotel is an excellent 4-star hotel in a delightful situation at Coral Bay. With its shingle and rock beach it offers a wide range of guest amenities and well-equipped comfortable accommodation. Just over six miles from the attractive resort of Paphos with its selection of shops, bars and restaurants, the hotel is also convenient for visits to the beautiful and remote Akamus Peninsula to the north.

Note: Adults Only hotel from May to October

PRICE PER PERSON INCLUDES:

- ✓ Return midweek flights from Gatwick, weekend flights at a supplement. A supplement will be payable if travelling from the following airports: Heathrow, Manchester, Birmingham, Stansted, Luton, Glasgow, Exeter, Leeds, Bradford, Aberdeen and Edinburgh.
- ✓ 4 weeks on Half Board the **4* Ascos Beach Hotel**, in a delightful situation at Coral Bay, near Paphos.
- ✓ Comfortable air-conditioned/heated rooms all have en suite bathroom and a **balcony**. They all feature satellite TV, radio, direct dial telephone and hairdryer. Side seaview and seaview rooms are available at a supplement.
- ✓ All UK & Cyprus airports taxes & passenger taxes.
- ✓ All airport security fees.
- ✓ Service of a Mercury Direct representative in resort.
- ✓ Return transfers in Cyprus.
- ✓ Full ATOL protection of your holiday.

PLUS:

- ✓ Good range of amenities include Outdoor and Indoor swimming pools.
- ✓ Other durations are available.

DEPARTURE DATES AND PRICES:

Board Basis: Half Board	7 nights	11 nights	14 nights	21 nights	28 nights
Dec '08 fr.	£239	£299	£359	£459	£599
Jan '09 fr.	£239	£299	£355	£445	£549
Feb '09 fr.	£259	£325	£369	£459	£569
Mar '09 fr.	£295	£369	£415	£499	£655
Apr '09 fr.	£399	£499	£599	£799	£999

Board Basis: All-Inclusive	7 nights	11 nights	14 nights	21 nights	28 nights
May '09 fr.	£565	£725	£825	£1119	£1419
Jun '09 fr.	£599	£799	£935	£1295	£1649
Jul '09 fr.	£649	£855	£995	£1349	£1699
Aug '09 fr.	£689	£895	£1035	£1389	£1739
Sept '09 fr.	£639	£839	£969	£1299	£1625
Oct '09 fr.	£575	£699	£789	£999	£1199

Prices are per person. fr. = from

Check your answer

- Did you think about the place?
- Did you think about the prices?
- Did you think about time?

Activity 2

This activity asks you to sort out attitudes towards three different things by looking carefully at the implications of what is reported.

Read the text below and then answer the following:

What attitudes are revealed about:

a the Council b old people c recycling?

Support the points you make by references to details from the text.

Daily Mail

By **Andy Dolan**

How a frail 97-year-old beat the wheelie bin police
013261

Defiant: Jenny Mapson, clutching her entire weekly rubbish in one hand, next to one of the council's wheelie bins.

FOR more than 25 years, she put out her rubbish in bin bags without giving it a second thought.

And in recent times Jenny Mapson has been only too happy to separate her waste into paper, tins and plastic to help the environment.

But when the council tried to force the frail 97-year-old to use two wheelie bins that were almost as big as her, she knew the time had come to put her foot down.

With no space to store the bins outside her tiny two-bedroom terraced home – even if she could move them – Miss Mapson refused to abide by the new regime.

Yesterday the spinster was celebrating the end of a four-month stand-off and a victory for common sense after being told she could carry on using her bin bags after all.

'This was the last straw'

The retired hairdresser was saddled with the bins in November as part of a so-called 'new and improved' waste scheme. It saw the local authority revert to alternate fortnightly collections of recycled and household waste using wheelie bins.

A black wheelie bin for normal waste and a green one for recycled waste were soon dropped outside her garden gate in Droitwich, Worcestershire.

Her 12ft by 10ft front garden has been professionally landscaped with shrubs and bushes – which leaves no room for a wheelie bin – so the pensioner called Wychavon District Council to explain her predicament.

Miss Mapson, who uses a walking stick, told them there was no room in her garden and wanted to continue using bin bags.

But she was told she had missed the deadline to apply for exemption and would have to make do.

Miss Mapson said: 'I said to the council, "Don't you know I'm an old woman of 97 and I live by myself and have difficulty getting in and out of the front door?"

'All he said was, "That's beside the point", and that the council want the bins to stay.'

The new regime was introduced on November 22.

Up until then, Miss Mapson's household waste was collected in bin bags every week, with paper waste collected in purple bags on one week, and a clear bag for plastics and tins collected on the alternate week.

Binmen continued to collect the plastic bin bags until February 24, when they suddenly refused to take Miss Mapson's purple bags.

Miss Mapson, who is hard of hearing and going blind, enlisted her niece Mandy Boswell to contact the council again on her behalf.

Mrs Boswell, an IT consultant, said: 'Nobody should be forced to house these huge bins in their front garden, let alone a frail old lady who lives alone.

'Her treatment has been very bad and I was told on the phone it wasn't the council's problem and we'd just have to get on with it.

'I was astonished. There are countless cases where these bins have been set alight or have been thrown through people's windows.

'Jenny has put her rubbish out in bin bags for more than 25 years and has had them collected with no issues at all. She is a very keen recycler and has done her best – but this was the last straw for her.'

A council spokesman said that following an investigation into her circumstances, Miss Mapson can continue using her bin bags.

The council apologised if she felt she had been badly treated.

Check your answer

- Did you find different attitudes?
- Did you notice the emotive language?

This lesson will help you to:

- practise an exam-style question
- assess your answer by looking at other responses.

Assessment practice

Now you are going to have a go at an exam-style question. Attempt the article in the time suggested and then complete the Peer/Self-assessment activity that follows.

Activity 1

Read the article below and then take 15 minutes to answer the following questions:

1 What assumptions are made about the readers of this article?

2 What is the attitude of the writer to the EU?

THE INDEPENDENT

So who says the EU is

Margot Wallstrom

TOMORROW is Europe Day, and let us be honest, there are, in most people's minds, more important events to be recalled today. It is, for example, Billy Joel's birthday, according to one calendar. Also, no less a source than the History Channel tells us that on 9 May 1998, 'Sex change singer Dana International won the Eurovision Song Contest for Israel with the song "Diva". ...'

Wikipedia does however note that on 9 May 1950 a French Minister announced to the press a plan for managing coal and steel production between Germany and France. To those people with a passion for mineral and industrial management (you know who you are) this was very significant, but for the rest of us...

The man was named Robert Schuman, and he had looked at Europe, devastated by war, and decided that there had to be a better way. But how? They could try to ban weapons, but that rarely works. The winners don't want to give them up, and the losers tend to get bitter about not having any. So instead, Schuman thought that if the leaders of Europe could not control who had weapons, they could control what makes weapons. Steel. And what do you need to make steel? Coal. Pooling production would make any war between France and Germany impossible according to Schuman.

It was a visionary plan, and it began the process that created today's European Union. The EU now has 27 member states. Two generations of Europeans have grown up without knowing what it is like to have a war in their country. (And this on a continent which played host to two world wars and innumerable others over the centuries.) I look around Europe today and ask myself, what happened to all those authoritarian governments that there used to be? Where are the dictators, communists and colonels? They have gone, hopefully for good.

So what? Many people say. They see a blue flag with 12 stars. Does it evoke passion? In a small minority, perhaps. Some see it as a symbol of good, a tiny minority detest it, but to most, it is a symbol that is just not relevant to them. The EU is a bit like the insulation in your house – it's good to know it's there but the average person does not go around thinking or worrying about it all the time. And yet, maybe that is its greatest success.

The EU doesn't really do passion. If you tried to market the EU as an aphrodisiac, it would rate up there with a nice pair of socks. If anything, the EU flag stands for boring reason over passion, for doing boring things like setting acceptable chemical levels in herring or discussing cross-border iPod warranty issues.

boring?

Where are Europe's dictators? They have gone, hopefully for good.

And yet the EU does stuff that is highly relevant to us. Like reducing the cost of using mobile phones abroad. Like creating millions of jobs via the single market. Like paving the way for cheaper air fares by opening up Europe's skies to competition. Like enabling students to study in another country.

So, this is my Happy Europe Day card. No need to wave a flag. But when you think about the positive and useful everyday work that European countries now do together, maybe it's a nice idea to remember the day in 1950 when one man, looking out over a continent that had been the world's greatest battlefield only five years previously, suggested that he might have a way of making sure it never happened again.

The writer is Vice-President of the European Commission

Peer/Self-assessment activity

1 Check your answer to Activity 1. Did you:

- make a range of points about assumptions
- use a range of implications to deduce the attitude of the writer
- support your points by reference to the details of the text?

2 Now assess your answer to Activity 1 using the criteria below. You will need to be careful and precise in your marking. Before you do this, you might like to read some sample answers to this activity on pages 36 and 37.

Good

- clear and effective attempt to engage with both parts of the article
- range of relevant points
- material chosen to focus on assumptions about readers and attitudes of writer.

Very strong

- detailed response to both parts of the question
- materials absorbed and shaped for purpose
- good understanding of material.

Excellent

- full, detailed, conceptualised response
- material fully absorbed and shaped for purpose
- full understanding of material.

GradeStudio

Here are two student answers to the activity on page 34:

1 ***What assumptions are made about the readers of this article?***

2 ***What is the attitude of the writer to the EU?***

Read the answers together with the comments. Then check what you have learnt and try putting it into practice.

Extract from an answer rated 'Excellent'

Extract from Student A

The writer assumes that the reader knows about the EU, who Billy Joel is, what the Eurovision Song Contest is, what Wikipedia is, what the History Channel is, and when Europe was devastated by war. She also assumes that the readers travel abroad. The educated reader recognises the writer to be opposed to dictators and communists, to understand that different people have different attitudes to the EU such as love, hate or apathy and that it is a good thing that the EU is unobtrusive. The writer is in favour of the EU because it affects ordinary people's lives for the better, reducing mobile phone costs abroad, creating jobs and prompting cheaper air fares.

Teacher comment

This is a very good, full answer, succinctly expressed and well put together. It includes a wide range of assumptions and attitudes.

Extract from an answer rated 'Good'

Extract from Student B

The writer assumes that the reader knows about the EU, Billy Joel and what Wikipedia is. She also assumes that the reader knows about the History Channel on TV. She realises that the EU doesn't excite many people but explains why it was a visionary plan. ~~She~~ explains that the EU does many things relevant to our daily lives, such as creating jobs.

Teacher comment

Although there are other points that could also have been made, this answer is detailed and contains supported points both about assumptions and implications. It answers both parts of the question clearly and systematically.

Implications and assumptions

To improve your answer, you need to make a wider range of points and make sure that you answer all parts of the question if there is more than one part to it. This is clearly shown in the difference between Student B who answers both parts of the question and Student A who gives a full and detailed answer including almost all of the possible points that could be made.

What have I learnt?

Discuss or jot down what you now know about:

- finding assumptions in a text
- finding implications in a text
- supporting your points by reference to the text's details
- what makes the difference between a good answer and an excellent one.

Putting it into practice

- You can practise this skill with several of the texts you come across.
- Ask yourself what the text:
  - assumes the reader knows
  - doesn't assume the reader knows
  - implies about something rather than directly stating it.
- Give yourself 10 minutes to practise this skill.

My learning

This lesson will help you to:
- identify and name language and grammar features
- comment on the effect of language and grammar features.

Getting started with language and grammar

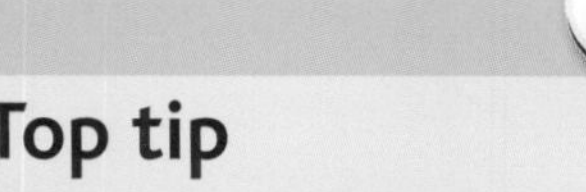

Language

You know a great deal about language because you have been studying it since you started school. In the exam, though, students often forget about some of the basic things they know about, such as:

- **nouns** (often names of things), e.g. *book, page*
- **verbs** (often doing words), e.g. *read, run*
- **adjectives** (words describing a noun), e.g. *bright, green*
- **adverbs** (words describing a verb), e.g. *quickly, slowly*
- **pronouns** (words used instead of a noun), e.g. *I, you, she, he, it.*

There are lots of other things you know about, too, because you have come across them frequently, such as:

- **first person**, e.g. *I, we*
- **second person**, e.g. *you*
- **third person**, e.g. *he, she, it, they*
- **metaphor**, e.g. *the room is a prison*
- **simile**, e.g. *the room is like a prison*
- **alliteration**, e.g. *grimy green gunk*
- **repetition**, e.g. *location, location, location*
- **rhyme**, e.g. *soar, roar*
- **slang**, e.g. *bling*
- **puns**, e.g. *the footballer kitted his kitchen out.*

Some of you will have looked at some other language techniques, such as:

- **onomatopoeia** (where the sound of the word is like the sound of the thing), e.g. *click*
- **paradox** (where two apparently opposite things are both true), e.g. *a huge mouse*
- **assonance** (repetition of the same vowel sounds in different words), e.g. *how now brown cow*
- **jargon** (specialist language), e.g. *mouse, browser, link* all have special meanings when you are talking about computers.

You will only have time to write about a few of these in the time in the exam, though. What is important is that you can quickly identify a range of language features so that you can use some of them as the basis for commenting on their effect on the reader.

Top tip

In the exam you are likely to be asked to:
- identify language and grammar features and comment on their effects.

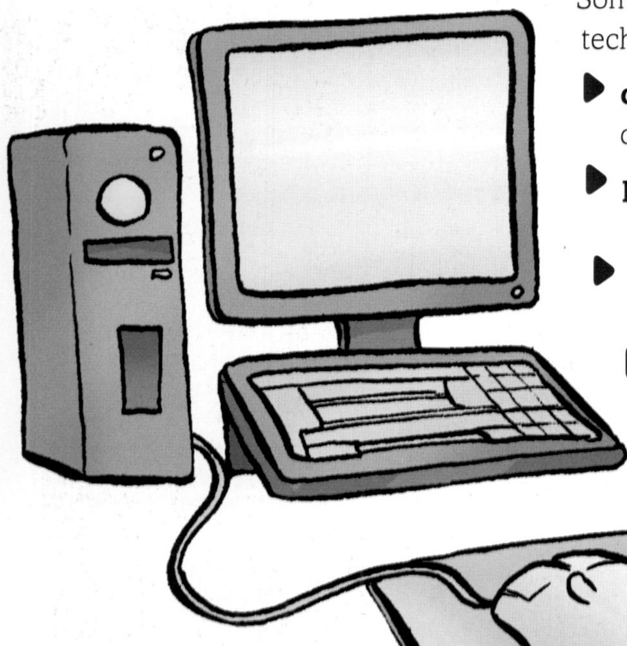

Grammar

In the exam you might also be asked to comment on grammar. Grammar is the construction which makes the sentence hang together properly. There are four basic kinds of sentence which are frequently used:

Simple sentence

This is a sentence (usually a short one) with a subject and a main verb. For example:

subject → I; verb → went

I went shopping.

Compound sentence

This is a series of two or more simple sentences joined together (usually with 'and' or 'but'). For example:

conjunctions → and, but

I went shopping and bought Bill a birthday present but I then decided to have lunch.

Complex sentence

This is a longer sentence with one part dependent upon another (using what is called a subordinating conjunction such as 'although', 'because', 'until'). For example:

subordinating conjunction → because

I went shopping because I needed to buy Bill a birthday present.

Minor sentence

This is a sentence which breaks the rules of grammar because it doesn't have a verb in it! These are often used for dramatic effect, to provide contrast to what has gone before or to jolt the reader. For example:

Gutted!

You can also identify and comment on particular kinds of sentences, such as questions, exclamations, rhetorical questions and any sentences that have unconventional grammar which breaks the rules or a deliberate grammatical mistake. Common examples of this are starting a sentence with a conjunction like 'and' or 'but' in order to sound informal or to make the reader sit up and take notice.

Top tips

When you are answering a question on language and/or grammar make sure you:

- name the feature
- give the example from the text
- make a comment.

Activity 1

Read the text opposite and then complete these questions.

1 Identify the following features:
   - minor sentences
   - a complex sentence
   - a compound sentence
   - two different uses of inverted commas
   - an informal contraction
   - a simple sentence
   - slang.

2 Then for each example you have chosen comment on what effect its choice has on the reader.

The Sunday Telegraph

PROFILE **ALAN BENNETT**

A writer who endures an embarrassment of talents

Big glasses. Big name. Big prospects. Alan Bennett was 75 yesterday, but his work is far from done.

There is simply too much ordinariness in the world for Bennett, our Mozart of the mundane, our Picasso of the prosaic, to consider quitting now.

Behind the shaggy sheepdog countenance, the old brain buzzes along as busily as it always has done – revelling in those plain slices of life that other playwrights tend to pass by. You can argue whether or not Bennett qualifies as a national institution, but there is no doubt that what we know as 'the Alan Bennett Character' (ABC) is one. Typically, the ABC will plod forth from the Northern lower middle classes, socially inept and consumed, behind a veneer of lace-curtained, allotment-tending respectability, by melancholy and dyspepsia. 'It'll take more than Dairy Box to banish memories of Pearl Harbour,' says Mrs Beevers, worried by the arrival of a Chinese waiter in the TV play *Afternoon Off*.

'Alan has got a very bleak view of human nature,' says his friend and fellow playwright Michael Frayn. 'He doesn't see people, on the whole, as finding very much enjoyment in life.' Bennett left the North a long time ago, and but for the chronic shyness that tends to keep him out of the limelight (he refuses to be interviewed) could now be counted among the cream of London's literati. Yet his appreciation of the great British art of being a total loser comes almost entirely from his early days as a Co-op butcher's son in Yorkshire. There, as he recalls, the hotels and restaurants were 'theatres of humiliation', and his family, unsteady in its steps up the social ladder, lived in dread of 'discovery, exposure and ignominious expulsion'.

In *The Lady in the Van*, a reminiscence he published in 1989, Bennett tells of his bizarre relationship with Miss Shepherd, an elderly madwoman who took up residence in a rusting van outside his house in a Camden Town crescent. Eventually, he invited her to move into his garden (an elevation she apparently took as a cue to stand for Parliament), where she remained for 15 years. 'There was,' he writes, 'a gap between our social positions and our social obligations. It was in this gap that Miss Shepherd was able to live.'

The gap was, perhaps, not as wide as it might have seemed. For Bennett has lived his whole life – in spirit if not in reality – among the oddballs. What might be called the eccentricity of ordinariness finds in him a natural chronicler, and his ear is constantly tuned to the possibilities of new material. The late George Melly recalled Bennett enacting a conversation he heard between two women on a bus. 'One said to the other something like, "What did the doctor say to your feet, Doris?", and she replied: "He said they'd not be much use to me in the future. Not as feet". That's the sort of thing he writes down. The sort of thing he uses.'

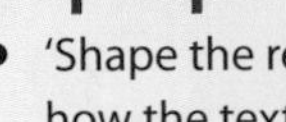

Activity 2

1 Read the article below and quickly identify and jot down as many language and grammar features as you can find.

2 Now answer the following question:

How does the writer of this text use language and grammar to shape the reader's response?

Top tips

- 'Shape the reader's response' means how the text makes you think and feel when you read it. So you are being asked here to look at specific aspects of language and grammar and then say how each of them makes you think and feel something in particular.
- In Activity 2, for example, you might start by mentioning the alliteration and the slang as well as the pun in 'bit of a buzz' in the first sentence. You could then say how this makes the reader interested in a catchy story and makes them smile when they grasp the pun on 'buzz'.

METRO

The fantastic Mr Fly

By ROSS McGUINNESS

A NEW musical talent has spread his wings and is already generating quite a bit of a buzz.

Meet Mr Fly, a piano-playing, guitar-bashing, musical genius from the insect world.

When he's not on stage or throwing up over his own food, he enjoys skateboarding, cycling and flying his kite.

Mr Fly is the unlikely muse of Belgian amateur photographer Nicholas Hendrickx.

Like his near namesake Jimi, the 21-year-old has torn up the rule book in his chosen field.

Nearly all the photographs of Mr Fly, whose first name is Gerald, were taken in Mr Hendrickx's bedroom, using mostly natural light and a small eight megapixel camera.

'I met Gerald Fly in my garden as I was shooting some flowers,' Mr Hendrickx said. 'There he was, staring at me with his big mosaic eyes, begging me for help. I offered him a job as my new model. That night we had a good drink and talked about potential photo shoots.'

'Surprisingly, he proved himself a lovely pianist and guitar player.'

In reality, Gerald is one of a number of flies which Mr Hendrickx photographs using props. 'It took quite some time. Some flies were great to work with, while others were very frustrating.'

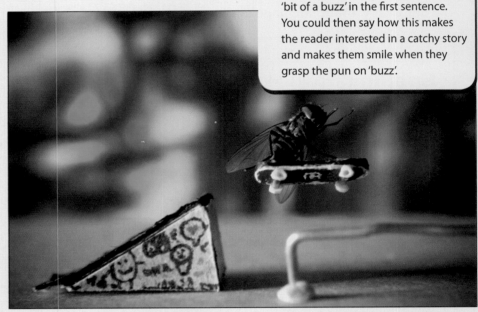

Multi-talented: Mr Fly shows off in a skate park before tinkling the ivories.

'I guess it's normal – flies and humans aren't made to work together. Flies are made to annoy us with their buzzing and pooping on stuff.' In explaining why he chose to put flies in front of the camera, Mr Hendrickx said: 'I guess I just wanted people to enjoy the little things in life and to give them a refreshing view on insect macro-photography.' He insists most of the shots feature live specimens, but how he gets a bug to read the paper on a deckchair is anyone's guess.

As for Gerald, he is reportedly seeking fame with his band The Buzzes, winging it through (very) small venues throughout Europe.

Check your answer

Did you:

- find several language and grammar features
- for each one, name the feature, give an example and make a comment on how it shapes the reader's response?

Range and effectiveness of language and grammar features

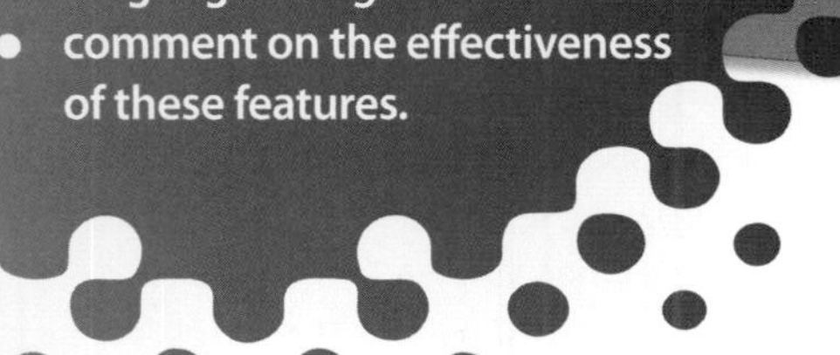

This lesson will help you to:

- identify and comment on a range of language and grammar features
- comment on the effectiveness of these features.

Some texts are denser and more complex than the 'Fantastic Mr Fly' article you read on page 41. Whereas the writer of that article was writing for a wide audience, the writer of the text in the following article is well-known for his articles about uses of language and so he is probably writing mainly for an audience interested in issues of language use.

Activity 1

Read the text below and then answer the following question:

How does the writer use language and grammar to illustrate what he has to say about language use?

THE TIMES

Spelling Philip Howard

LoL, Molly, LoL. You tap it out to Gabi on my laptop. Lots of Love. It is shorthand spelling. I do not advise it for our Spelling Bee. But it is an interesting example of an old phenomenon. The techies call it SMS. This stands for 'short messaging system', reflecting the service provider's point of view, and that of the user.

SMS represents a large slice of telecommunicated conversation among young people. It saves time, and digital fumbling or erosion of fingertips. You can tap out the msg on a tiny screen using only your thumb. It provides shortened forms of words and phrases, often omitting the vowels, as in TXT for text. It uses numbers for their sound values: CUL8R represents 'see you later'. Sometimes SMS just represents the first letters of words of a formula. BTDT stands for 'been there, done that'. I agree that acronyms and abbreviations are a modern plague, intended to demonstrate professionalism and efficiency, but in practice spreading darkness and irritation. (An acronym makes a word that you can say, such as Nato and Unesco. If you can't say it as a word, e.g. SMS, then it's officially an abbreviation or abbrev.) As usual in orthography, this is a snafu (situation normal all fouled up).

We do not need to get our Kns in a Tw over SMS. It is just a high-tech example of the ancient pleasure of sharing a private code. For example, argot is the secret language of thieves and tramps, serving to veil their meaning. Children have always had their private codes. SMS is just a mobile phone example, demonstrating the English adaptability for puns and homophones. It does not mean the end of English literacy.

There have been many attempts to simplify and abbreviate English spelling before SMS. In his famous 18th-century spelling book for Americans, Noah Webster listed many words that could lose a letter or two from their conventional spelling with no loss of identity, for example: relm, hed, giv, frend, bred and bilt. In 1906 the Simplified Spelling Board recommended 300 shortened spellings, including: thru, thoro, tho, prolog, altho. President Teddy Roosevelt endorsed them as US government style. But he was quickly overruled. Since then advertisers have launched trimmed spellings such as sox, thru, nite and lite. But only 'lite' appears in standard prose. English spelling is peculiarly resistant to change. Please spell it LIGHT for our Spelling Bee, dear girl.

Check your answer

Did you:

- find a range of language features to comment on
- find a range of grammar features to comment on
- comment on both language and grammar features?

In addition to being asked to comment on the effect of language and grammar, you might also be asked to evaluate the effectiveness of the writer's techniques. In order to be able to do this you need to follow the same preparation method – identify the feature, give the detail, say what you think the intended effect was and then comment on how effectively the feature does its job.

Activity 2

Read the text below and then answer the following question:

How effectively do the writers of this text use language and grammar features?

Daily Mirror

SMASH AND DRAG

£75m jewels stolen by gang dressed as women

By PETER ALLEN in Paris

ROBBERS dressed as women stole £75million worth of jewellery in an audacious lightning raid.

Four men in wigs and armed with shotguns and pistols burst into celebrity jewellers Harry Winston in Paris.

After just five minutes, they escaped with gems, gold, pearls and cash in one of the most lucrative heists in criminal history.

Their loot included single diamonds worth £100,000.

Forcing security guards and staff against a wall, they filled swag bags as they rifled displays and safes.

Two were in drag while the others covered their faces with ski masks. They are believed to have disabled some of the store's CCTV cameras.

Police suspect the robbers, who spoke in French and another unspecified language, had inside help. They knew the names of staff, barking orders at them as they went along.

Fifteen people, including guards, were in the store at the time. Nobody was seriously hurt but victims told how they feared for their lives. One said: 'It was terrifying. The raiders acted violently and shamelessly. Once they had pushed the customers into a corner they turned on the staff.

'They were hit around their heads and upper bodies with rifle butts. They were really knocked about. It was very nasty.'

A source at the BRB, France's elite anti-bandit brigade, said: 'It was a well planned brutal robbery. This is one of the most glamorous stores in Paris, and they knew it would be full of hugely expensive stock.

'We are particularly concerned that they appeared to know some of the staff, using them to get into the displays and the safes. They also seemed to know exactly where some of the most expensive pieces were hidden.'

The raiders struck at the American-owned store just after 5.30pm – closing time – on Thursday. The jeweller's, known for its upmarket clientele, is directly opposite the swanky Plaza Athénée hotel – used by celebrities including Madonna and Britney Spears. It often lends expensive items to stars for events such as the Cannes Film Festival.

Yesterday the store, which lost around £9million jewellery and cash when it was raided by three armed men a year ago, put up a £330,000 reward for information.

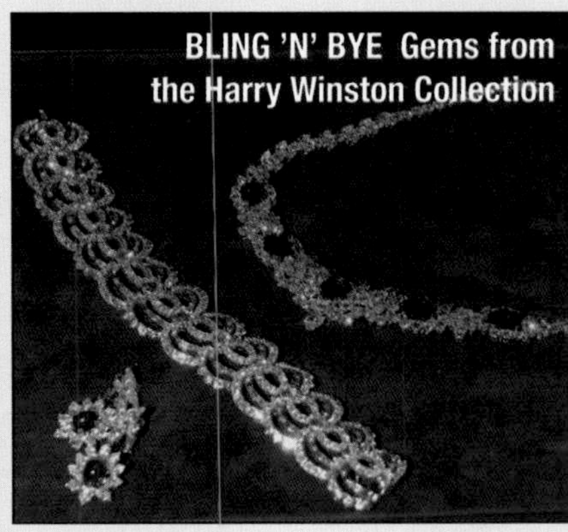

BLING 'N' BYE Gems from the Harry Winston Collection

Check your answer

Did you:

- comment on a range of language features
- comment on a range of grammar features
- comment on how effectively each of these was used?

This lesson will help you to:

- practise an exam-style question
- assess your answer by looking at other responses.

Assessment practice

Now you are going to have a go at an exam-style question. Attempt the activity in the time suggested and then complete the Peer/Self-assessment activity that follows.

Activity 1

This activity asks you to identify language features and to comment on the effect of each of them. Make sure that you find a range of features to comment on and that you comment on the effect of each of them.

Look closely at the text below and then spend 20 minutes answering the following question:

How does Germaine Greer use language to reveal her ideas and attitudes in this article?

ArtsComment

Germaine Greer I'd be happy if the new laureate blew all her money on the horses or invested in fetish gear

Dear Carol Ann Duffy, congratulations, I think. I was surprised when you accepted the laureateship because I had you down as a republican. You're probably fed up with being hailed not only as the first woman to hold this thankless job, but the first Scot, the first bisexual, the first lesbian, the first single mum, the first Catholic and, for all I know, the first capricorn. If you'd been black and disabled, you'd have ticked all the boxes.

'We all love and trust you, but you owe us nothing' ... Carol Ann Duffy.

What I hope is that you're the first republican to take it on. Not that I expect you to take the mickey out of the royal family. That's been going on for so long already, I doubt there's any mickey left in them to take.

I would like you to be clear about something. You're the laureate. You're the one with the crown of laurels. The queen's the one with the Koh-i-Noor and the Cullinan Diamond. And she doesn't even pay your miserable annual stipend of nearly £6,000: less than £500 a month for being a full-time poet is an insult. Of course, you can use the dosh to fund a prize for the best poetry collection of the year, but I'd be just as happy if you blew it on the horses or invested it in fetish gear. You shouldn't be feeling that you have to fund a poetry prize out of your meagre emolument.

What I'm keen to have you know is that you don't have to write a poem about Prince Harry's latest triumph on the party circuit or Kate Middleton's thong. Wordsworth, who was probably still a republican when he took the job, made it a condition of his acceptance that he wouldn't have to hymn the monarch or the proliferating royal family, and that has been accepted ever since. Ted Hughes didn't have to do it either; it was part of his genuine strangeness that he chose to, for Prince Andrew and Fergie's wedding. He actually chose to celebrate the place where Andrew proposed, but The Honey Bee and the Thistle's rolling versets are festooned with witchy nonsense about lay lines and the destiny that was supposed to have tied the place to those two thoroughly undistinguished people. Andrew Motion should have refused, but when he got badgered by the media he capitulated, and wrote stuff he's now ashamed of.

When the tabloids pursue you, just say no. You don't have to write anything about any of the royals, if you don't want to. Here I am, an old woman scowling in the gay springtime, hoping against hope that you don't want to. They, needless to say, will not care whether you do or not.

Top tips

- In the exam you are allowed to think what you like, as long as it is based closely on the text and supportable from the text's details.
- If, for example, you are asked to comment on the effects of language features, the examiner doesn't have the 'right answer' about what the effect is. The examiner just wants to see you comment on what you think it is.

The Guardian

They spend more time killing birds in large numbers than they do reading poetry.

My vote would have been for Alice Oswald, because she is a poet of country. I'm using the word the way Aboriginal people do, to mean the land; its associations, its in-dwelling spirits, its history, and now its desperate fragility. You write about people, about feelings, about our gropings in the dark towards each other, our evasions and fantasies – and I love what you do. But I wanted Oswald because I wanted someone who could make our hearts ache for the irreplaceableness of everything we are losing, the filthiness of our sky and our poisoned sea and the silent struggles of our trees. In my distorted view, the responsibility of the national poet is to the land and its inhabitants, not to its rulers.

I read that you see the history of the royal family as intertwined with the British national identity, which is strange because so few of them have been British. I'd love it, we'd all love it, if you wrote a sequence for the poor old Princesses of Wales, a sort of pendant to your The World's Wife. All the wives of Princes of Wales, bar one, have come to sticky ends. If anyone can drive futile ambitions to be princesses out of the minds of a generation of girls in pink, it's you. You're the one who knows how to bring females, big and small, to their senses – in every sense of senses.

There's a whole generation that has grown up with you, reading you for GCSE and A-level, and I've looking on as you performed your poetry for them, dangerously deadpan, in your sweet lisping brogue. We all love you and trust you, but you owe us nothing. Try to get some fun out of your new ridiculous job. I'd like to read your account of the Queen sending herself a telegram when she turns 100 – but you really, truly don't have to write it. Try as I might, I can't discover whether you've taken the job for 10 years, as Motion did. I'd make it less.

Cheers (three).

PS: Would you like me to make you a laureate hat, maybe a green balaclava with a crocheted garland of leaves? Given the bumpiness of the road ahead, you might be better off with a crash helmet.

Peer/Self-assessment activity

1 Check your answer to Activity 1.
Did you:
- find several language features
- show how language revealed ideas
- show how language revealed attitudes.

2 Now assess your answer to Activity 1 using the criteria below. Before you do this you might like to read some sample answers to this activity on pages 46 and 47.

Good
- clear and effective attempt to engage with activity
- range of effective points about language
- language features related to ideas and attitude.

Very strong
- full and detailed grasp of language features
- material absorbed and shaped for purpose
- good understanding of the material.

Excellent
- full, detailed and conceptualised
- material fully absorbed and shaped for purpose
- full understanding of the material.

GradeStudio

Here are two student answers to the activity on page 44:
How does Germaine Greer use language to reveal her ideas and attitudes in this article?
Read the answers together with the comments. Then check what you have learnt and try putting it into practice.

Extract from an answer rated 'Good'

Extract from Student A

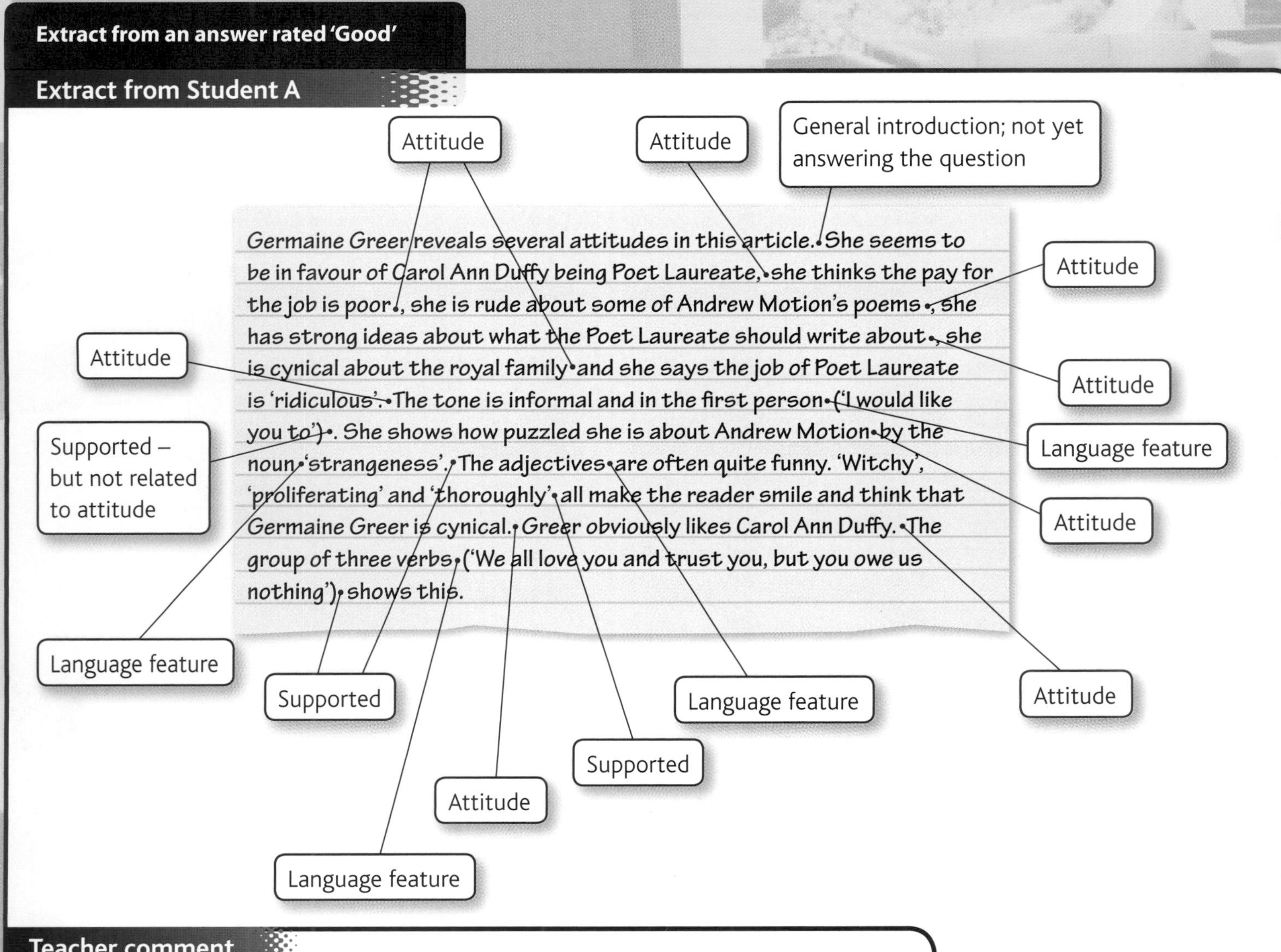

Attitude
Attitude
General introduction; not yet answering the question
Germaine Greer reveals several attitudes in this article. She seems to be in favour of Carol Ann Duffy being Poet Laureate, she thinks the pay for the job is poor, she is rude about some of Andrew Motion's poems, she has strong ideas about what the Poet Laureate should write about, she is cynical about the royal family and she says the job of Poet Laureate is 'ridiculous'. The tone is informal and in the first person ('I would like you to'). She shows how puzzled she is about Andrew Motion by the noun 'strangeness'. The adjectives are often quite funny. 'Witchy', 'proliferating' and 'thoroughly' all make the reader smile and think that Germaine Greer is cynical. Greer obviously likes Carol Ann Duffy. The group of three verbs ('We all love you and trust you, but you owe us nothing') shows this.
Attitude
Attitude
Attitude
Supported – but not related to attitude
Language feature
Attitude
Language feature
Supported
Language feature
Attitude
Supported
Attitude
Language feature

Teacher comment

This answer begins with a very general statement and then lists six attitudes. However, the answer doesn't show how language reveals these attitudes. The second part of the answer from 'The tone is informal ...' does deal with language and two of the points are clearly tied to attitudes, but they are rather different points than those made in the second sentence. It's the method that doesn't quite work here. The student has written about attitudes first and then language, so that the answer as a whole doesn't consistently show how Greer's language reveals her attitudes.

Extract from an answer rated 'Very strong'

Extract from Student B

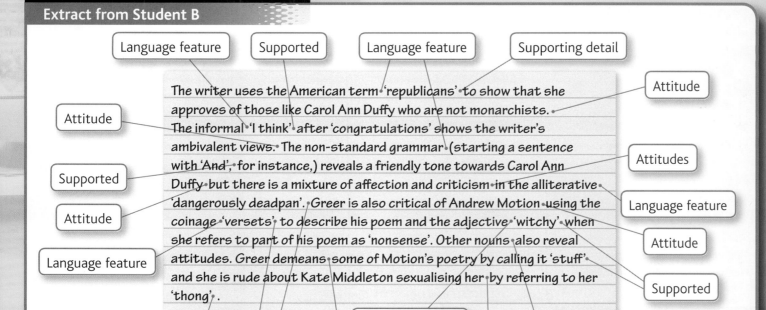

The writer uses the American term 'republicans' to show that she approves of those like Carol Ann Duffy who are not monarchists. The informal 'I think' after 'congratulations' shows the writer's ambivalent views. The non-standard grammar (starting a sentence with 'And', for instance,) reveals a friendly tone towards Carol Ann Duffy but there is a mixture of affection and criticism in the alliterative 'dangerously deadpan'. Greer is also critical of Andrew Motion using the coinage 'versets' to describe his poem and the adjective 'witchy' when she refers to part of his poem as 'nonsense'. Other nouns also reveal attitudes. Greer demeans some of Motion's poetry by calling it 'stuff' and she is rude about Kate Middleton sexualising her by referring to her 'thong'.

Teacher comment

This answer includes a wide range of language features and gives quick brief examples of them. Each one is related to an idea or an attitude. The whole answer covers what is required, though it doesn't have an overview of what Greer's ideas and attitudes are.

Language and grammar features

To improve your answer, make sure you identify features in the activity before you read the text. Then for each feature that you mention, name the feature, give an example and make a comment. If you are asked about the effectiveness of the language and/or grammar, then think about the intended effect of each feature you choose to write about and then comment on its effectiveness. Make sure that you look at the question carefully to see if you are being asked about presentational features, structure or both.

What have I learnt?

Discuss or jot down what you now know about:

- finding language and grammar features
- commenting on the effect of language and grammar features
- commenting on the effectiveness of language and grammar features
- answering the question
- what makes the difference between a good answer and a very strong one.

Putting it into practice

- You can practise these skills with any text you come across.
- Take a few minutes to identify some language features.
- Take a few minutes to identify some grammar features.
- Practise writing sentences where you name the feature, give an example and make a comment.

My learning

This lesson will help you to:
- identify and name presentational and structural features
- comment on the effect of these features.

Introducing presentation and structure

When you read something that has been published, someone has written the text and someone has decided how it's going to look – the presentation.

There are lots of different features that you can use, but broadly they fall under two headings:

- **Presentational features** such as:
  - size, font
  - bold, italic, underlining
  - headlines, subheadings, pictures, graphics, charts, graphs, logos, website addresses, colour.
- **Structural features** such as:
  - paragraphs, bullet points, sections, boxes
  - introduction, conclusion, summary, repetition
  - discourse features, such as *first*, *secondly*, *in conclusion*, numbering.

Top tip

In the exam you are likely to be asked to:
- identify structural and presentational features and comment on their effects.

Activity 1

Read the article opposite, from the *Metro* newspaper, and then complete the following activity.

1 Look carefully at the article. Identify and list as many presentational and structural features as you can. You can use the lists above to help you make a start.

2 Now answer the following question:

How do the designers of this text use presentational and structural devices to interest the reader?

For each feature that you choose to write about when answering the question, you should:
- name the feature
- give a detail
- make a comment about how it interests the reader.

Check your answer

Did you:
- find several presentational and structural features
- name the feature, give an example and make a comment on how it interests the reader?

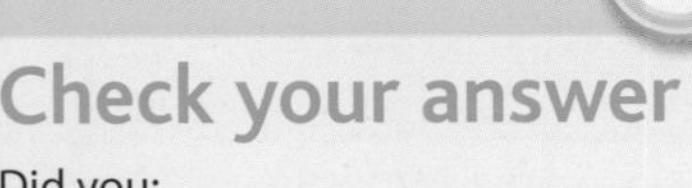

METRO

Golf, basketball, ten-pin bowling… parakeet AJ has mastered them all

The above-par birdie

By **Ross McGuinness**

IF THERE was an Olympic Games for birds, this sporty parakeet would be favourite for golds galore.

AJ is such a good all-rounder he can putt a golf ball, slam dunk a basketball and perform gymnastic routines.

Thousands of fans have watched a video of the sporty bird demonstrating his skills on the internet.

In the 1min 14sec clip, the green and yellow parrot's personal trainer shouts words of support from the sidelines with comments such as 'good bird' and 'good job'.

AJ also psyches himself up by repeating: 'Put the ball in the basket. Put the ball in the basket.'

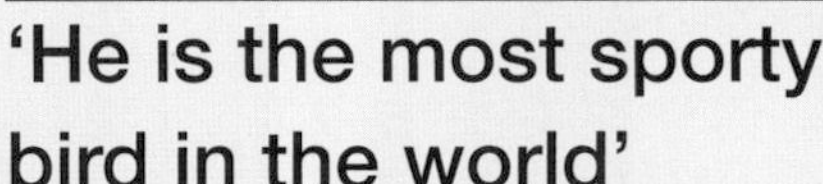

'He is the most sporty bird in the world'

The 18-year-old Indian ringneck parakeet starts his routine by playing dead and jumping to his feet as his trainer says: 'Get up.'

He then uses a high bar to perform more remarkable flips before flying to his £2,000 miniature golf course.

The sporty bird then swings a club in his beak and the ball slides into the hole – possibly for a birdie.

Owner Dave Cota, from Florida, believes his parakeet is probably the most sporty bird in the world.

'It seems he can play anything I show him,' said the 40-year-old.

Wildlife expert Chris Packham explained the parrot species had a natural ability to learn human behaviour.

He said: 'The parrot's beak and claws, designed to grasp and open fruit, gives it a dexterity not found in all birds. Bring that together with its ability to learn and mimic and you can see why these birds are so popular.'

Top of the tree: AJ the sporty parakeet holds a mini golf club in his beak to putt a hole-in-one to shouts of 'good job' from his trainer.

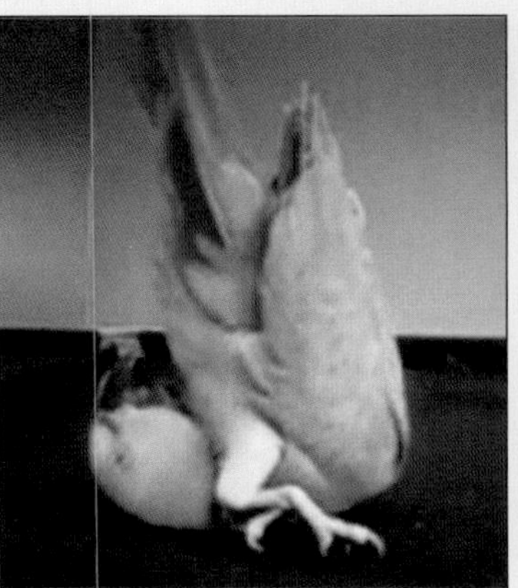

Flying high: The bird has also learnt how to play basket ball, roll over sideways and play tenpin bowling.

Not all texts are as effective in their use of structural and presentational devices as others. They might, for example:

- have too much text to allow the reader to pick out the main points
- have something missing which makes them not really fit for purpose
- be too dense or too cluttered.

What you think about a text in an exam is entirely up to you. If you think the effect is something negative, then that is fine for you to say. The marks are not for your judgement but for how you arrive at that judgement.

Because the Assessment Objective asks you to 'evaluate', you have to use your own judgement in order to consider the extent to which a text is effective. While the examiners are looking for you to consider a range of presentational and structural devices, commenting on several different ones, they don't mind which you choose. There are always going to be a lot more in the text than you will have time to comment on. So you will have to select.

Very good answers will comment on different features. In the same way, different students will have different views about how effective these features are. This is fine. Examiners are not expecting everyone to say the same thing. It's the explanation of why you think something is or is not effective which matters.

Activity 2 is asking you to:

- identify and comment on the effect of presentational features
- identify and comment on the effect of structural features
- comment on how effective you think each of these is.

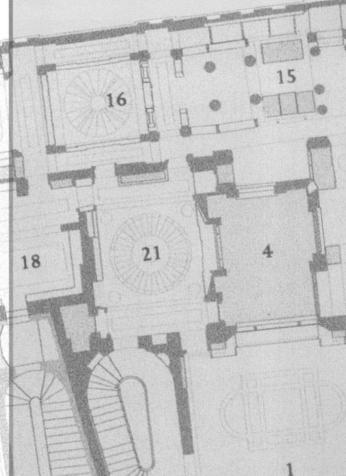

Activity 2

Read the text opposite which is the last page of a booklet about Sir John Soane's museum in London, and then answer this question:

How effective are the presentational and structural features in this text in getting information across and influencing the reader?

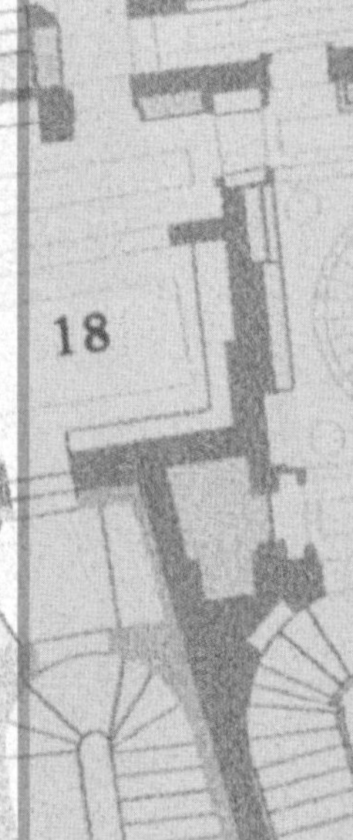

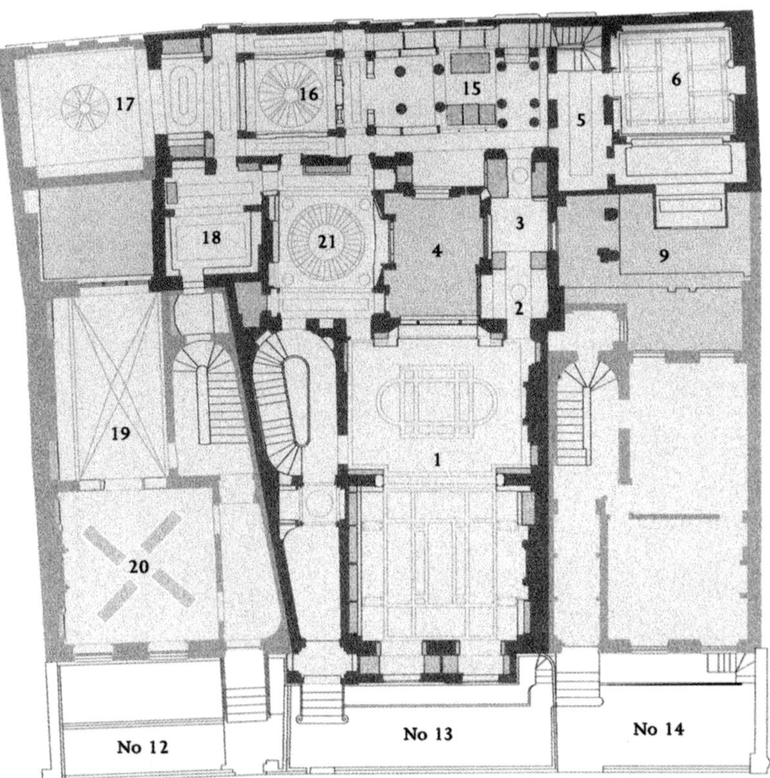

Plan of the Ground Floor (for Plan of Basement see overleaf)

Sir John Soane's Museum is open free: Tuesday to Saturday inclusive, 10am – 5pm. Also on the first Tuesday of each month, 6 – 9pm. Closed Sunday, Monday, Bank Holidays and Christmas Eve. Public lecture tour every Saturday at 11am, except as above. 22 tickets are available from 10.30am at a cost of £5 each, free to students.

Group visits to the Museum must be booked in advance and the group may be no more than 20 in number. Group visits may not be booked for Saturdays or for the first Tuesday of the month evening opening. Access to the Research Library and collections of manuscripts and architectural drawings is by appointment.

The Museum welcomes the support of individuals who can help in different ways. The Development Department organises a varied programme of lectures, private views, visits to private collections and social events for Soane Patrons and Soane Supporters. If you would like information on these groups or details of how it is possible to help the Museum, please contact Mike Nicholson on 0207 440 4241 or mnicholson@soane.org.uk

Sir John Soane's Museum 13 Lincoln's Inn Fields London WC2A 3BP
Tel: General Enquiries 020 7405 2107 Research Library: 020 7440 4251
Group bookings: 020 7440 4263 or email jbrock@soane.org.uk
Registered Charity No: 313609 Website: www.soane.org Fax: 020 7831 3957

Plans drawn by Christopher Hawkesworth Woodward (1996). Designed by Libanus Press. Printed by Hampton Printing, Bristol. Revised January 2008

Check your answer

Did you:

- find a range of features to comment on
- comment on both presentational and structural features
- make a comment about the effectiveness of each of the features you chose?

My learning

This lesson will help you to:
- identify presentational and structural features
- comment on how effectively these features are used.

Commenting on presentation and structure

In the previous lesson you identified presentational and structural features in two texts. You also started to comment on how effective those features were. In this lesson you will look at a more complex text and evaluate its use of presentation and structure.

Activity 1

The text opposite is from a 'World factfile' which devotes one page to each of the countries in the world. This is one page from it. Its purpose is to provide as much useful information about the country as possible on one page.

Read the text and then answer the following question:

How effectively do the designers of this text use presentational and structural features?

Look back at the lists on page 48 if you need to be reminded about some of the presentational and structural features.

Check your answer

Did you:
- comment on a range of presentational features
- comment on a range of structural features
- comment on how effectively each was used?

World factfiles

The Guardian

Pakistan

Potted history
Pakistan, created by the partition of India in 1947, has been under military rule for most of its existence. A US ally throughout, it has lurched from crisis to crisis, including three wars with India. In 1998, the country successfully test-fired a nuclear bomb. Its decision to join the US war on terror after the September 11 attacks was significant, fuelling an Islamist rebellion at home.

Political pressure points
The country is riven by ethnic, sectarian and civil–military tensions. The Punjab province is dominant, to the great resentment of the other three provinces. Democratic governments, when they have existed, have lived in constant fear of military takeover. Sensitive foreign and security policy remains in army hands.
Population mix Punjabi 44.68%, Pashtun 15.42%, Sindhi 14.1%, Saraiki 8.38%, Muhagirs 7.57%, Balochi 3.57%, other 6.28%
Religious makeup Muslim 96% (majority Sunni)
Main languages Urdu and English (official), Punjabi, Pashtu, Sindhi, Saraiki
Living national icons Mohsin Hamid (author), Imran Khan (politician and former cricketer), Mehdi Hassan, Ghulam Ali (Ghazal singers), Abdul Sattar Edhi (philanthropist), Iftikhar Arif (poet), Younis Khan (cricketer)

Landscape and climate
Deserts in the south, fertile plains in the Punjab. Three mountain ranges in the north – the Hindu Kush, the Karakoram and the Himalayas, include the world's second-highest peak, K2. Pakistan has hot, humid summers in the plains, with pleasant winters. In the mountains, it snows heavily.
Highest point K2 8,611 metres
Area covered by water 9,737.5 square miles

Healthcare and disease
Healthcare is generally poor in public hospitals, with many suffering filthy conditions. There are private hospitals and clinics where it is possible to pay for a better standard of care. Doctors tend to be good but aftercare is deficient. Polio recently returned in some areas, as a result of Islamic extremists stopping vaccinations against it.
Average number of children per mother 3.6
Maternal deaths per 100,000 live births 320
Infant deaths per 1,000 births 97
HIV/Aids rate 0.1%
Doctors per 1,000 head of population 0.8
Adult literacy rate 54.9% (m 68.7%; f 40.2%)

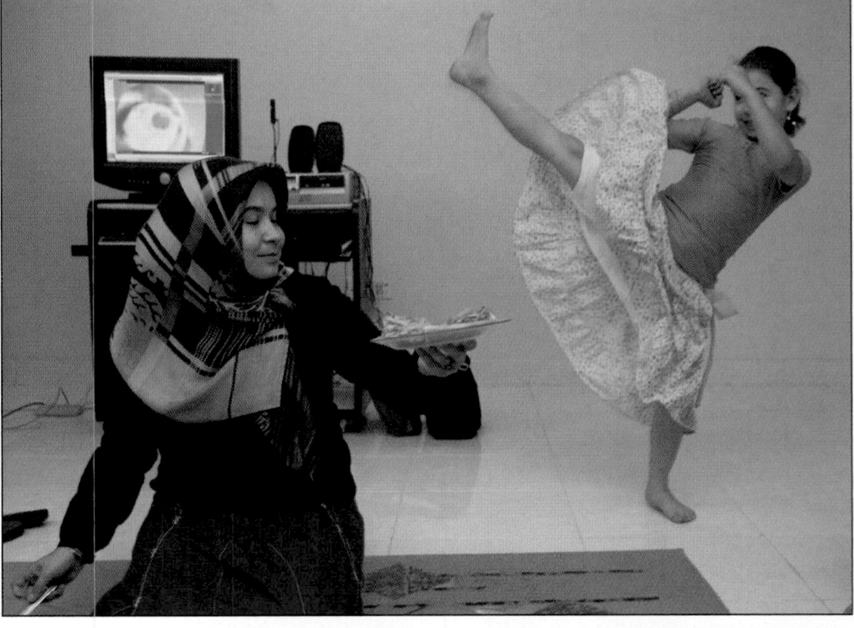

At a glance
Location South Asia
Neighbours Afghanistan, Iran, India, China
Size 307,374 square miles (excluding disputed territories of Kashmir, Jammu, Junagardh, Manavadar)
Population 158,700,000 (6th)
Density 516.3 people per square mile
Capital city Islamabad (population 780,000)
Head of state President Asif Ali Zardari
Head of government Prime minister Yousaf Raza Gillani
Currency Pakistani rupee
Time zone Pakistan standard time (+5 hours)
International dialling code +92
Website pakistan.gov.pk

Economic outlook
Mounting instability has meant that international investment has dried up since 2007 and even local businesses are reluctant to commit capital. There are chronic power shortages, high inflation and high interest rates, along with a poorly educated workforce.
Main industries Petroleum, textiles, automobiles, electrical goods, agriculture
Key crops/livestock Wheat, sugar cane, rice, cottonseed, dry onions
Key exports Textiles, vegetable products
GDP £64,773m (46th)
GDP per head £408
Unemployment rate 5.3%

Average life expectancy (m/f)
65/66
Proportion of global carbon emissions
0.43%
Media freedom index (ranked out of 173)
152

Blessed be the sacred land / Happy be the bounteous realm / Symbol of high resolve / Land of Pakistan / Blessed be thou citadel of faith
National anthem

Most popular tourist attractions The Karakoram highway, which runs from Islamabad to China, is an engineering miracle that opens up much of Pakistan's mountains.
Local recommendation Sufi religious festivals show the more tolerant, colourful side of Pakistan. The biggest is the three-day festival at Sehwan Sharif, an oasis town in Sindh, in late summer or autumn each year.
Traditional dish *Kadai* (curry)
Foreign tourist visitors per year 850,600

Did you know…
The Badshahi mosque is one of the world's largest, holding 100,000 worshippers.

This lesson will help you to:

- practise an exam-style question
- assess your answer by looking at other responses.

Assessment practice

Now you are going to have a go at an exam-style question. Attempt the activity in the time suggested and then complete the Peer/Self-assessment activity that follows.

Activity 1 asks you to identify presentational and structural features and to comment on the effect of each of them. Make sure that you find a range of features to comment on and that you comment on the effect of each of them.

Top tips

- In the exam you are allowed to think what you like, so long as you can support your ideas with details of the text.
- If, for example, you are asked to comment on the effects of a language feature, the examiner doesn't have the 'right answer' about what the effect is. The examiner just wants to see you comment on what you think it is.

Activity 1

Read the text below closely and then complete the following.

1 Identify and list all the presentational features and the structural features that you can find.

2 Then take 15 minutes to answer this question:

How are presentational and structural features used in this advertisement, and what are their effects?

A wild kind of fish

Alaska has long managed its plentiful wild fish sustainably, and it's some of the healthiest and tastiest you can find. By **Bart Johnson**

Sustainable fishing is a modern mantra... part of helping to save the world's resources. Yet sustainable fishing has been a way of life in Alaska for 50 years, where sustainably managed seafood is part of the country's constitution.

Yet even though this is part of one of the most advanced nations in the world, Alaska remains one of the last great wildernesses. Of its 586,400 square miles, only about 250 are populated. The rest is made up of snow-capped mountains, glaciers, forests, clear waters and green plains. There are more than 3 million lakes, 3,000 rivers and 34,000 miles of coastline. Little wonder, then, that fish is so abundant, particularly salmon, which thrives here.

It's not just salmon that is so nurtured. All Alaska seafood has to be maintained sustainably, and the state is a leader in sustainable fisheries. Added to that, all Alaska fish and other seafood is wild. So, swimming freely off Alaska's coast, the salmon builds up firm, lean flesh, high in protein, calcium and vitamins, and low in cholesterol. It is also rich in omega-3 oils, which, as part of a balanced diet, may help maintain a healthy heart.

FREE RECIPE BOOK

Discover for yourself the delights of wild Alaska seafood with a collection of more than 50 delicious recipes from the Alaska Seafood Marketing Institute. To receive one of 500 copies of *Wild Wonderful Alaska Seafood* (pictured on the right), send a postcard with your name and address to ASMI/Stella, c/o The Dialogue Agency, 8 Oak Lane, Twickenham TW1 3PA. Or call 020 8607 0349 or email alaskaseafood@dialogueagency.com

*Wild, Natural & Sustainable**

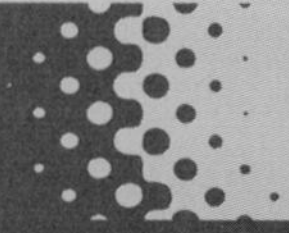

Peer/Self-assessment activity

1. Check your answer to Activity 1.
   Did you:
   - find several presentational features
   - find several structural features
   - comment on the effect of each of them?
2. Now assess your answer to Activity 1 using the criteria below. Before you do this you might like to read some sample answers on this activity on pages 56 and 57.

Good

- clear and effective attempt to engage with activity
- range of relevant points
- both structural and presentational features covered
- comments on both structural and presentational features.

Very strong

- full and detailed grasp of structural and presentational features
- material absorbed and shaped for purpose
- good understanding of the material.

Excellent

- full, detailed and conceptualised
- material fully absorbed and shaped for purpose
- full understanding of the material.

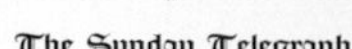

Wild Alaska salmon colcannon with lemon and chive butter

50g butter; finely grated zest and juice of 1 lemon; 1tsp Dijon mustard; 1 tbsp fresh chives, chopped; 1kg potatoes, peeled and cut into chunks; 4 x 125–150g wild Alaska salmon fillets; 150g Savoy cabbage, finely shredded; 6 spring onions, finely sliced; salt and freshly ground black pepper; snipped fresh chives to garnish.

Mix together butter, lemon zest, mustard and chives. Refrigerate. Cook potatoes in lightly salted boiling water for 20 minutes, until tender. After potatoes have been cooking for 10 minutes, preheat grill. Arrange salmon on grill rack and sprinkle with lemon juice. Cook for about 8 minutes, turning once, until done – flesh will be opaque and should flake easily. While fish is cooking, boil cabbage and spring onions for about 5 minutes, then drain. Mash potatoes and mix in cabbage and spring onions. Season, then share between 4 warmed plates. Arrange salmon fillets on top of mash, then share lemon and chive butter between them. Garnish with snipped fresh chives. Serve.

Cook's tip: try using parsley or thyme in the flavoured butter instead of chives.

GradeStudio

Here are two student answers to the activity on page 54:
How are presentational and structural features used in this advertisement, and what are their effects?
Read the answers together with the comments. Then check what you have learnt and try putting it into practice.

Extract from an answer rated 'Excellent'

Extract from Student A

This strange advertisement attracts the reader by a large, colourful, mouth-watering picture of a salmon dish and entices the reader further with a small square inset picture of beautiful Alaska. The large bold headline suggests that the article is going to be about salmon and the recipe, with its bold heading, italicised ingredients, block of instructions and italicised cook's tip at the end, does the same. The company's logo, though, in the middle of the page at the bottom, with its stylised ship and blue water and sky lets the reader know that the advert is really for a company called Alaska Seafood, which the rest of the page doesn't give away. The reader is enticed by the offer of a free recipe book, this being the only bold capitalised headline on the page.

The page is divided into several sections. The large picture at the top is interrupted by the small inset picture and this links, because of its angle with the salmon recipe below, printed on a coloured background. The main text, after a bold headline and subheading is plain, but the free offer section in the middle of the page is introduced as something separate by its upper case bold headline. The final element in the composition is the logo, central and striking with its angled lettering and touch of colour.

Annotations: Presentational feature; Supported; Supporting detail; Effect; Three presentational features; Two presentational features; Supported; Presentational feature; Effect; Supported; Supported; Presentational feature; Three presentational features; Two effects; Structure; Effect; Effect

Teacher comment

This student clearly didn't think the advertisement was effective but each comment on effect is clearly supported. That is what gains the marks. This outstanding answer is very full and detailed throughout. It covers a very wide range of points, supported quickly and efficiently, and makes several comments about effect. It continues to support the structural points with details of presentational features.

Peer/Self-assessment activity

1 Check your answer to Activity 1.
Did you:
- find several presentational features
- find several structural features
- comment on the effect of each of them?

2 Now assess your answer to Activity 1 using the criteria below. Before you do this you might like to read some sample answers on this activity on pages 56 and 57.

Good
- clear and effective attempt to engage with activity
- range of relevant points
- both structural and presentational features covered
- comments on both structural and presentational features.

Very strong
- full and detailed grasp of structural and presentational features
- material absorbed and shaped for purpose
- good understanding of the material.

Excellent
- full, detailed and conceptualised
- material fully absorbed and shaped for purpose
- full understanding of the material.

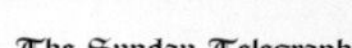
The Sunday Telegraph

Wild Alaska salmon colcannon with lemon and chive butter

50g butter; finely grated zest and juice of 1 lemon; 1tsp Dijon mustard; 1 tbsp fresh chives, chopped; 1kg potatoes, peeled and cut into chunks; 4 x 125–150g wild Alaska salmon fillets; 150g Savoy cabbage, finely shredded; 6 spring onions, finely sliced; salt and freshly ground black pepper; snipped fresh chives to garnish.

Mix together butter, lemon zest, mustard and chives. Refrigerate. Cook potatoes in lightly salted boiling water for 20 minutes, until tender. After potatoes have been cooking for 10 minutes, preheat grill. Arrange salmon on grill rack and sprinkle with lemon juice. Cook for about 8 minutes, turning once, until done – flesh will be opaque and should flake easily. While fish is cooking, boil cabbage and spring onions for about 5 minutes, then drain. Mash potatoes and mix in cabbage and spring onions. Season, then share between 4 warmed plates. Arrange salmon fillets on top of mash, then share lemon and chive butter between them. Garnish with snipped fresh chives. Serve.

Cook's tip: try using parsley or thyme in the flavoured butter instead of chives.

GradeStudio

Here are two student answers to the activity on page 54:
How are presentational and structural features used in this advertisement, and what are their effects?
Read the answers together with the comments. Then check what you have learnt and try putting it into practice.

Extract from an answer rated 'Excellent'

Extract from Student A

This strange advertisement attracts the reader by a large, colourful, mouth-watering picture of a salmon dish and entices the reader further with a small square inset picture of beautiful Alaska. The large bold headline suggests that the article is going to be about salmon and the recipe, with its bold heading, italicised ingredients, block of instructions and italicised cook's tip at the end, does the same. The company's logo, though, in the middle of the page at the bottom, with its stylised ship and blue water and sky lets the reader know that the advert is really for a company called Alaska Seafood, which the rest of the page doesn't give away. The reader is enticed by the offer of a free recipe book, this being the only bold capitalised headline on the page.

The page is divided into several sections. The large picture at the top is interrupted by the small inset picture and this links, because of its angle with the salmon recipe below, printed on a coloured background. The main text, after a bold headline and subheading is plain, but the free offer section in the middle of the page is introduced as something separate by its upper case bold headline. The final element in the composition is the logo, central and striking with its angled lettering and touch of colour.

Supported
Supporting detail
Effect
Presentational feature
Three presentational features
Two presentational features
Supported
Presentational feature
Effect
Supported
Supported
Presentational feature
Three presentational features
Two effects
Structure
Effect
Effect

Teacher comment

This student clearly didn't think the advertisement was effective but each comment on effect is clearly supported. That is what gains the marks. This outstanding answer is very full and detailed throughout. It covers a very wide range of points, supported quickly and efficiently, and makes several comments about effect. It continues to support the structural points with details of presentational features.

Extract from an answer rated 'Good'

Extract from Student B

The colourful picture of a salmon dish makes you want to read the article and the angled inset picture shows you how beautiful Alaska is. The large bold headline introduces the topic of the article. The page is in sections – a picture, an inset, a story and a recipe.

Teacher comment

This answer begins well on presentational features, several being mentioned and supported with comments on their effect. Only one point is made about the structure and, although it is supported, there is no comment on effect.

Presentational and structural features

To improve your answer, make sure you identify features in the activity before you read the text. Then for each feature that you mention, name the feature, give an example and make a comment. This will keep you on track throughout your answer and the more of these you can do in the time allowed (which will be about 10 minutes) the better. Practise seeing how many of these three-part sentences you can do in 10 minutes. Also make sure that you look at the question carefully to see if you are being asked about presentational features, structure or both.

What have I learnt?

Discuss or jot down what you now know about:

- finding presentational features
- commenting on presentational features
- finding structural features
- commenting on structural features
- answering the question
- what makes the difference between a good answer and an excellent one.

Putting it into practice

- You can practise these skills with any text you come across.
- Take a few minutes to identify some presentational features.
- Take a few minutes to identify some structural features.
- Practise writing sentences where you name the feature, give an example and make a comment.

7 Collate and compare

My learning ▶

This lesson will help you to:
- make comparisons within and between texts
- select material to answer the question.

Introducing collating and comparing

Collate

Collate means putting more than one thing together. If the exam question is aimed at the 'collate' part of this Assessment Objective, you might be asked to choose your own material from several texts and then answer an activity based on the material you have chosen.

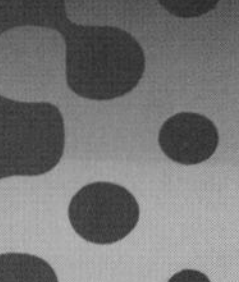

Top tips

In the exam you are likely to be asked to:
- compare material in two texts
- make a comparison by choosing which texts to compare.

Compare

One of the questions in the Reading paper is very likely to ask you to **compare**. This means:

- find similarities
- find differences
- find similarities within differences
- find differences within similarities.

You don't know before you see the question paper what you are going to be asked to compare. It might be, for example:

- how information is presented in more than one text
- the purpose of and audience for more than one text
- how language is used
- presentational devices
- the similarities and differences between two similar stories.

Note: if the question asks you to make 'cross-references' – this means make comparisons.

Top tips

- Always find your material in the two texts first. Then find some clear similarities and some clear differences.
- These words and phrases are sometimes useful when you are comparing:
  both texts... *each text...*
  on the other hand... *however....*

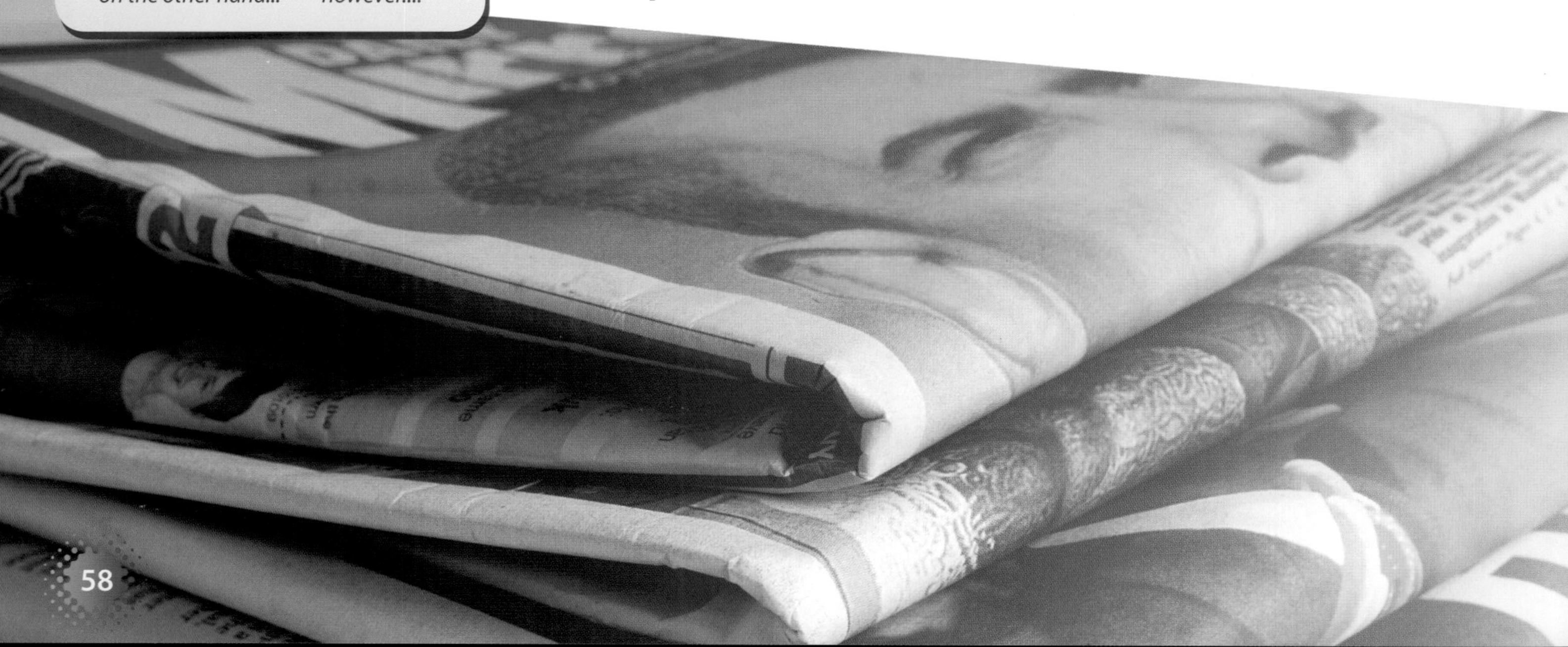

The most straightforward compare activity is when you have one short text and are comparing two things in it. Activity 1 is an example of this sort of activity.

Top tip

- In Activity 1, you could start by looking at the kinds of words used and then find some similarities and/or differences.

Activity 1

Read the text below and then answer the following question:

Compare the language used in the first seven paragraphs with the language used by Sarah Colclough and Nigel Pickard. What are the effects on the reader of these differences?

DAILY STAR

KIDS TV GETS TOUCHY-FEELY

Tots tune in to Hippy-Tubbies

TV's new Tellytubby-style characters are a bunch of tree-hugging hippies.

The touchy-feely series *Waybuloo* sees fluffy family the Piplings doing yoga and embracing each other.

The show for toddlers stars four animated characters, Lau Lau, De Li, Nok Tok and Yojojo.

Each character, representing a particular quality or emotion, bounces through a cartoon countryside trying to achieve a state of happiness called Buloo.

Simple

If they feel truly happy or make their pals feel better they begin to float.

They even interact with children – known as Cheebies – by addressing toddlers and parents at home.

■ by **VICTORIA RICHARDS**

Those watching are encouraged to join in with 'yogo' exercises, which are simple yoga moves for two to five-year-olds.

Sarah Colclough, executive producer for CBeebies, said 'We were looking for a concept that would bring together that elusive notion of children's emotions.

'It is an extremely distinctive programme in that way. Each show teaches about friendship, co-operation and citizenship,' she added.

'The heart of the programme is about encouraging children to be happy. At the launch the children watching were utterly mesmerised.'

Nigel Pickard, director of family entertainment at programme maker RDF, said Waybuloo would show children how they can 'work together to become positive and content'.

OLD SCHOOL: Tellytubbies

Check your answer

Did you:

- find several language features to compare
- make some clear comparisons
- write about the effect on the reader?

In Activity 1 you made comparisons within a text. A different kind of comparison is where you compare how the material in two different texts about the same topic is presented.

Activity 2

Read the texts opposite then answer the following question:

Compare the ways the writers present attitudes to women in these two articles.

Begin by:

- identifying attitudes to women in the two texts
- thinking about similarities and differences between these attitudes.

There may well be more than one attitude in each text because there may be attitudes from different people.

THE TIMES

Jeanette Winterson

The new laureate shows how far we have come

The story goes that when Ted Hughes died in 1999 and Britain needed a new poet laureate, Tony Blair stepped in and told the mandarins who decide these things that the people were not ready for Carol Ann Duffy.

She was, and still is, a woman. She was, and still is, gay. Too much all at once for Little Britain. The laureateship went to Andrew Motion. He has done a lot for poetry over the past ten years, and we should celebrate him, but he was a safe pair of hands. Duffy will be wilder, stranger, and pretty exciting.

The poet laureate is a political appointment as well as a poetical one. Not only does the laureate have to write poems to order – and Duffy, like Hughes, will no doubt have to do a royal wedding – he, and now she, becomes part of the Establishment.

Motion, as a tall white male, well mannered and uncontroversial, left-wing but not radical, fitted the politics of the past decade – the Blairite love of consensus. That Duffy can now be both part of the Establishment and a popular choice is an indicator of how we British have become used to difference. Female, gay and, let's not forget, from the North of Britain, never used to tick the boxes. Now it does.

We are used to concentrating on how bad everything is – the economy, the state of politics, education, social fragmentation, but the fact is that we are becoming more tolerant and more inclusive.

Our cultural attitudes are changing. When David Cameron admitted that he had taken drugs in his youth, nobody really worried about it – that wasn't how to judge him. Such tolerance would have been unthinkable even ten years ago. It's a cause for celebration that we, as a nation, can take the broader view of someone's character and their achievements. In particular, gender and sexuality are no longer the barrier that they were.

Duffy published her first collection of poetry, *Standing Female Nude*, in 1985, the same year that I published *Oranges Are Not the Only Fruit*. To be a woman, to be gay, and to have serious literary ambitions was in itself a challenge to the status quo.

Immediately you were in a niche – women's poetry, lesbian fiction – horrible little reductive categories designed to keep women in their place, and our place, creatively, was a long way below the men.

Nearly 25 years later such attitudes, while still around, are not everywhere, and not interesting. Women have made enormous leaps forward in every field, and gay is getting to be less and less of a defining statement, and more like background information, which is right.

These days we all know someone who is gay, just as we all know someone who is a single parent, divorced, in a mixed marriage. Even *Daily Mail* readers seem to be able to cope.

Poetic justice: a gay woman is the people's choice

There are still pockets of resistance. Sandi Toksvig tells a story of an old buffer at the BBC coming up to her and saying: 'So how does it feel to be a woman and the presenter of *The News Quiz*?' She replied: 'Well I've been a woman for 50 years, so that feels fine…'

Duffy is 54. She is a role model for older women, creative women, successful women and aspiring women. This ends the male domination of poetry, and it buries any lingering doubts about women's creativity somehow not being quite up to the male mark. As a political appointment it is a sign that we have come a long way in a short time.

Carol Ann Duffy turned out to be the people's poet after all. Her work is first rate, but she has the popular touch. No more gay ghettos, no more 'women's writing'. Just the best person for the job.

That's poetic justice.

Daily Mail

Psst! Heard the news?

Women really listen only to gossip and other people's conversations

Daily Mail Reporter

IF YOU want to gain a woman's full attention, make sure you've got a juicy piece of scandal to pass on.

According to a survey, more than two-thirds of women admit they pay full attention to conversations only when they are gossiping.

The same proportion, 67 per cent, think they hear most intently when they are trying to eavesdrop on tittle-tattle taking place nearby.

By contrast, only half of men said they listen intently to gossip, while a mere 41 per cent admitted to listening closely to others' conversations.

A survey of 2,000 respondents also found that only 21 per cent of men reckon they always listen carefully to every word, with just 19 per cent of women saying the same. Five per cent of women admitted to hearing only the odd word here and there.

Women are also more likely to switch off when listening to their work colleagues, with the average woman catching what even the boss says only two-thirds of the time.

They really hear only 70 per cent of the conversations they have with their partner.

But when it comes to talking to their best friend, women give their full attention to more than three-quarters of what is spoken.

Researchers also revealed that 84 per cent of Britons think they are good listeners, with 20 per cent saying they listen to every word.

And 58 per cent think speaking face to face is the best form of communication.

The research was carried out for Siemens Hearing Instruments, which found that 66 per cent of women admitted they had never had a hearing test – compared with 55 per cent of men. And 46 per cent of both sexes confessed they sometimes struggle to hear what others are saying.

Audiologist Wendy Davies said: 'You don't have to be old to lose your hearing – loud clubbing and high volume on your MP3 can damage ears, so it's important to have regular tests.

'If it *is* hearing loss, don't panic. Hearing aids are very different to the beige bananas that granny used to wear.

'Today, you can get funky models the size of a chilli bean.'

Check your answer

Did you:

- find several different attitudes
- find some points of similarity
- find some points of difference
- find similarity within difference
- find difference within similarity
- make clear comparisons throughout your answer?

Planning for a 'compare' question

This lesson will help you to:
- plan an answer to a 'compare' question
- compare texts across several criteria.

In the exam you might be given a comparison where there are several things to do and you are given a list of bullet points to cover. This means that your planning needs to be more detailed in order to make sure that you have covered all the bullets.

Activity 1

1 Read texts A and B and then read the following question:

Compare these texts in terms of the following:
- **their purpose and audience**
- **their language**
- **their use of presentational devices.**

2 Make a plan to answer the question above by copying and completing the following table:

	Text A	Text B
Purpose		
Audience		
Language features		
Presentational features		

In the exam you would probably annotate the text itself on the question paper. You might want to use a code for annotating your texts, such as:

P for purpose
A for audience
L for language
Pr for presentational features

In the exam you might also want to note the name of the features in the margins as you go along.

3 Now answer the question in 1 above.

A

THE TIMES

Sport of Queens

There is democratic glory and no shame in being a royal also-ran at the Festival

Come on Barbers Shop. You were in there with a chance, but you dropped back over the last three fences. The Queen's colours were fluttered in the Cheltenham Gold Cup for the first time yesterday. And even the ranks of Ireland could scarce forbear to cheer. When they inherited George VI's stable, the Queen took the Flat, and her mother the Jumps. The Queen, an infrequent visitor, was last at Cheltenham six years ago to unveil the bust of her mother. She had ring-fenced her engagements yesterday in order to watch Barbers Shop, whom she inherited from her mother, jump well: but just not well enough.

Horses and royals go together like divorce and marriage. For racing is the one sport where the monarchy plays on a fairly level track beside its subjects. Both horses and royalty depend on bloodlines. Both royalty and horses rely on the affection of the punters and the support of the bookies, or ministers. Both are constrained to run down constitutional rails between prescribed limits with regular turns, jumps or hurdles.

Boadicea was the first equestrian queen to be recorded in the form book, though the Roman Jockey Club considered the scythes on her chariot wheels an early example of nobbling. Henry VIII imported the royal stud; Charles II wrote the rules for racing at Newmarket; Queen Anne invented royal Ascot, and rode down the course in her best hat to start the meeting. Democracy has replaced absolute monarchy. But hippocracy – horses rule, OK? – is still a British peculiar.

Yesterday the Queen experienced Cheltenham: to race, to jump, to bet and not to win. But has she caught the spring fever of a national celebration? Better luck next year, Ma'am.

B

DAILY STAR

UNION JACKASSES

8ft pole too dangerous to fly flag for hero Brit troops

■ by JERRY LAWTON

BUREAU-PRATS have banned the Union flag from flying in honour of our troops because the 8ft pole is too dangerous to climb.

For 453 years a flag has proudly flown over the Town Hall in Bourne, Lincs, to mark Armed Forces Day and the Queen's birthday.

But now the council has banned it on health and safety grounds.

Town hall bigwigs say it is too risky for a member of staff to climb a ladder to unfurl the flag.

They have also banned the flag of St George on patron saint's day.

Fury erupted last night as residents and war veterans condemned the move.

Former mayor Brian Fines, 72, a former Army Lieutenant Colonel, raged: 'What a sad and sick society we're becoming.

Life

'This despotic government's health and safety laws have prevented the council flying a flag from the building that's the hub of our town.

'We are told they're not allowed to use a ladder to access the mast. It's annoying and upsetting a lot of people.'

Councillor Fines spent 30 years with the Royal Electrical and Mechanical Engineers before running engineering firms in the private sector.

He said: 'I've been in charge of engineering businesses employing hundreds of people. Health and safety has been my bread and butter.

'But it shouldn't be about someone sitting in an office and saying no.

'It seems it's permeating every aspect of life. It's like a cancer.'

Mayor Shirley Cliffe said: 'I just don't understand it. A lot of the public are upset.

'It's the first time the flag won't be flown. It's disgusting. It's essential that we fly the flag to help celebrate occasions such as these.'

Local decorator Phil Sargent, 47, added: 'If climbing ladders is so dangerous I'd have been out of business or dead years ago.'

A spokesman for South Kesteven District Council insisted: 'The process involves our site manager climbing an 8ft ladder which rests on a plinth overlooking a spiked gate. We think this is too risky.'

POLAXED! It's 'too risky' to fly flag in Bourne

Check your answer

Did you:

- find more than one thing to say about each bullet
- support your points by referring to the details in the texts
- make clear comparisons throughout?

Assessment practice

This lesson will help you to:
- practise an exam-style question
- assess your answer by looking at other responses.

Now you are going to have a go at an exam-style question. Attempt Activity 1 in the time suggested and then complete the Peer/Self-assessment activity that follows. Activity 1 asks you to make comparisons and also to link your comments on content, language and presentation to purpose and audience. This means that you need to find your material on content, language and presentation first, so that you can link it to purpose and audience and at the same time compare the two articles.

Activity 1

Read texts A and B on pages 64–66. They are on the same story, published on the same day but in different newspapers. The first (A) was published in *The Guardian*, the second (B) was published in *Metro*, a free newspaper. Note: 'gravy train' means making money without much effort.

Now take 15 minutes to answer the following question:

Compare these two accounts, showing how choices of content, language and presentational devices are linked to purpose and audience.

A

The gravy train must stop – PM orders expenses shakeup

Eve of budget move to reform MP payments amid backlash fears

Patrick Wintour
Political Editor

Gordon Brown's sudden announcement yesterday that he intends to rush through reform of the much-criticised system of MPs expenses came after he was warned by Labour whips that the party would lose support unless he acted within weeks.

He was told that the publication in July of about 1m expenses claims dating back four years would generate a wave of public anger and a damaging backlash against the government and politicians in general.

Yesterday's move infuriated some backbenchers and was criticised as 'half-baked' by a former cabinet minister, but the package – disclosed on the eve of today's budget – is likely to be pushed through the Commons next week as opposition leaders recognise the danger of resisting change.

The scrapping of the much-abused £24,000-a-year second home allowance is the biggest reform among a raft of measures that Brown hopes will cut costs.

Instead, MPs would be able to claim an allowance based on daily attendance at Westminster, which could be worth up to £150 a day tax-free – prompting concern from the Liberal Democrat leader, Nick Clegg, about bringing the 'Brussels gravy train' to Westminster.

The clocking-on proposal, aired via a surprise posting by Brown on YouTube, will be pushed through the Commons next Thursday. The prime minister will hold talks with the opposition leaders, David Cameron and Clegg, and it looks as if the two men will have little choice but to accept the package foisted on them yesterday.

The whips warned Brown that the electoral damage looming in July could only be contained if the whole system of MPs' expenses had been radically reformed by then.

Brown had been working to a more leisurely timetable, but the whips said the whole system needed to be overhauled before the claims were released.

He had initially asked Sir Christopher Kelly, the chairman of the committee on standards in public life, to report on a new system after the election, later asking him to report by the end of this year.

Kelly, who was only told of the prime minister's speedier plans yesterday morning, insisted 'an in-house quick fix by politicians' will not satisfy the tide of public anger. Due to launch his inquiry tomorrow, Kelly insisted any agreement reached by MPs next week should only be seen as an interim solution.

Brown's new scheme will consist of a 'simpler and less generous' system of perks, including a daily fixed-rate attendance allowance based on MPs being at Westminster or in their ministerial offices.

The level of that daily allowance will be fixed by the senior salaries review body, and may not even be known when MPs vote next week. Downing Street insisted the overall effect of the reform will be that, on average, MPs receive less money, and that the overall cost to the taxpayer will also be lower, partly because as many as 80 London-based MPs will not receive an attendance allowance.

To achieve savings, the allowance will have to be well below £150 for each day the Commons sits.

The reform, Brown said, would show voters that MPs were 'there to serve the public, not there to serve themselves', adding that he no longer met any young people who wanted to go into politics.

Those MPs who live within a reasonable distance of Westminster will be given a flat rate supplement of £7,500 a year on top of their salary of £63,291, and office costs, so in effect requiring them to commute to Westminster each day.

No second homes allowance will be available to ministers with access to grace and favour homes. In addition, all staff taken on by MPs, including family members, will become 'direct employees' of the House of Commons which will be responsible for their terms, conditions and salaries.

All receipts for claims, no matter how small, will have to be published.

In an attempt to wrong-foot the Tories, Brown also proposed that all MPs would have to publish the exact income they receive from outside directorships and jobs, whether they relate to their parliamentary duties or not.

Cameron faced a revolt in his shadow cabinet when he proposed the reform: as many as a third of Tory MPs have outside consultancies.

Yesterday, Cameron welcomed the proposals as a significant U-turn. But both Cameron and Clegg also expressed serious reservations about whether introducing a 'Brussels-style' attendance allowance was the best way to restore public faith that MPs were not milking the system. Clegg said: 'MPs will be getting a blank cheque just for turning up to work in the morning.'

One former cabinet minister also condemned the reforms as 'half-baked', saying it would mean MPs hanging around the Commons until Thursday morning, clocking on and then rushing back to their constituencies. He also predicted it would create real difficulties for young MPs.

John Mann, a Labour backbencher who has angered his colleagues by calling for reform, claimed the changes could save as much as £20m a year for the taxpayer, insisting MPs had to take a hit in a recession.

Ministers will be whipped to support the government measures, but backbenchers will be free to vote as they wish next week.

Gordon Brown at No 10 yesterday. The prime minister was warned expenses could cost Labour support

B

METRO

'Gravy train' is arriving for MPs

By **Fred Attewill**

MPs could make even more money under emergency proposals to scrap their controversial second home allowance in favour of a daily payment.

They may be in pocket if they turn up every day, despite losing the £24,000-a-year handout under new rules Gordon Brown said would be 'simpler and less generous'.

Their daily attendance allowance is likely to be similar to the £174 paid to Lords who have to stay in the capital overnight. If they make it to all 143 sittings of parliament in a year they will collect a total of £24,882.

MPs will be paid thousands of pounds more if the figure is set nearer the £247 a day given to members of the European parliament, who simply have to turn up to sign a register, without showing they stayed all day.

MPs will be paid simply for turning up at work

Liberal Democrat leader Nick Clegg – himself a former MEP – said the new system risked 'bringing the Brussels gravy train to Westminster'.

Mr Brown was stung into action by an investigation into home secretary Jacqui Smith, who since 2001 has claimed £150,304 for the cost of running her 'second home' in her Redditch constituency while listing her main home as a London flat she shares with her sister.

Last month, Mr Brown had insisted MPs' allowances were an issue for sleaze watchdog, the Committee on Standards in Public Life.

But his apparent U-turn came as he outlined the changes in a YouTube video. His proposals also included making MPs' staff employees of the Commons and a tightening of the rules on declaring other incomes.

Earlier, communities secretary Hazel Blears gave a sneak preview of the plans when she left a cabinet meeting with the paperwork on show.

Mr Brown said the Commons could vote on the issue as early as next week as he admitted 'the country has lost confidence in the current system'.

He will meet Conservative leader David Cameron and Mr Clegg today to discuss the plans. But Mr Clegg said: 'The great danger is… you are giving MPs a cheque simply for turning up for work and the MPs don't have to prove they need that money.'

Peer/Self-assessment activity

1 Check your answer to Activity 1.
Did you:
- find several points about content
- find several language features
- find several presentation features
- link each point to purpose and audience?

2 Now assess your answer to Activity 1 using the criteria below. Before you do this you might like to read some sample answers to this activity on pages 68 and 69.

Good

- clear and effective attempt to engage with activity
- range of relevant points
- content, language and presentational devices all covered
- clear links to purpose and audience.

Very strong

- full and detailed grasp of content, language and presentation
- material absorbed and shaped for purpose
- good understanding of the material
- material consistently linked to purpose and audience.

Excellent

- full, detailed, conceptualised comparisons
- material fully absorbed and shaped for purpose
- full understanding of the material
- comparative material coherently linked to purpose and audience.

GradeStudio

Here are two student answers to the activity on page 64:
Compare these two accounts, showing how choices of content, language and presentational devices are linked to purpose and audience.
Read the answers together with the comments. Then check what you have learnt and try putting it into practice.

Extract from an answer rated 'Very strong'

Extract from Student A

These two articles take a very different angle on the same basic story. The shorter one in *Metro*, aimed at the general reader, explains how MPs could be much better off under the new system by getting a daily attendance allowance, but the one in *The Guardian* is aimed at the reader of a quality newspaper and explains how the expenses system needs to be changed and includes a great deal more detail. The *Metro* story uses some dramatic phrases such as 'stung into action' and 'sleaze watchdog' whereas *The Guardian* one seems to rely on more clichés such as 'much-criticised', 'damaging backlash', 'much-abused', 'pushed through', 'foisted on them', 'damage looming' and 'interim solution'. The article in *The Guardian* is a long and detailed account of Gordon Brown's proposed reforms, but the *Metro* shows how changing the system of paying allowances will make them even better off. The article in *The Guardian* seems to be praising and supporting the Prime Minister whereas the one in *Metro* only mentions him very briefly. Both headlines use the phrase 'the gravy train' but while *The Guardian* says it must stop, *Metro* says it is arriving. The Labour-supporting *The Guardian* has a large picture of the Prime Minister but *Metro* has no pictures. Its use of quotations only from Mr Clegg suggests that it supports the Liberal Democrat position.

Comparison of content

Supported

Comparison of language supported

Precise comparison of content

Comparison of attitude

Comparison of language

Supported

Comparison of presentation

Comparison of purpose and audience

Teacher comment

This answer concentrates mainly on content but makes an effective and detailed comparison of language, linking it to purpose and audience.

Extract from an answer rated 'Excellent'

Extract from Student B

Both political reports are about reform to MPs expenses. The one in *The Guardian* seems to support the Prime Minister, focusing on his reforms, whereas the one in *Metro* takes the angle that MPs will be much better off after the proposed reforms. The traditionally Labour-supporting *The Guardian* features a large picture of the Prime Minister, but *Metro* has no such illustrations. Both have the colloquial 'gravy train' in their headline; *The Guardian* says it must stop but *Metro* says it is just arriving, suggesting that *Metro* is not supporting Labour or the Prime Minister, particularly as it quotes his own words ('simpler and less generous') to suggest that he is a hypocrite. *The Guardian*'s use of the same words is much more favourable to Mr Brown. There is some informal language and jargon in *Metro* ('scrap', 'handout', 'stung into action', 'U-turn', 'sneak preview') and some in *The Guardian* ('backlash', 'raft') but *The Guardian*'s sentences are more complex and less emotive, again supporting its backing of Mr Brown, as opposed to *Metro*'s criticism. Both articles are aimed at educated readers who like reading political articles, but the *Metro* has less political bias.

Comparison of purpose

Comparison of presentation

Supported

Comparison of purpose

Comparison of language

Language

Purpose

Comparison of language and purpose

Compared and supported

Comparison of language

Comparison of purpose

Language

Comparison of audience

Teacher comment

This answer is focused directly on the task and relates its comments about language and presentation to purpose and to audience at the end. All the bullets are covered and there is some well-observed supporting detail.

Collate and compare

To improve your answer, read the question carefully to make sure you are clear about exactly what you have to compare. Find the material in the texts and be sure to cover all parts of the question. Make comparisons throughout your answer.

What have I learnt?

Discuss or jot down what you now know about:

- making comparisons and comparing purpose and audience
- comparing content, language and presentation
- answering the question.

Putting it into practice

- You can practise these skills with any text you come across.
- Take a few minutes to compare texts.
- Practise finding detailed and precise points of comparison.

Section B Writing

Introduction

This section aims to encourage you to develop your writing skills. The teaching, texts, activities and tips are all focused on helping you improve your writing.

This part of your course encourages you to write for different purposes and audiences and to make some choices about how you write. Successful writers make all kinds of choices: not just who they are writing for and the purpose of the text, but what kind of language would be best to use, and what kinds of presentational devices would help the reader to take in what is written.

We write all the time, but what we write isn't always formal. We write lists, notes for people, text messages and emails to friends. But these also have their own conventions and they are no use if they can't be understood by the person reading them.

The different chapters look at specific aspects of writing, one at a time. But we don't often write like this. We need to have in mind all the different skills all the time and that is what this book is aiming to help you to do.

In the exam you will have to do two pieces of writing, most probably for different purposes and maybe for different audiences, so practising the skills individually in the following chapters will help you to have all the different skills in place when the day of the exam comes.

Assessment Objectives

The Assessment Objectives underpin everything you will learn about and be tested upon. It is vital that you understand what these are asking of you. So, here are the Assessment Objectives that relate to the Writing part of your exam together with comments to help you understand what they are.

- Write to communicate clearly and effectively using and adapting forms and selecting vocabulary appropriate to task and purpose in ways that engage the reader.
- Organise information and ideas into structured and sequenced sentences, paragraphs and whole texts, using a variety of linguistic and structural features to support cohesion and overall coherence.
- Use a range of sentence structures for clarity, purpose and effect, with accurate punctuation and spelling.

This Assessment Objective asks you to make what you have to say clear and to write in such a way that the readers will be interested in what you write because you have chosen appropriate and interesting language.

This Assessment Objective means that the whole text needs to hang together. Paragraphs, particularly links between paragraphs, will help you to do this as will writing which is clearly organised and sequenced. You are writing in timed conditions in the exam, but you always need to think about how long your text needs to be to do the job properly, so that it ends up just the right length for the readers to take in what you need them to take in.

This final Assessment Objective is about technical accuracy and variety. This is where many students fail to do as well as they could because they don't proof read their writing carefully enough. Remember that in the exam it's the quality and accuracy of the writing that matter. Crossings out are fine if you find during your checking that you can make improvements and corrections.

Examiner and student concerns

To help you improve your writing it is helpful to know what concerns examiners and students most about the Writing section of the exam. Below is a list of some of the concerns that they have.

What concerns examiners?

- Clear focus on the task throughout. Some answers have too much material which is not necessary; others don't develop their points.
- Technical errors such as spelling and punctuation.
- It's not always easy to see where the writing is going.
- Students sometimes write all they can think of rather than selecting what is going to be most effective.

What concerns students?

- How much should I write?
- I don't have time to check.
- Teachers always tell us to plan but there's not enough time.
- I have so much to say I just want to get it all down.

My learning

This lesson will help you to:
- plan, write and check effectively in different forms and for different audiences
- adapt the level of formality in your writing.

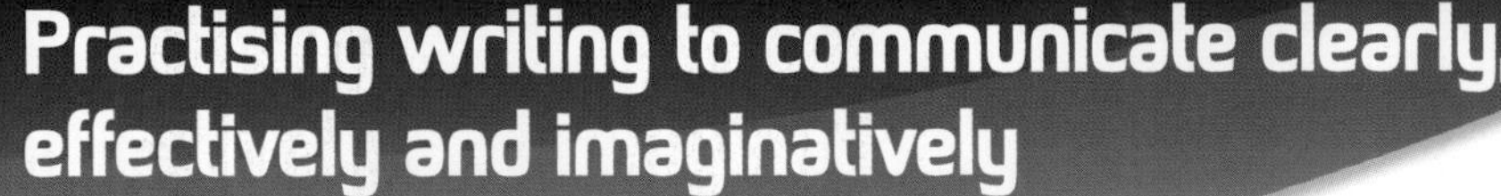

Practising writing to communicate clearly, effectively and imaginatively

There are several things you need to consider when you are doing a writing activity in the exam. You need to think about:

- what exactly the question is asking you to do
- the purpose of the text you are writing
- the audience it is for
- how to structure your answer
- how to use appropriate language
- what presentational devices you need to use
- how to interest the reader in what you write.

Activity 1

Here is some information, in a random order, about Hampton Court. Read the information then complete the activity below.

Write a short entry about Hampton Court for a tourist guide. Make sure that you:

- **plan carefully so that you can give information in a clear and logical order**
- **interest the reader by using your own words when you want to**
- **persuade the reader that Hampton Court would be a good place to visit.**

You don't have to include all the information given opposite; choose what you think is appropriate for your purpose and audience.

Hampton Court

- It was extended in the late 17th century for William and Mary.
- The new buildings were designed by Sir Christopher Wren.
- George II had a suite made in the middle of his palace for his son, the Duke of Cumberland, which he moved into at the age of 11.
- Hampton Court was one of the first buildings in England to be built with running water, drawn from a spring a few miles away.
- It was a model of modern hygenic living, all waste matter being taken by sewers to be dumped into the Thames.
- Henry VIII rebuilt and enlarged the palace after 1530.
- Hampton Court is by the Thames in Hampton in south west London.
- Queen Victoria opened the palace to the public in 1838.
- It was built by Cardinal Wolsey and begun in 1514.
- The original chimney pots are all different from each other.
- The nursery rhyme 'Mary, Mary, quite contrary' refers to the rebuilding of Hampton Court for Queen Mary.
- The original Tudor kitchens are well worth a visit.

Check your answer

Did you:
- think carefully about the audience and purpose of your text
- present the information clearly
- use some persuasive language?

- Wren had several of his favourite artists working at Hampton Court – Jean Tijou (who designed the wrought iron Trophy Gates), Grinling Gibbons (one of the greatest woodcarvers the world has ever known), Antonio Verrio (who painted the Grand Staircase and several ceilings) and James Thornhill (best known for painting the inside of the dome of St Paul's Cathedral and the Painted Hall in Greenwich).
- Queen Mary was a keen gardener and had the gardens at Hampton Court redesigned.
- The maze dates from 1714.
- The palace is huge and even though you can only visit a small part of it, a thorough visit takes a whole day.

Activity 2

The way you write will depend very much on the audience and purpose of your text. This means that you might well choose different kinds of language and sentence structures if the audience is different.

Now draw from the same information in Activity 1, to write for a very different audience (a specific one this time) and a different purpose.

Imagine that a relative is planning to visit London for a few days and that he or she has asked you to recommend somewhere interesting to visit. Write an email to your relative explaining why you think he or she should visit Hampton Court.

Top tips

- Because this is an email to a relative you might well want to use some less **formal language**. How **informal** your language is will, of course, depend on what your relative is like and how he or she would expect you to write. For example, to a relative you know well you might write: 'You've got to see Hampton Court – it's cool!' Whereas, a more formal example might be: 'You really should visit Hampton Court as it is one of London's best attractions.'
- You don't have to include all the information about Hampton Court this time. Select what you think is appropriate but make sure that you explain why your relative should visit.

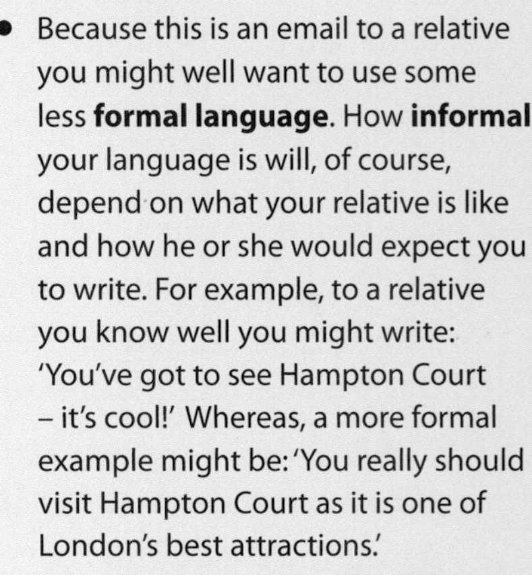

Check your answer

Did you:

- select material appropriate for your chosen relative
- explain why they should visit
- use a range of sentence structures
- use interesting vocabulary
- check your work for accuracy in punctuation, spelling and grammar?

This lesson will help you to:

- communicate effectively, clearly and imaginatively
- assess your answer by looking at other responses.

Assessment practice

In the exam you will be asked to write two pieces, each of which will take you about 30 minutes. It may be that you are asked to write pieces of different lengths – perhaps a shorter piece which will take about 20 minutes and a longer one which will take about 40 minutes.

While you are preparing for the exam you will need plenty of practice of writing to time. Remember that your writing will be much better if you plan first and decide what information you are going to use, and in which order. So 5 minutes should be spent planning and you need to allow a few minutes when you have finished for checking, finding and correcting any errors you might have made.

Attempt Activities 1 and 2 to give yourself practice in writing two texts in exam-style conditions and then complete the Peer/Self-assessment activity that follows.

Activity 1

In the activities in the previous lesson you used the same information to create two different kinds of text – one which informed and persuaded and one which informed. Now you are going to use your own experience and information which you have in your head to create a text advertising a place which you know well.

Spend 25 minutes doing the following activity:

You have been asked to create a part of a tourist information leaflet persuading people to visit somewhere you know well.

You need to:

- **give information about the place**
- **detail its attractions**
- **explain how to get there**
- **persuade people to visit.**

If you decide that you need presentational devices, you don't need to draw them in detail. Just show what you want the advertisement to look like by using a labelled diagram. For instance, you could draw a box and then say what you want to appear in it.

Activity 2

Now attempt the following activity. You are allowed 30 minutes, 5 of which should be spent planning and 3 of which should be spent checking carefully.

'People talk far too much about the dreadful effects of climate change. They should just enjoy its benefits.' Write an article for a magazine arguing for or against this view.

Peer/Self-assessment activity

1 Check your answer to Activity 2. Did you:
- argue for or against
- plan and sequence your ideas effectively
- write it as an article
- make clear which magazine you were writing for
- write clearly, accurately and stylishly?

2 Now assess your answer to Activity 2 using the criteria opposite. You will need to be careful and precise in your marking. Before you do this you might like to read some sample answers to this activity on pages 76 and 77.

Communication and organisation

Good
- form, content and style are generally matched to purpose and audience
- increasing sophistication in vocabulary choice and phrasing
- well structured
- effective paragraphing with links between paragraphs.

Very strong
- form, content and style consistently matched to purpose and audience
- evidence of conscious crafting
- coherently structured
- fluently linked sentence structures and paragraphs.

Excellent
- form, content and style assuredly matched to purpose and audience
- controlled and sustained crafting
- highly effective and delightful vocabulary choices
- distinctive and consistently effective.

Sentence structure, punctuation and spelling

Good
- uses a range of sentence forms for effect
- generally accurate spelling of commonly used words and of more complex words
- generally accurate punctuation.

Very strong
- uses full range of sentence structures accurately
- high level of technical accuracy in spelling of commonly used and complex words (with occasional lapses)
- high level of technical accuracy in range of punctuation marks (with occasional lapses).

Excellent
- uses full range of sentence structures accurately and effectively
- near perfect technical accuracy in spelling of wide range of complex words
- near perfect technical accuracy in punctuation.

GradeStudio

Here are two student answers to the activity on page 74:
'People talk far too much about the dreadful effects of climate change. They should just enjoy its benefits.' Write an article for a magazine arguing for or against this view.
Read the following answers together with the comments. Then check what you have learnt and try putting it into practice.

Extract from an answer rated 'Excellent'

Extract from Student A

For *Shout* magazine
Celebs: Who Cares about the Climate?
Earlier this week there was an uproar in every normal, working-class home in the world.
Or was there?
I certainly hope so. During an interview with racing driver L J Bennett and mega stars Candydolls, a gathering of some of the hottest people alive, they were all asked about what their suggestions were for climate change.
Now I can totally bring myself to understand why they were all quiet for a few moments, but when sports sensation Bennett answered on a chat show, LIVE, I have to be honest with you girls, I wasn't impressed. His exact words were:
'People talk far too much about the dreadful effects of climate change. They should just enjoy its benefits!'
He's perhaps one of biggest names in the sporting industry right now. He spends his life inside a car. What sort of climate change is he looking forward to?
Now if any of you had seen the reaction of pop wonders Candydolls, I hope you were listening when they said that it's laid back chumps like Bennett who make climate change an even bigger problem. Thankfully someone had their head screwed on.
You girls have been reading my articles for months. You're well aware of how passionate I get with important issues. So listen up.
The human race is the ultimate race; we rule, men and women alike. So when the climate started to change, when floods and heatwaves increased, who was to blame? Us. Millions of people started dying prematurely. When people die of climate change in the future, who will be to blame? Us.
Just because you girls didn't start it, it doesn't mean you're not responsible for the chain of events which follows. Because of what my generation did it's down to you girls. And guys of course. Because things really are that bad. A fuss is necessary, girls.
The celebs failed you this week...
Don't fail the planet.

Challenging start – clear article following headline

Effective vocabulary for chosen magazine

Quotation correctly punctuated

Variety of sentence structure; paragraphs effective for magazine article

Range of rhetorical devices

Very well structured

Punchy ending

Teacher comment

This is a clear article with language, sentence structures and content thoroughly appropriate for the readership. The paragraphing, headline and structure are all perfectly matched to the purpose and audience. It is technically accurate.

Extract from an answer rated 'Good'

Extract from Student B

Since the earth was created it has been changing and evolving, creating new plants and new life.
It is believed that we humans were evolved from chimps and with evolution, plus our superior minds, comes development.
Whether it was fate, destiny or even God, humans were inevitably going to be the most dangerous animals on the planet.
If we have caused climate change today, then what caused climate change millions of years ago? I'm pretty sure that we didn't have gas guzzling four by fours and jumbo jets at the time when dinosaurs roamed the earth.
What caused the ice age, then? Or CO2 emissions? Who knows.
I believe that the earth will always be changing no matter what we do, so all we can do is accept it.
~~OK.~~ So, yeah, I suppose we could do a bit of recycling now and again and getting proper insulation wouldn't hurt us, but as always, things have to end ~~sometime,~~ its not a question of how can we stop it. But when will it happen?
So I say don't worry, ~~chill, sit back and relax~~ because the earth will heal in time and plants will evolve and animals will evolve and WE will evolve. It will be tough, but trust me when I say, be glad that you're along for the ride and everything will work out for the best.
Now I'm not saying that life itself will have a fairy tale ending, but ~~also, it~~ won't be wiped out with scientists making new discoveries and developments every single day, we just have to be patient and carry on living our lives.

Unnecessary word

Appropriate vocabulary; idea neatly expressed

Rhetorical questions turned into real ones. Range of rhetorical devices

Missing apostrophe

Comma splice

Comma splice

Effective link between paragraphs

Misplaced comma

Comma splice

Teacher comment

This is effectively organised and structured. Form, content and style are generally matched to purpose and audience. There are some effective links between paragraphs. Paragraphs are appropriate for an article. There is some effective vocabulary and phrasing. Spelling is generally accurate. There are sentence forms for effect. Unchecked punctuation errors prevent it from going higher on the second mark.

Writing clearly, effectively and imaginatively

To improve your answer, the closer you can match your writing to purpose and audience the better. Make sure your meaning is always clear. Choose your language and sentence structures carefully to interest the reader.

What have I learnt?

Discuss or jot down what you now know about:

- what the examiners are looking for
- what a mark scheme looks like
- what you are being assessed on in your writing.

Putting it into practice

- You can work through the skills one by one in the chapters that follow.

Organise information and ideas

My learning

This lesson will help you to:
- plan your writing
- sequence your information and ideas.

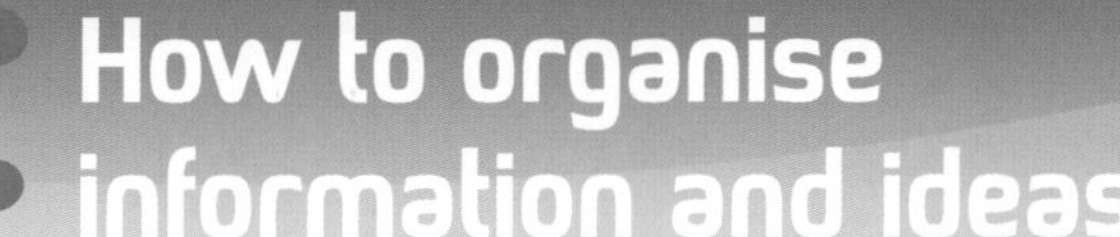

How to organise information and ideas

Successful writing

There are four key stages towards a successful piece of writing:

1 thinking

2 planning

3 writing

4 checking.

Most students have done a lot of work on all four of these when they are preparing for the exam, but when the day comes, often they only do one of them. They write. But thinking your ideas through first and then sequencing and organising them is the real key to success. If you have your ideas ready then you can concentrate on writing them as well as you can and you can make choices about your words, sentences and paragraphs.

Sentence structures

Page 112 looks specifically at using four different kinds of sentence structures:

- simple sentences
- compound sentences
- complex sentences
- minor sentences.

You need to be able to use all four of these in your exam. So if you are not yet confident with sentence structures look carefully at this page.

Paragraphing

Paragraphs help the reader to follow what you are saying because you are dividing your writing into sections. Effective paragraphing:

- divides the writing into sections to make for easy reading
- introduces new aspects of the topic in new paragraphs
- has links between the paragraphs to help the reader follow what you are writing.

How you use paragraphs depends on what kind of text you are writing. For example:

- tabloid newspapers tend to use short paragraphs
- broadsheet newspapers tend to use longer paragraphs
- other articles vary the length of their paragraphs.

So first of all you need to think about what kind of text you are writing. Then you need to develop your ideas. You can do this in the form of a list or a spidergram. Activity 1, on page 80, gives you the opportunity to practise these points.

Beginnings and endings

Your first and last sentences are really important. You want to grab the reader's attention with your first sentence to make the reader want to read on. For example:

> *Banish the lard and get fit.*

is a much more interesting opening sentence than:

> *In this article I am going to write about being healthy by losing weight.*

In the same way the last sentence needs to round off your topic and give the reader something to remember. For example:

> *Blueberries and tofu it is, then, rather than pizza and chips.*

is much more memorable than:

> *Eating healthy food will do you a lot more good than eating a lot of fatty foods.*

Activity 1

Imagine that you have been asked to write a magazine article for a weekend colour supplement about living a healthy lifestyle. Planning is vital because it will help you to decide where your paragraphs are going to be. This activity is mostly about planning – until the very end when you write your article.

1 Decide on your audience(s) – who you are writing for. This will be mainly adults because the magazine comes with a Sunday newspaper. However, there are significant differences in the style and content of the Sunday colour supplements. *The News of the World*, for example, is very different in content, tone, presentation and language from *The Independent on Sunday*. So decide which colour supplement you are going to write for and your writing will be more effective.

2 Develop your ideas on the different aspects of the topic which you can cover. Do this either in the form of a list or a spidergram.

Opposite are some possible ideas to begin with. Add your own to the spidergram.

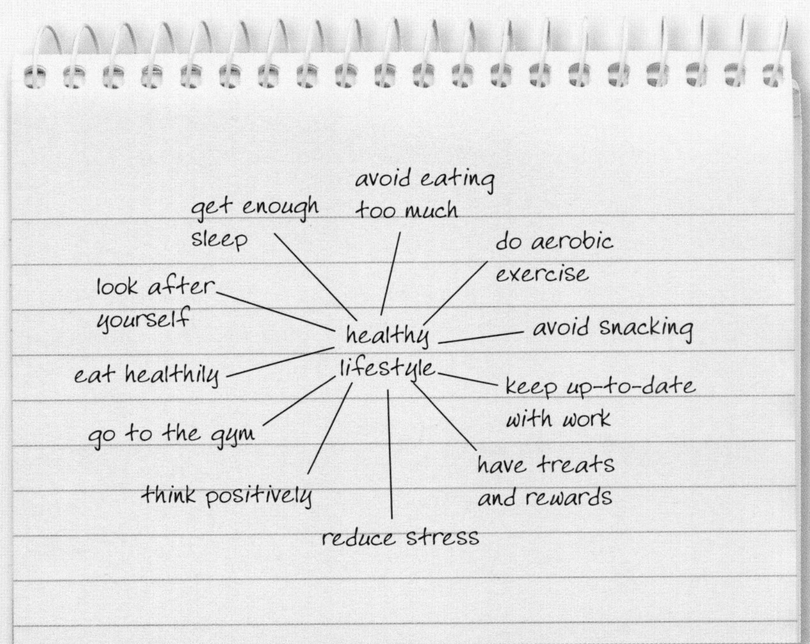

3 Decide which of the ideas in the spidergram you are going to use and then decide the order in which you are going to present your ideas. Number the points in your plan. This will give you the sequence of your paragraphs. Ask yourself:

- which ideas go together
- which can I combine
- which show different aspects of the topic?

4 Decide on your headline. Make sure it's suitable for the magazine you are writing for. You might want to leave some space to put in your headline at the end.

5 Because this is going to be a magazine article you must decide whether you need any other presentational devices such as pictures, graphics, subheadings, boxes, etc. If this activity was in an exam, you would not be expected to draw the graphics, but a box telling the reader what you want where would be a good idea. Decide whether the sort of article you are writing needs subheadings. It's an issue to think about before you start to write.

6 Decide on:

- your first sentence to grab the reader's interest
- your last sentence.

Make sure that you can grab the reader's interest in the first sentence and think about a catchy way to end the article. You can, of course, revise your first and your last sentences when you are checking your writing at the end.

7 Now that you have completed all your planning, write your article about living a healthy lifestyle.

8 When you have finished, check your writing. Can it be improved in any way? Have you corrected any spelling, punctuation or grammar errors?

Top tips

- Include your own ideas in the plan that you write.
- Sequence your ideas by numbering them.
- Decide on your heading before you begin to write.

Check your answer

Did you:

- plan carefully enough
- sequence your ideas
- find links between your paragraphs
- check your article when you had finished writing
- correct any errors of spelling, punctuation, grammar and sentence structure?

My learning

This lesson will help you to:

- improve your answering technique in the exam
- develop your planning, sequencing and linking skills.

Planning exam answers

Answering the question

The process that you go through when you are faced with a writing task in the exam is:

- thinking
- planning
- writing
- checking.

Your initial thinking will create a lot of ideas. In your planning, from all these ideas, you need to decide what you are actually going to use in your answer. The highest marks will be gained by those who match their material most carefully to the demands of the specific task. You must answer the question exactly as it is asked – not as you think it should be phrased.

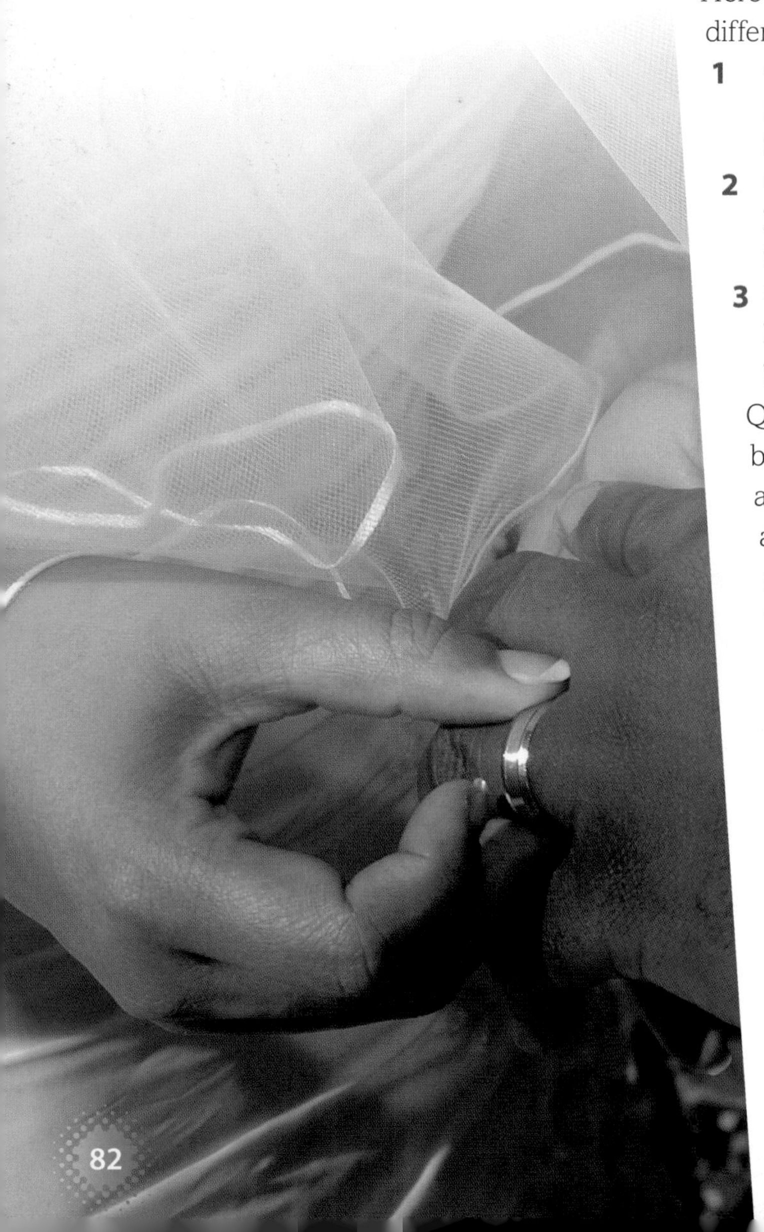

Here are three questions on the same topic which demand different kinds of answers.

1. **'Society would be better and more stable if we all had a system of arranged marriages.' Argue in favour of this view.**
2. **'Society would be better and more stable if we all had a system of arranged marriages.' Argue against this view.**
3. **'Society would be better and more stable if we all had a system of arranged marriages.' How far do you agree with this view?**

Question 1 means that all the material you choose should be in favour of the proposition. You would only use arguments against the view in order to be able to counter and demolish them.

Question 2 means that everything you choose has to be against the proposition. Again, you would only use arguments in favour of the proposition in order to counter them.

Question 3 means that you have to be able to think of arguments for and against the proposition and then to argue your own case. Some students think that this sort of question means you have to sit on the fence and not come to any conclusion, but that is far from the case. It asks 'how far?' That means that you have to make a decision and to support the extent of your agreement or disagreement appropriately.

Activity 1

Imagine that in the exam you have been asked to complete a writing task on the topic of arranged marriages. You will be asked to respond to society being 'better and more stable if we had a system of arranged marriages'.

1 First, jot down all your initial ideas on the topic, either as a list or spidergram. You need to make sure that you plan links between:
   - society being better (you have to define what you think this means) and
   - society being more stable (you have to decide in what ways).
2 Write a plan, sequencing and finding links between points, to the following question:

   'Society would be better and more stable if we all had a system of arranged marriages.' Argue in favour of this view.
3 Write a plan, sequencing and finding links between points, to the following question:

   'Society would be better and more stable if we all had a system of arranged marriages.' Argue against this view.
4 Write a plan, sequencing and finding links between points, to the following question:

   'Society would be better and more stable if we all had a system of arranged marriages.' How far do you agree with this view?

10 Use language and structure

My learning

This lesson will help you to:
- use a range of language features
- structure your writing.

Introducing language and structure

Language

The **language** you use needs to suit your purpose and audience. If, for example, you are writing a letter to an editor of a newspaper, you need to plan it carefully and write it in Standard English. If, on the other hand, you are writing to a friend, you might well use informal English and probably won't plan it carefully.

Structure

The simplest way to think about **structure** is to think about:

- a beginning
- a middle with several stages
- an end.

If you plan your writing, then you can decide what each of these stages is going to be.

Activity 1

Read the advertisement opposite. It is from a brochure put out by the National Trust advertising the trust's attractions in Cornwall. Each page of the brochure is devoted to a different place.

1 Identify each of the different sections and say what its purpose is.
2 A different structural device has been used for each section. Identify the device and say what you think its effect is.
3 Look at the section with bullet points. Identify the words in this section which are designed to persuade the reader that Lanhydrock would be a great place to visit.

Lanhydrock

(in woods and park) Map ref: 9

- Magnificent late Victorian country house, atmospheric home of the Agar-Robartes family
- Fifty rooms to explore, revealing fascinating aspects of life & the inner workings of this wealthy well-run household
- Highlights incl. great kitchen, evocative nursery wing & 17th-century Long Gallery with plaster ceiling depicting biblical scenes
- Large formal & woodland garden incl. Victorian parterre, stunning magnolias, camellias & rhododendrons
- Superb parkland setting in the Fowey valley, with miles of walks through woods & along the river

Gift Aid Admission: Adult £9.90, child £4.95, family £24.75, family (1 adult) £14.85. Groups adult £8.40. Garden & grounds only: adult £5.60, child £2.80.
Nr Bodmin PL30 5AD
E lanhydrock@nationaltrust.org.uk
T 01208 265950 (estate 265211)
Bodmin Parkway 1¾ miles, lovely walk

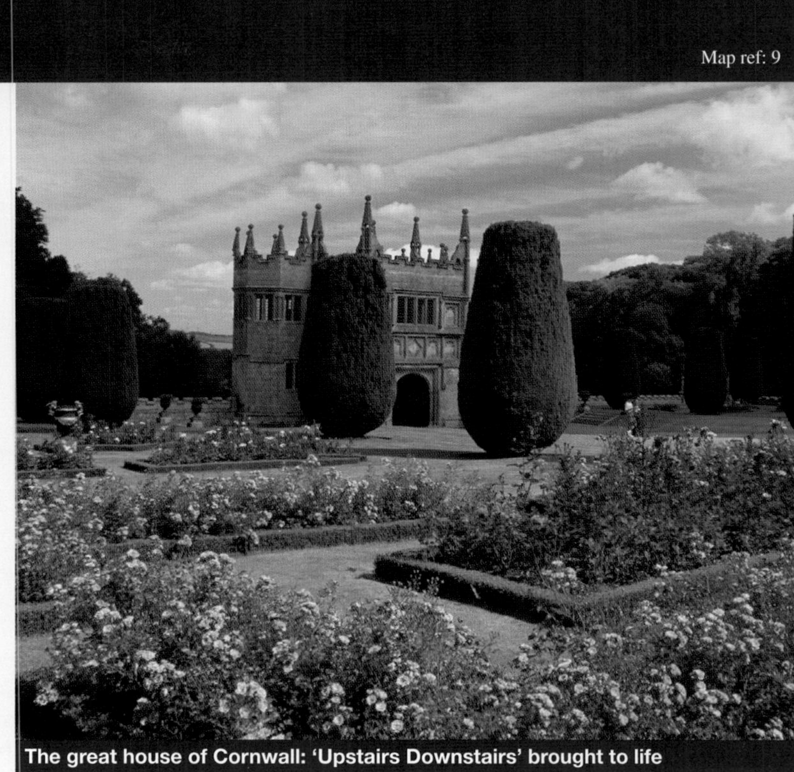
The great house of Cornwall: 'Upstairs Downstairs' brought to life

Opening arrangements 2008			NB: Bold – open
House	15 Mar–2 Nov	11–5.30 (5 from 1 Oct)	M **T W T F S S**
Garden	All year	10–6	**M T W T F S S**
Shop & refreshments	5 Jan–3 Feb	11–4	M T W T F **S S**
	9 Feb–14 Mar	11–4	**M T W T F S S**
	15 Mar–2 Nov	11–5.30 (5 from 1 Oct)	**M T W T F S S**
	3 Nov–24 Dec	11–4	**M T W T F S S**
	27 Dec–31 Dec	11–4	**M T** W T **F S S**

Also open BH Mons & Mons in August. Plant sales open daily 1 Mar – 2 Nov. Refreshments available from 10.30 in main season. Shop & refreshments are inside tariff area. Tel. for specific details of restaurant opening.

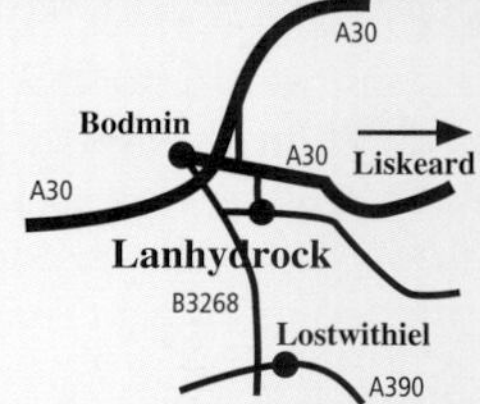

Activity 2

Now choose your own place and write a one page advertisement for it, using as many of the following as you can:

- illustrations
- persuasive language
- factual information
- details of the attractions
- useful directions
- any other revelant information.

Top tips

- Plan your page carefully before you begin to write.
- Divide the page into sections.
- Use a range of language devices.
- Use a range of structural devices.
- Use a range of presentational devices.

Check your answer

- how clear and attractive is your page?
- how wide a range of information have you included?
- did you remember to include persuasive language?

This lesson will help you to:
- understand writers' techniques
- apply these techniques to your own writing.

Writer's techniques

It is always useful to have some models in mind when you are creating your own text. This is why all the texts in the Reading section of this book can be useful to you when you are writing your own texts. You can increase your own stylistic repertoire by thinking carefully about the techniques used by writers in their own published texts.

Activity 1

Read the following letter, written to a newspaper by a fireman, explaining why his work is worth the £30,000 a year he is paid.

The Guardian

Am I worth £30,000?

Am I worth £30,000? In my career I have been taught skills to save life, prolong life and to know when to walk away when there is no life left. I have taken courses to fight fire from within, above and below. I can cut a car apart in minutes and I can educate your sons and daughters to save their own lives.

No matter what the emergency, I am part of a team that always comes when you call. I run in when all my instincts tell me to run away. I have faced death in cars with petrol pouring over me while the engine was ticking with the heat. I have lain on my back inside a house fire and watched the flames roar across the ceiling above me. I have climbed and I have crawled to save life and I have stood and wept while we buried a fellow firefighter.

I have been the target for yobs throwing stones and punches at me while I do my job. I have been the first person to intercept a parent who knows their son is in the car we are cutting up, and I know he is dead. I have served my time, damaged my body and seen things that I hope you never will. I have never said 'No, I'm more important than you', and walked away.

Am I worth £30k? Maybe now your answer is no. But when that drunk smashes into your car, or the candle burns down too low, or your child needs help, you will find I'm worth every last penny.

Jay Curson
Firefighter, Nottingham

This text is full of structural and linguistic techniques, many of them derived from the classic tradition of 18th century sermons. Find an example of each of the following and decide what effect each has on the reader.

1. Rhetorical question
2. Repeated later for structural cohesion
3. Repeated use of first person (I)
4. Repeated use of 'I have'
5. Triplets (groups of three) – used throughout
6. Verbal patterning – repeating words both within sentences and in related sentences
7. Sophisticated accurate grammar (e.g. 'I have lain')
8. Play on words – 'run in' ... 'run away'
9. Slang for dramatic effect
10. Emotional appeals to the reader
11. Use of cliché
12. Ambiguous resonances (e.g. 'served my time')
13. Images to transcend time (e.g. 'candle burns down too low')
14. Four clear sections

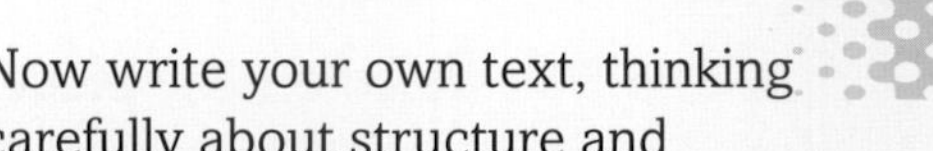

Activity 2

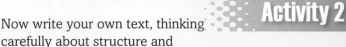

Now write your own text, thinking carefully about structure and language. You can choose either to write the script for:

A speech to be given to your year group, persuading them to support the charity of your choice.

or

A speech to be given to your year group, persuading them to take an interest in the sport or cause of your choice.

Here are some ideas to help you.

- Gather your ideas on your chosen subject in a list or spidergram.
- What can you say to persuade your audience? Think of how to structure your speech. You need:
  - an interesting opening
  - several stages
  - precise details about your subject
  - how your audience could help or be involved
  - a catchy conclusion.
- When you are writing include some of these:
  - groups of three
  - direct address to your audience using second person (you)
  - identification with your audience by using first person plural (we)
  - repetition
  - contrast
  - emotive language
  - images for effect
  - wordplay for effect.
- Think each sentence through before you write it.
- Imagine the words being read aloud.
- Make sure you are always persuading and interesting your listener.
- Ask yourself what the impact of each sentence on the reader will be.

My learning

This lesson will help you to:

- practise writing for different purposes and audiences
- practise writing in different forms.

Relating language to form, purpose and audience

The structure and the language you use for your text will depend very much on:

- its purpose
- the intended audience
- where the piece is to be published.

When the form, the purpose and the audience change, so will your language.

Activity 1

Look closely at the images opposite. They are all from a Creative Hairdressing competition. Then undertake two or more of the writing tasks that follow, concentrating on the language you use and the structure of what you write. In each case spend some time planning before you write and then checking your work when you have finished.

1. Decide which image you think deserves first, second and third prize, and write a news report for your local newspaper. The actual news story would carry the picture of each of the three winning styles.
2. As Chair of the judges for the 'Beautiful Facial Hair' competition in London, you have been asked to write a short explanation of why the first, second and third prize winners gained their prizes.
3. Write an informal email to a friend, poking fun at some of the entries for the 'Facial Hair' competition you attended at the weekend.
4. Write a brief feature article for *Hairdressing Monthly* drawing attention to the most recent styles. You are allowed three illustrations (which you do not need to draw!).

Check your answer

Did you:

- vary your language appropriate to the purposes and audiences
- structure your text clearly and effectively
- maintain an appropriate and consistent tone?

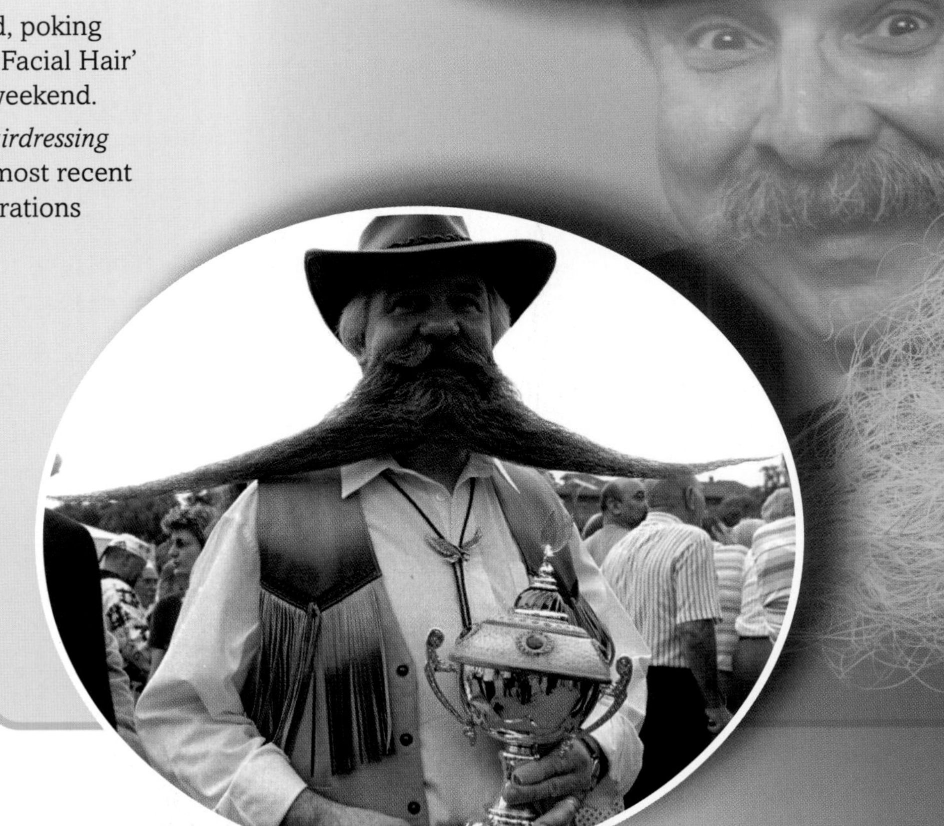

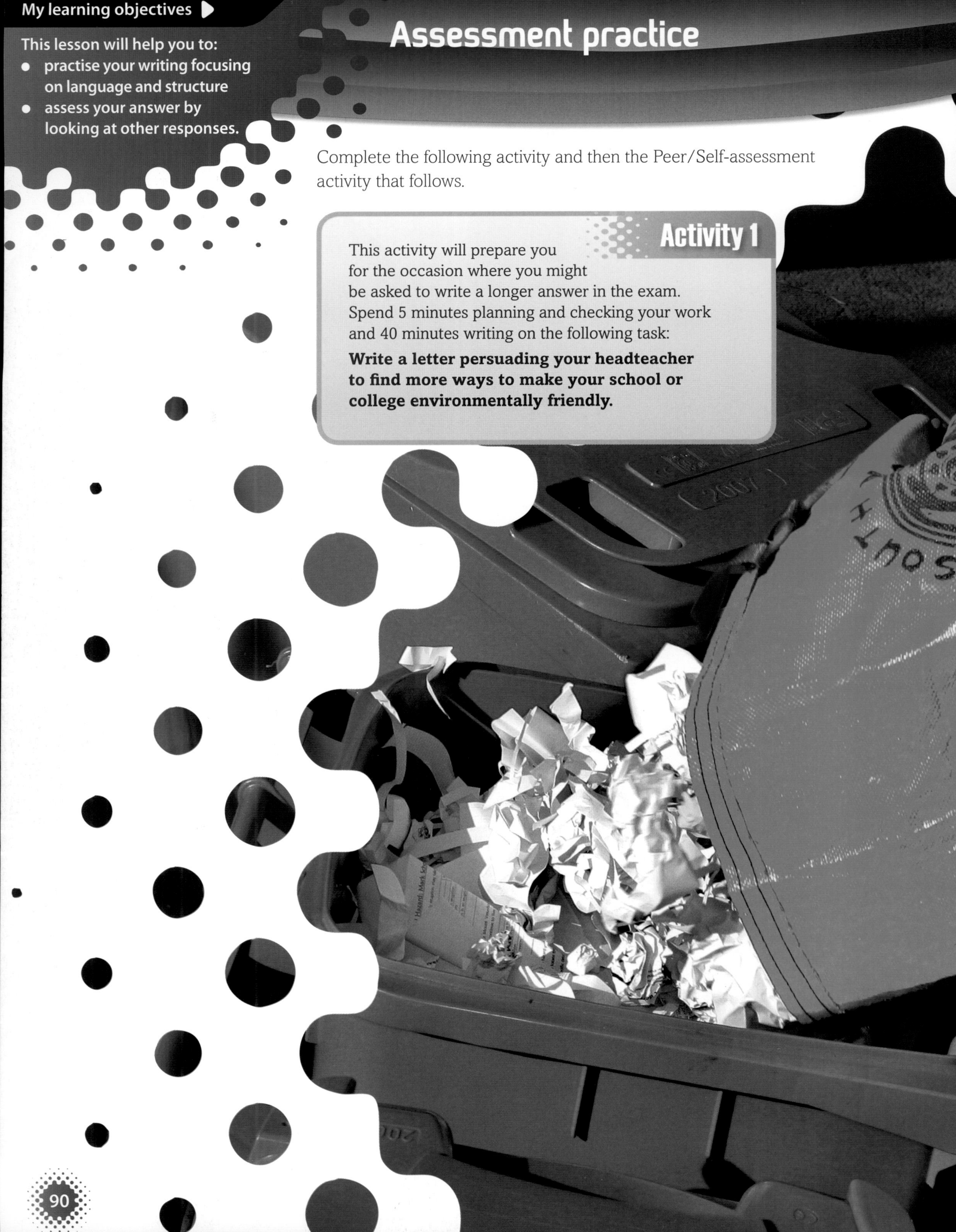

My learning objectives

This lesson will help you to:

- practise your writing focusing on language and structure
- assess your answer by looking at other responses.

Assessment practice

Complete the following activity and then the Peer/Self-assessment activity that follows.

Activity 1

This activity will prepare you for the occasion where you might be asked to write a longer answer in the exam. Spend 5 minutes planning and checking your work and 40 minutes writing on the following task:

Write a letter persuading your headteacher to find more ways to make your school or college environmentally friendly.

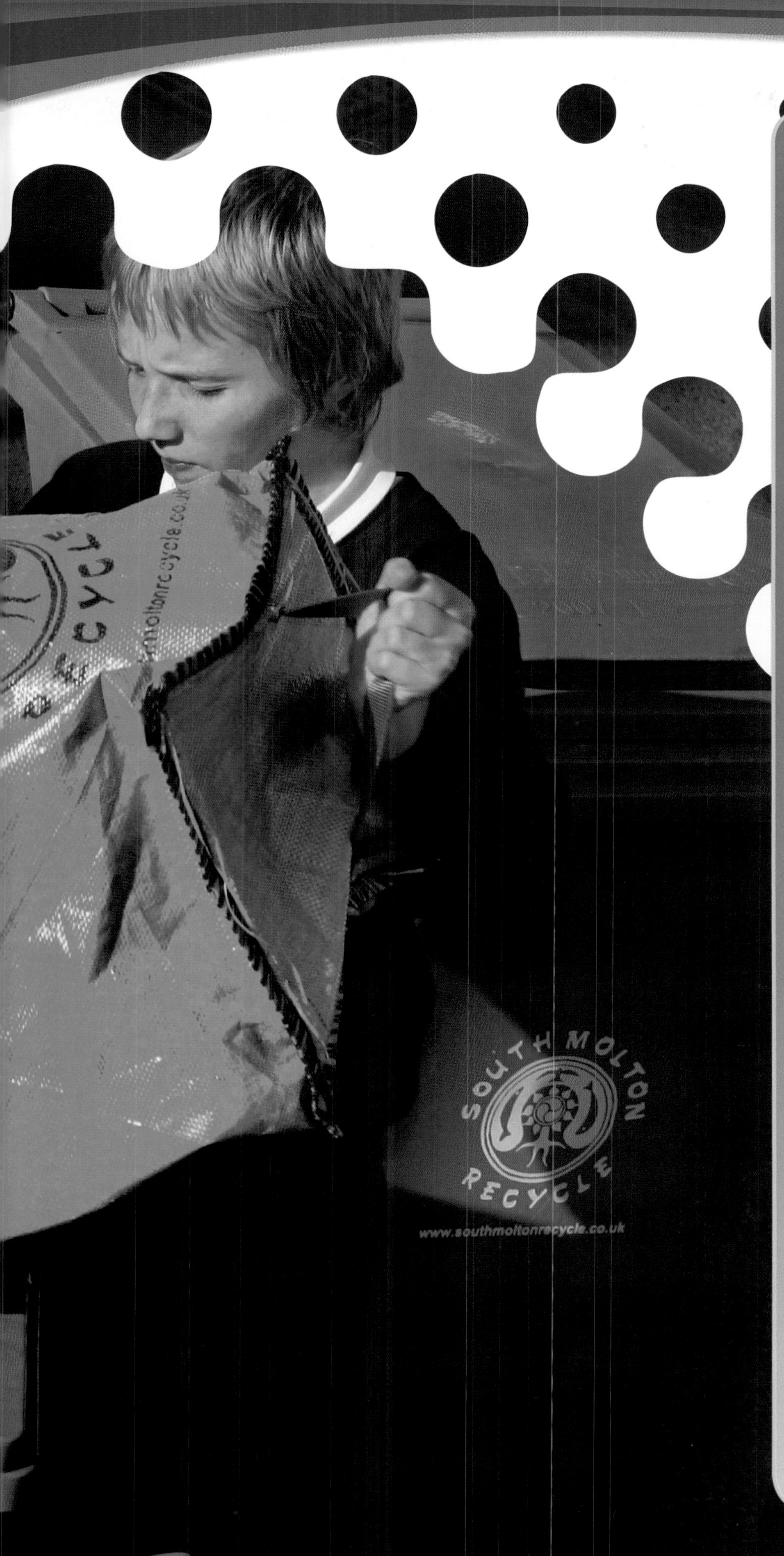

Peer/Self-assessment activity

1 Check your answer to Activity 1. Did you:
   - plan first
   - maintain an appropriate and consistent tone
   - structure your ideas effectively
   - make links between paragraphs
   - have an interesting opening and ending
   - include interesting and varied language throughout?

2 Now assess your answer to Activity 1 using the criteria below. You will need to be careful and precise in your marking. Before you do this, you might like to read extracts from two sample answers to this activity on pages 92 and 93.

Good
- well structured
- use of paragraphs to enhance meaning
- increasing sophistication in vocabulary and phrasing.

Very strong
- coherently structured
- fluently linked sentence structures and paragraphs
- evidence of conscious crafting.

Excellent
- controlled and sustained crafting
- highly effective and delightful vocabulary choices
- distinctive and consistently effective.

GradeStudio

Here are two student answers to the activity on page 90:
Write a letter persuading your headteacher to find more ways to make your school or college environmentally friendly.
Read the answers together with the comments. Then check what you have learnt and try putting it into practice.

Extract from an answer rated 'Good'

Extract from Student A

10 The High Street
Manchester
M36 8ZQ
3 February 2010
Dear Mr Dust,

As headteacher of Lowood School you must know more than most about the current problem of climate change. Everyday, students in your school are learning about the effects our lifestyles have on the environment. But they are learning this in a school that uses enough energy to melt at least a metre of the Polar Ice Caps every term. Is that the sort of headline you want on your next school newspaper? Should this fact be addressed in the school prospectus? I think the answer to both of these would be a NO.

But what, you may be thinking, can I do to make a difference?

Well, Mr Dust, there are many answers to this. Being the Beacon School that you are, you have now 12 computer suites, each with 40 computers. If my calculations are correct, that is 480 computers left on all day everyday, even when not in use. If these computers were simply turned off when not being used, this would save approximately 9180 joules a day. But what is that? That, Mr Dust, is £410 a week knocked off your electricity bill. Is the whole idea of an environmentally friendly school now beginning to appeal?

Your most recently refurbished sports stadium. A fantastic attribute, but why not make the 12 flood lamps solar powered? This would save yet more money!

Mr Dust I am sure you do not need me to tell you what needs to be done. Lowood School could be the first environmentally-friendly school in the area and this could be down to you.

Yours,
Natalie Graham

Appropriate address, date, salutation

Every day should be two words; redundant comma

Rule breaking for dramatic effect

Hyperbole for effect

'In' would be better

Might have been more effective without the rhetorical questions being answered

Two words

Presumably Mr Dust isn't a school!

Effective arithmetic; paragraph could be more succinct

The repetition of the name has now become amusing!

No obvious effect gained by this minor sentence

Missing comma

Nothing useful gained by the exclamation mark

'Yours sincerely' would be expected here

Teacher comment

There is a clear structure here, although the range of suggestions is not extensive. There is a clear sense of audience throughout and the rhetorical questions work well. The language is appropriate throughout and there is some variation in tone.

Extract from an answer rated 'Very strong'

Extract from Student B

Appropriate address, date and salutation

Clumsy phrase

Effective minor sentence riposte

Effective variety of sentence structures and vocabulary

64 Penny Lane
Puddington
Totnes
Devon
SK32 9BB
1 April 2010
Dear Mrs Smith,

I am writing this letter in accordance with the monstrosity that this school is when it comes to recycling. We need a more environmentally friendly place to grow up in. Why deprive us of trying to do our bit for the world?

To start off, we could allocate recycling bins or bags to different parts of the school which would allow our litter to be disposed of effectively. Why shouldn't the school have to do this? We have to where I live. It would be a strategic way of enlightening the younger children about recycling.

Introduce energy efficient lightbulbs. Each one lasts longer than a pupil's stay in the school and it would save on maintenance costs. Can it be possible that what I have heard is true? That in the holidays lights and computers are left switched on? Why? What do you achieve? Nothing except waste. Let's save the world instead of damaging it. It is futile that we work hard to save the planet while you mock us by squandering fuel when we're not here.

Make some changes, Mrs Smith, and help us to be friends of the environment. We still have our lives to live.

Yours sincerely,
Harry Featherstone

Teacher comment

This answer is consistently matched to purpose and audience. There are many sentence forms for effect and the response is succinct, effective and technically accurate.

Language and structure

To improve your answer, you need to:

- match your writing to purpose and audience
- think about the form of your response (the text for a letter here)
- vary your sentence structures
- vary your language
- make the reader interested in what you write.

What have I learnt?

Discuss or jot down what you now know about:

- planning and structuring your writing
- using language for effect.

Putting it into practice

- You can practise this skill with anything you write.
- You can get efficient at making plans.
- You can begin to sequence effectively.

My learning ▶

This lesson will help you to:
- understand the different forms you need to write in
- write letters using the correct features.

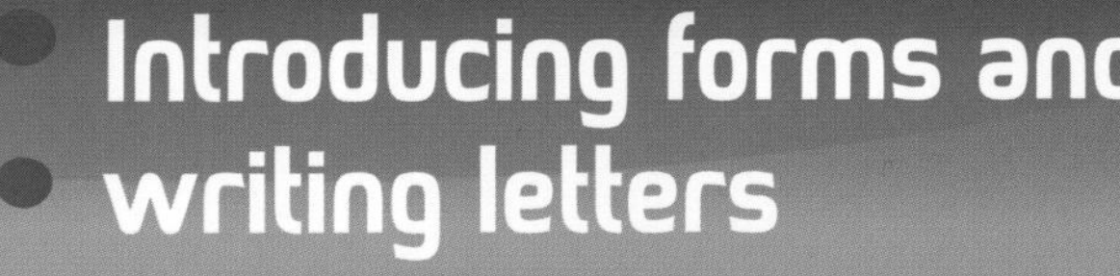

Introducing forms and writing letters

Introducing forms

We don't write everything in the same way. How we write depends very much on purpose and audience, but each time we write we make choices about:

- form
- sentence structures
- language
- presentational features such as paragraphs, bullet points and headlines.

In your course you look at a wide range of forms of non-fiction and media texts. Many of these will have been to prepare for the Reading part of the exam. There are lots of different forms of text in the Reading section of this book. The features used in these texts are useful to you in preparing for your own writing.

Some main forms that you may be asked to write in are:

- reports
- letters
- advice sheets
- articles
- information sheets
- emails.

You may be asked to write in any two of these forms in the exam.

Letters

Remind yourself of some of the key features of letters:

- what addresses you put in
- where the address or addresses go
- the date
- how you start the letter (the 'salutation')
- how you finish the letter (the sign off).

All these will depend on the purpose of and the audience for the letter. The letter opposite is an example of the beginning of a formal letter written to a company:

12 Lake Street
Headingley
Leeds
LS6 3PY

1 December 2009

Customer Services Manager
Moneyworks
24 Broad Street
Birmingham
B1 4RW

Dear Sir/Madam

The address of the company/person you are writing to lower down and on the left

Your address top right

The date, beneath your address

In this instance, as the name isn't known, Dear Sir/Madam is used – the letter would end 'Yours faithfully'

Remember:

- If you are writing to someone whose name you know, then you start 'Dear Mr or Mrs…' and end 'Yours sincerely'.
- If you are writing to someone who lives at the address you are sending the letter to, you don't include their address in your letter.
- A letter to a friend would be much less formal and might start 'Dear Chris', ending with 'Love' or 'Cheers'.

There are many different conventions which the professional world uses for letters – hence the wide variety of layouts on formal letters from companies and organisations. However, whatever the design decisions, there are some features that are essential:

- the address of the sender (including the postcode)
- the date
- the salutation
- the sign off
- the name of the sender.

Activity 1

1 Write the beginning and the ending of a letter to each of the following:
   - a letter to a friend
   - a business letter to someone whose name you don't know
   - a letter replying to one from Mrs R Singh at the local tax office
   - a formal letter of application for a job.

2 Now choose one of the above and write out a full letter. Make sure your language is appropriate, in terms of formality, for the purpose and audience.

Check your answer

Did you use the following correctly:

- Dear Sir/Madam, Dear Mr/Mrs, Hi mate, etc.
- Yours sincerely, Yours faithfully, Love
- your own address
- the address of the person the letter was going to
- the date?

My learning

This lesson will help you to:

- understand the features of reports and emails
- use these features in your own writing

Reports and emails

Reports

In the workplace people are often asked to write reports: perhaps minutes of meetings; perhaps a briefing paper for people who have not been involved in the discussions about something that you have been; perhaps a summary of different points for action; perhaps a summary of the main issues about a topic.

These are usually written in formal Standard English and include headings and bullet points. It is a useful skill to be able to write reports.

Top tips

Make a list of all the points you are going to include and sequence them before you begin to write. Decide:

- whether you are going to number your points
- whether you use paragraphs and, if so, what length they should be.

Check your answer

- Is the information clear?
- Is it easy to follow?
- Is the format consistent?
- Do the Conclusion and Recommendations follow on from what you have already included?

Activity 1

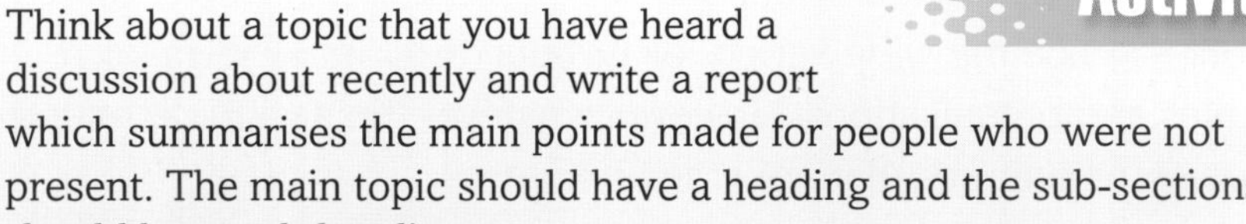

Think about a topic that you have heard a discussion about recently and write a report which summarises the main points made for people who were not present. The main topic should have a heading and the sub-sections should have sub-headings.

For example, you might have been involved in a school council discussion about whether there should be more revision classes for GCSE. You might use this heading:

Revision Classes

and these sub-headings:

- Advantages
- Disadvantages
- Possible Times for Classes
- Conclusion
- Recommendations.

You could use this structure and format for many different topics.

Now choose a topic, a purpose and an audience for your report on any topic of your choice and write it using the structure given above.

The address of the company/person you are writing to lower down and on the left

12 Lake Street
Headingley
Leeds
LS6 3PY

Your address top right

1 December 2009

The date, beneath your address

Customer Services Manager
Moneyworks
24 Broad Street
Birmingham
B1 4RW

Dear Sir/Madam

In this instance, as the name isn't known, Dear Sir/Madam is used – the letter would end 'Yours faithfully'

Remember:

- If you are writing to someone whose name you know, then you start 'Dear Mr or Mrs…' and end 'Yours sincerely'.
- If you are writing to someone who lives at the address you are sending the letter to, you don't include their address in your letter.
- A letter to a friend would be much less formal and might start 'Dear Chris', ending with 'Love' or 'Cheers'.

There are many different conventions which the professional world uses for letters – hence the wide variety of layouts on formal letters from companies and organisations. However, whatever the design decisions, there are some features that are essential:

- the address of the sender (including the postcode)
- the date
- the salutation
- the sign off
- the name of the sender.

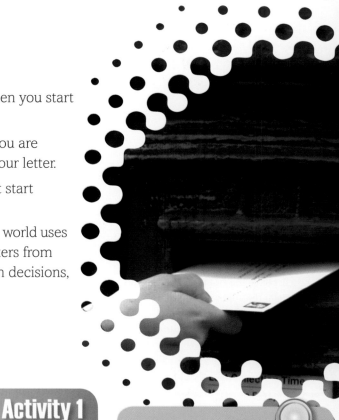

Activity 1

1 Write the beginning and the ending of a letter to each of the following:
   - a letter to a friend
   - a business letter to someone whose name you don't know
   - a letter replying to one from Mrs R Singh at the local tax office
   - a formal letter of application for a job.

2 Now choose one of the above and write out a full letter. Make sure your language is appropriate, in terms of formality, for the purpose and audience.

Check your answer

Did you use the following correctly:

- Dear Sir/Madam, Dear Mr/Mrs, Hi mate, etc.
- Yours sincerely, Yours faithfully, Love
- your own address
- the address of the person the letter was going to
- the date?

My learning

This lesson will help you to:

- understand the features of reports and emails
- use these features in your own writing

Reports and emails

Reports

In the workplace people are often asked to write reports: perhaps minutes of meetings; perhaps a briefing paper for people who have not been involved in the discussions about something that you have been; perhaps a summary of different points for action; perhaps a summary of the main issues about a topic.

These are usually written in formal Standard English and include headings and bullet points. It is a useful skill to be able to write reports.

Top tips

Make a list of all the points you are going to include and sequence them before you begin to write. Decide:

- whether you are going to number your points
- whether you use paragraphs and, if so, what length they should be.

Activity 1

Think about a topic that you have heard a discussion about recently and write a report which summarises the main points made for people who were not present. The main topic should have a heading and the sub-sections should have sub-headings.

For example, you might have been involved in a school council discussion about whether there should be more revision classes for GCSE. You might use this heading:

Revision Classes

and these sub-headings:

- Advantages
- Disadvantages
- Possible Times for Classes
- Conclusion
- Recommendations.

You could use this structure and format for many different topics.

Now choose a topic, a purpose and an audience for your report on any topic of your choice and write it using the structure given above.

Check your answer

- Is the information clear?
- Is it easy to follow?
- Is the format consistent?
- Do the Conclusion and Recommendations follow on from what you have already included?

12 Lake Street
Headingley
Leeds
LS6 3PY

1 December 2009

Customer Services Manager
Moneyworks
24 Broad Street
Birmingham
B1 4RW

Dear Sir/Madam

Your address top right

The address of the company/person you are writing to lower down and on the left

The date, beneath your address

In this instance, as the name isn't known, Dear Sir/Madam is used – the letter would end 'Yours faithfully'

Remember:

- If you are writing to someone whose name you know, then you start 'Dear Mr or Mrs…' and end 'Yours sincerely'.
- If you are writing to someone who lives at the address you are sending the letter to, you don't include their address in your letter.
- A letter to a friend would be much less formal and might start 'Dear Chris', ending with 'Love' or 'Cheers'.

There are many different conventions which the professional world uses for letters – hence the wide variety of layouts on formal letters from companies and organisations. However, whatever the design decisions, there are some features that are essential:

- the address of the sender (including the postcode)
- the date
- the salutation
- the sign off
- the name of the sender.

Activity 1

1 Write the beginning and the ending of a letter to each of the following:
   - a letter to a friend
   - a business letter to someone whose name you don't know
   - a letter replying to one from Mrs R Singh at the local tax office
   - a formal letter of application for a job.

2 Now choose one of the above and write out a full letter. Make sure your language is appropriate, in terms of formality, for the purpose and audience.

Check your answer

Did you use the following correctly:

- Dear Sir/Madam, Dear Mr/Mrs, Hi mate, etc.
- Yours sincerely, Yours faithfully, Love
- your own address
- the address of the person the letter was going to
- the date?

Reports and emails

My learning

This lesson will help you to:

- understand the features of reports and emails
- use these features in your own writing

Reports

In the workplace people are often asked to write reports: perhaps minutes of meetings; perhaps a briefing paper for people who have not been involved in the discussions about something that you have been; perhaps a summary of different points for action; perhaps a summary of the main issues about a topic.

These are usually written in formal Standard English and include headings and bullet points. It is a useful skill to be able to write reports.

Top tips

Make a list of all the points you are going to include and sequence them before you begin to write. Decide:

- whether you are going to number your points
- whether you use paragraphs and, if so, what length they should be.

Check your answer

- Is the information clear?
- Is it easy to follow?
- Is the format consistent?
- Do the Conclusion and Recommendations follow on from what you have already included?

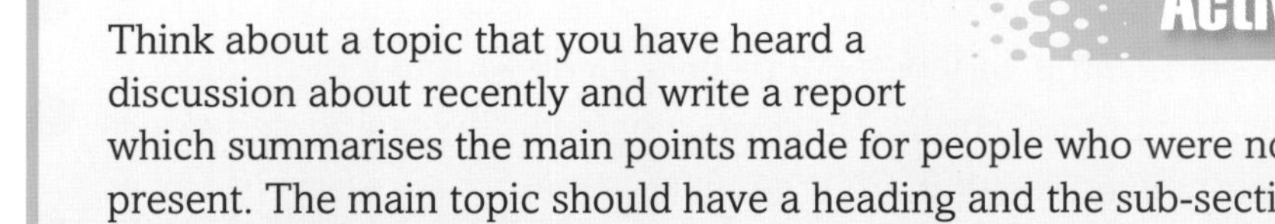

Activity 1

Think about a topic that you have heard a discussion about recently and write a report which summarises the main points made for people who were not present. The main topic should have a heading and the sub-sections should have sub-headings.

For example, you might have been involved in a school council discussion about whether there should be more revision classes for GCSE. You might use this heading:

Revision Classes

and these sub-headings:

- Advantages
- Disadvantages
- Possible Times for Classes
- Conclusion
- Recommendations.

You could use this structure and format for many different topics.

Now choose a topic, a purpose and an audience for your report on any topic of your choice and write it using the structure given above.

Email

Informal emails break many of the rules of Standard English. If you are emailing a friend then much of what you write may be like text messaging language, with abbreviations, symbols, missing apostrophes, few if any capital letters and mistakes uncorrected.

Email, though, is now also a primary means of business communication. Many people write dozens of emails a day but they must be certain that their message is clear and so they use many (sometimes all) of the conventions of Standard English. These formal emails are a more common means of communication than letters these days, but they obey the Standard English conventions. If you don't use Standard English then the person receiving the email might think you struggle with basic literacy skills.

A formal email often has these features:

- no addresses (because you are writing to a specific person and your email address and theirs is at the top)
- a salutation
- a sign off.

So a formal email is more like a letter than a text message, although it might be very brief and direct.

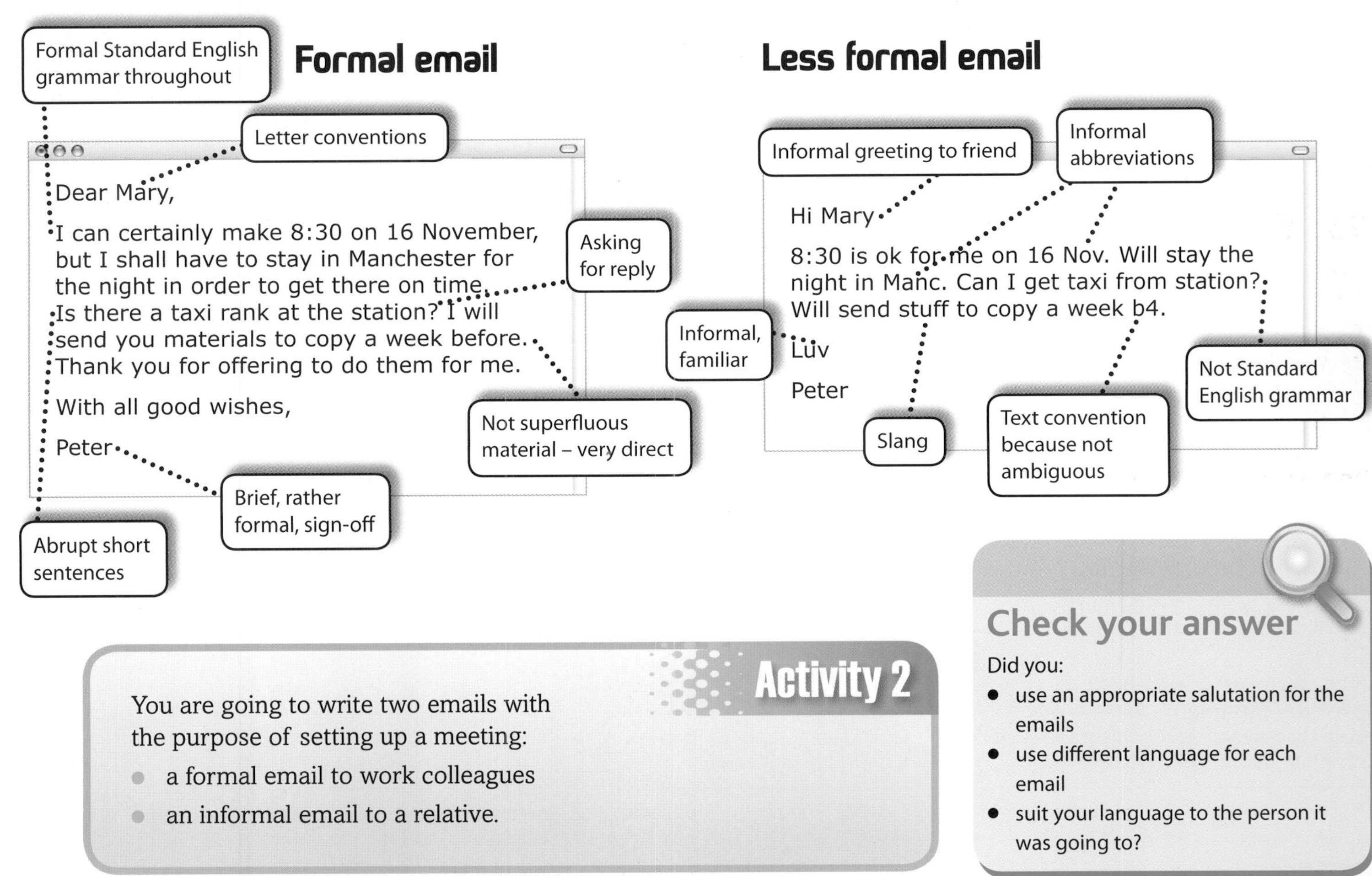

Formal email
Formal Standard English grammar throughout
Letter conventions
Dear Mary,
I can certainly make 8:30 on 16 November, but I shall have to stay in Manchester for the night in order to get there on time. Is there a taxi rank at the station? I will send you materials to copy a week before. Thank you for offering to do them for me.
With all good wishes,
Peter
Asking for reply
Not superfluous material – very direct
Brief, rather formal, sign-off
Abrupt short sentences
Less formal email
Informal greeting to friend
Informal abbreviations
Hi Mary
8:30 is ok for me on 16 Nov. Will stay the night in Manc. Can I get taxi from station? Will send stuff to copy a week b4.
Luv
Peter
Informal, familiar
Slang
Text convention because not ambiguous
Not Standard English grammar

Activity 2

You are going to write two emails with the purpose of setting up a meeting:

- a formal email to work colleagues
- an informal email to a relative.

Check your answer

Did you:

- use an appropriate salutation for the emails
- use different language for each email
- suit your language to the person it was going to?

This lesson will help you to:
- choose the right form for your response
- make choices about how to present your writing.

Articles and information/ advice sheets

Articles

Articles most often appear in newspapers and magazines and can be about a huge range of topics and issues. When writing an article, first you need to decide:

- where it might be printed
- its purpose
- the intended audience.

Here is an example of an article which also has in it some features of an information sheet.

General introduction

Picture to make it dramatic

Article writer's name

Top heading introduces topic

Jokey headline

Open wide: Eli Martinez, carefully places food into a tiger shark's mouth on the ocean floor

The diver bringing fish suppers to one of the ocean's great predators

Grabbing a bite to eat

by **Miles Erwin**

DIVING with sharks seems crazy enough but some adrenaline junkies have taken the sport one step further by feeding the fish by hand.

Eli Martinez says there is no greater thrill than getting up close and personal with one of the most dangerous predators known to man.

'Diving with sharks is what I do,' he said. 'Some may think it's a crazy idea, but I know what I'm doing. To be with them in the ocean, swimming around, is just mind blowing.'

The retired rodeo bull rider started feeding tiger sharks without protection two years ago, having first practised his technique on smaller species while wearing a chainmail suit.

Using bloody fish as bait, Martinez from Alamo, Texas, is able to entice the sharks amazingly close.

However, the father of four admits the sport is not without its risks after an Austrian died on an open water shark dive in the Bahamas last year.

'This was a very unfortunate accident that hopefully will never happen again,' he said.

He added: 'On several occasions, I have been chased out of the water when the sharks have got too excited but, if you let them calm down, you can get right back in again.'

>Tiger shark facts

- **Largest predatory shark after the Great White**
- Grows between 3.25m (10.5ft) and 4.25m (14ft) and weighs between 385kg (60st) and 900kg (142st)
- **Eats the most varied diet of any shark, including dolphins, snakes, turtles – and even tyres**
- Gets name from stripes on body which gradually fade with age

METRO

Main character of story introduced

Direct speech for authenticity

Tabloid paragraphs each with a slightly different angle

Extra information about tiger sharks

Activity 1

Write the first two paragraphs of an article on how to make the most of your money. Write for:

- your school magazine
- a tabloid newspaper
- an article in the financial section of a broadsheet newspaper.

Top tips

Sometimes in an exam the exact form and the exact audience isn't stated. You can choose. But it's good practice always to have a very specific audience and form in mind. For example, the question might ask you to write a magazine article. You will do best if you write for a specific magazine. The question might ask you to write to a friend. Think of a specific friend and your writing will seem more authentic. Then you need to make choices about:

- language
- headings, subheadings and any other presentational features
- paragraphs.

Information and advice sheets

These are designed to get specific information across to the reader clearly and directly. The layout of the information and advice is therefore key to the sheet's success. Such sheets often have:

- headings and subheadings
- different styles (bold, italic, capitals, underlining, print size)
- bullet points and other listing devices
- informative language for an information sheet
- persuasive language and conditionals for an advice sheet (e.g. could, should, ought to, must).

Although this is a holiday advertisement, it uses the features of an information sheet in order to cram a lot of information into a short space.

Check your answer

Did you:

- choose different headlines for each of the three articles
- think carefully about your audiences
- use language to interest each of your audiences?

Direct headline advertising holiday

Rhine Valley by Eurostar

theguardian reader offer

Includes rail to London

Generic picture of Rhine

Informs about length and price

Selected departures up to June 2010. Fully escorted price includes

- Return rail connections on selected dates from over thirty regional stations including Newcastle, Durham & Darlington, plus many others
- Return standard class reserved seat on Eurostar and TGV (French high-speed train) from Ebbsfleet or London St. Pancras International
- 6 nights bed and breakfast at excellent quality 3* hotels plus two dinners
- Visit to Aachen
- Tour of the romantic Rhine valley
- Guided tour of baroque Heidelberg, seat of one of Europe's oldest & most prestigious Universities
- Visits to the Black Forest and Colmar
- Tour of the scenic wine road in Alsace
- Guided tour of Strasbourg
- The services of an experienced tour manager

Information bullets

Not full sentences for clarity and directness

A little elaboration to tempt interest

Book at guardian.co.uk/holidayoffers (Code GDNRE)

Call 0330 333 6750

Email: guardian@rivieratravel.co.uk Calls to 03 numbers will cost no more than calls to national geographic numbers starting 01 or 02. Prices based on per person sharing a twin room, single rooms available at a supplement. Holiday organised by Riviera Travel, New Manor, 328 Wetmore Road, Burton upon Trent, Staffs DE14 1SP and is offered subject to availability. ABTA V4744 ATOL 3430 protected.

Clear information about how to book

Activity 2

You have been asked to produce some material about health and safety in your school or college.

1 Write an information sheet for students telling them what the issues are.

2 Write an advice sheet advising them how to keep healthy and safe while at school or college.

You will make a much better job of these if you do them on a computer. Then you can make choices about effective presentation, suited to the purpose and audience of the sheets.

Check your answer

Did you:

- think carefully about layout
- think carefully about presentation
- use sections, bullet points, underlining
- choose language to inform
- choose language to advise
- choose language suitable for your audience?

Assessment practice

My learning

This lesson will help you to:
- practise your writing, thinking particularly about form
- assess your answer by looking at other responses.

Complete the following activity and then the Peer/Self-assessment activity that follows.

Spend 30 minutes on the following activity:

Write an advice sheet for a newcomer to your school or college, advising them what to expect and how best to fit in.

Peer/Self-assessment activity

1. Check your answer to Activity 1.
   - Is your advice sheet clear?
   - Did it use appropriate layout features?
   - Did you provide advice on both what to expect and how best to fit in?
2. Now assess your answer to Activity 1 using the criteria below. You will need to be careful and precise in your marking. Before you do this, you might like to read some sample answers to this activity on pages 102 and 103.

Good
- clear and effective advice sheet
- form, content and style generally matched to purpose and audience
- well-structured range of relevant points and detail.

Very strong
- form, content and style consistently matched to purpose and audience
- well-structured range of relevant material
- evidence of conscious crafting.

Excellent
- form, content and style assuredly matched to purpose and audience
- controlled and sustained crafting
- distinctive and consistently effective.

GradeStudio

Here are two student answers to the activity on page 101:
Write an advice sheet for a newcomer to your school or college, advising them what to expect and how best to fit in.
Read the answers together with the comments. Then check what you have learnt and try putting it into practice.

Extract from an answer rated 'Good'

Extract from Student A

Welcome to Langbaine School!

So it's your first day and I guarantee you are worried about something, whether it is uniform, homework or teachers, this leaflet is going to get you through your first week, hassle free!

Uniform

You will have got all your uniform and have your shirt tucked in and your tie to the top button, but that is the way it should stay. Trust me, when a teacher says to you in the corridor 'Tuck that shirt in', do it straight away, no excuses, do it. There is no point in getting a 30 minute detention on your first day for not having a shirt tucked in.

Teachers

Yes they all seem daunting but don't worry they are fine when you get to know them. Be prepared for the odd day when they begin to rant and rave. They will have their 'days'.

Equipment

If you have a pen, pencil and ruler you will be fine, but have a pencil case on hand just in case you need it.

Breaktime and Lunch

Being in Year 7 means that you have to wait until all the other years have gone to the dinner hall, but there is a solution. Bring your own lunch! If you have your own lunch you can go straight in without having to queue up.

When you are walking from lesson to lesson expect there to be pushing and shoving as the whole school is marching around. Try and stay out of as many 'corridor crushes' as you can so that you don't get hurt.

I'm sure you will have heard of the 'High School Myth' that is 'swirlies'. This is aload of rubbish, no one has ever had their head put down the toilet so don't worry about it, it will not happen.

I hope this has been some help to you. Just as long as you talk to all the other students in your year and get the homework done, your five years with us will be great!

Appropriate opening

Comma splice

Useful introduction

Clear headings

Missing punctuation

Headings have disappeared

Two words

Comma splice

Useful conclusion

Rather odd; not linked to anything

Teacher comment

The headings are appropriate, but then disappear for no good reason. Form, content and style are appropriate to the audience, though it might make more sense to the reader if there were links between the sections. The advice is restricted mainly to very practical matters. There is some range of sentence structures. Spelling is accurate (apart from one error) but the comma splices should have been corrected during the checking stage.

Extract from an answer rated 'Very strong'

Extract from Student B

Three rhetorical questions, all minor sentences, immediately engage the reader

New to the school? Want to know how to fit in? Want to know what to expect when you start? Follow these rules and your introduction to St Peter's will be trouble free.

Firstly, probably the best advice I can give you is don't do anything silly in the first few days. Work out things for yourself and get your bearings. Then everything will fall into place for you.

Get to know the different groups and cliques in the year. Like any school, St Peter's has its own divisions but trust me, on the whole everyone gets on very well together. I think you should start off slowly and, let's say, attach yourself to the lads who play football at lunchtime. If you're a girl, go and sit and talk about... well, girl stuff I suppose.

If you think you're good enough to join a sports team, why not? Sports teams are a fantastic way of meeting new friends and talking to new people. To be honest, our football team could do with a new star player.

Finally, just be yourself. Trust me. If you are a nice person you will make friends. It's inevitable. Whether it be with the indie kids, the moshers, the chavs, the plastics or the – ahem – smokers, there will always be space for a new member. If the worst comes to the worst, you can always join the chess club. It's ok. There isn't a chess club at St Peter's.

Appropriate, clear introduction

Personal approach sustained and quite amusing

Fluent link between paragraphs

Encouraging and personable

A naughty touch to appeal to Year 7s

Nice joke to finish with

Teacher comment

This a clear set of advice, which concentrates on fitting in. Maybe a title would have been additionally effective. But it isn't too long to bore the reader. Form and style are consistently matched to purpose and audience; a Year 7 audience is kept in mind throughout. Sentence structure, punctuation and spelling all show a high level of technical accuracy, although nothing particularly ambitious is attempted.

Using and adapting forms

To improve your answer, you need to:

- include the correct information for your purpose
- think about your presentational features, and use them consistently
- use your paragraphs properly and try to make some links between paragraphs
- match your tone at all times to the purpose and audience of your text
- use sentence structure, spelling and punctuation appropriate to purpose and audience.

What have I learnt?

Discuss or jot down what you now know about:

- choosing the correct form and layout
- sequencing and writing to engage the reader.

Putting it into practice

- You can practise this skill with anything you write.
- Choose the best form for your purpose and audience.
- Sequence your ideas.
- Think about paragraphs and links between paragraphs.

My learning

This lesson will help you to:

- spell as accurately as you can
- identify errors with commas and full stops
- develop strategies to correct those errors.

Identifying and correcting spelling, full stop and comma errors

If you are hoping to gain the highest grades you will know how to spell accurately already. In the exam, though, because part of you will be thinking about what you are writing, rather than thinking about how you are writing it, it is possible that you might make a few mistakes. This is where checking your work for spelling in the writing activities is really important in the exam. Because you are unlikely to have made many mistakes, careful and accurate proofreading is essential.

It's usually much easier to find errors in something someone else has written than it is to find them in something that you have written. If you are looking at something you have just written then you are tempted to see what you ought to have written rather than what you have actually written.

Improving spelling

Spelling is very individual. There's no quick and easy way to spell everything correctly; it needs some hard work over a period of time.

The best thing to do is to keep a spelling notebook where you write down the correct spelling of all the words you often spell wrongly and the correct spelling of new words you come across which you might use some time. You can identify these from all your GCSE subjects.

You should:

- write down the words you misspell
- look up the correct spellings in a dictionary
- learn the correct spelling of words you often misspell.

Activity 1

This activity asks you to find and correct the errors in something someone else has written. It is an extract from an article about writing about literature.

Find the errors, look up the spellings in a dictionary and write out the correct spellings. There are three to find. If you are using a spelling notebook, and you didn't know how to spell these words, add them to your notebook.

Every subject has its own meta-language and English Literature is no exception. Students who are in the early stages of writing about literature think that their task is to use a lot of arcane words and then find examples of them in the text they are studying. This is not what the study of Literature should be about.

It's a low level skill to find examples of posh things and then give an example from the text, even if those things sound impressive, like onamatopeia, paradox, dipthong or oxymoron. Instead literary study should focus on how the writer encourages and stimulates the reader's response. This is called Reader Response Theory and went out of fashion for a while when post-modernist critical theory was all the rage. But it's back now because it's about what happens when you make meanings.

So banish thoughts of technique spotting and look at Litrature as an art, a craft.

Top tip

- Two of the words in this activity are part of the literature meta-language (words specific to a particular topic) and are difficult to spell. You would not be prevented from getting an A* by misspelling them. The third, though, is a word in much more common use and examiners would expect you to be able to spell it correctly. It's an example of a slip by an able student, but one which should be caught by careful checking.

Check your answer

Did you:

- find all three errors
- write down the correct spellings?

Introduction to punctuation

Items of punctuation which you should know how to use include the following:

- full stop .
- comma ,
- apostrophe (for possession and for missing letters) '
- question mark ?
- exclamation mark !
- colon (introducing a list) :
- semi-colon (separating clauses in a list or separating sentences which are interrelated and interdependent on each other for their meaning) ;
- brackets/parentheses ( )
- square brackets (usually used for a reference) [ ]
- dash -
- ellipsis (to indicate something that is missing) ...

Full stops and commas

It's rare to find students who don't know where to put full stops, but the most common mistake in writing in the exam is to put a comma where there should be a full stop. This is usually because while the writer is writing one sentence he or she is thinking about what will go in the next one and so places a comma at the end of the sentence rather than a full stop. These are called comma splices.

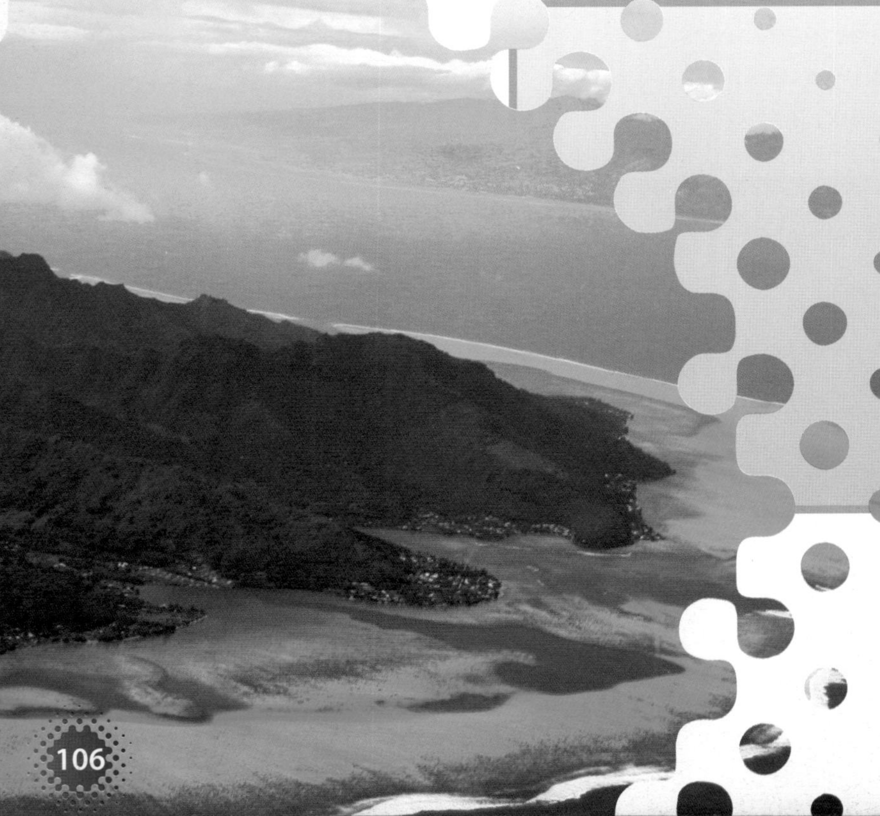

Activity 2

Find the four comma splices in the following extract. Then write out the offending bits so that the punctuation is correct. The two ways of doing this are:

- putting a full stop instead of the offending comma
- changing the grammar.

You should try both of these ways of correcting the errors.

There are twenty thousand islands in the South Pacific, they were created by the lava thrown up by powerful volcanoes under the sea. Coral reefs are eventually formed and the sea around these atolls is teeming with life. Hawaii is the most famous place created by these underwater volcanoes, land is being created there all the time. Some trees are attracted to the lava and when they start to grow exotic birds come to feed off the fruit of the trees.

Underground are enormous lava tubes, these are formed by the flows of lava but when the lava stops flowing these holes are left. There are all kinds of strange creatures living there, most, like spiders, crickets and translucent earwigs, have lost all their colour because they live in total darkness. The weirdly named small-eyed big-eyed hunting spider is the strangest. Totally blind, despite its name, it preys on other smaller creatures by sensing their whereabouts.

Check your answer

Did you:

- find all four comma splices
- replace the commas with full stops
- find an alternative solution by changing the grammar?

My learning

This lesson will help you to:
- identify errors with colons, semi-colons and other punctuation
- put it all together to spell and punctuate correctly.

Colons, semi-colons and other punctuation

Colons

The **colon** is used:

- to introduce a list. For example:
  - *If you go camping you will need: a tent, a sleeping bag, a torch and warm clothes.*
- to introduce a quotation. For example:
  - *A lady on the bus shouted after me: 'You have forgotten your bag!'*

You should be very confident about using the colon to introduce a list because I've used hundreds of lists in this book, each introduced by a colon. Most of the lists here are in bullet point form. I could have put them in continuous prose, though, in which case the colon would have introduced the list and then the items would have been separated by a comma except for the last two items which would have been linked by 'and'.

When you are introducing a quotation, you place a colon, leave a line and indent your quotation without inverted commas.

Semi-colons

The **semi-colon** is used:

- where a colon has introduced a list and the items in the list are grammatically full sentences. When this is the case these items in the list are separated by semi-colons rather than commas. For example:
  - *I have lots to do in town: I need to buy a dress; I have to meet my friend; I must post a letter.*
- where two sentences are closely linked in meaning. For example:
  - *I love eating spaghetti bolognaise; it is my favourite meal.*

Activity 1

Below are four sentences that need colons or semi-colons. Decide whether a colon or semi-colon should go in each place indicated by a number.

a There were many sides to William Shakespeare (1) actor, playwright, husband, father and property owner.

b There were many sides to William Shakespeare (2) he was an actor (3) he wrote plays (4) he was a husband and father and he was a property owner.

c Perhaps the most famous line in all English literature is Shakespeare's (5) To be, or not to be (6) that is the question.

d Shakespeare is sometimes referred to as the father of the English language (7) many of our common sayings were first recorded as being used in print by him.

Check your answer

Did you:

- use three colons
- use four semi-colons?

With punctuation, often there isn't just one right answer. Let's take question **c** in Activity 1. This could be correctly punctuated in the following ways:

- Perhaps the most famous line in all English literature is Shakespeare's:
  To be, or not to be; that is the question.
- Perhaps the most famous line in all English literature is Shakespeare's 'To be, or not to be; that is the question.'
- Perhaps the most famous line in all English literature is Shakespeare's: 'To be, or not to be; that is the question.'

Evolution, house style and fashion

Knowledge of the basic rules of punctuation is the building block for every writer. But rules are there to be broken. Once you are confident about using the rules you can break them in order to achieve a particular effect. But you need to know how to do it conventionally first!

For example, sometimes you see this in print:

> He asked her 'When will you marry me, then?'.

The final full stop is redundant because the question mark (and exclamation mark) carries the idea of a full stop within it. If you think about it, the bottom of the punctuation mark is a full stop.

As you become more experienced and confident as a writer you will develop preferences about some of these things. However, good qualities to aspire to in the use of punctuation are that it is:

- clear
- unambiguous
- as straightforward as possible
- consistent.

Other punctuation

At this level you should be confident using the following:

- apostrophes
- question marks
- exclamation marks
- inverted commas.

Just to check that you know when to use them properly, complete the following activity.

Activity 2

Write out the following correctly.

1 'Its it's,' he cried! 'It's its, not our's or theirs!'
2 'Have you read the book 'How many beans make five'?
3 'Help,' she cried. 'Help, help.'
4 Its never entirely clear what youre supposed to do is it.

Putting it all together – spelling and punctuation

Activity 3

The article below, which is about spelling and punctuation, appeared as a leader in *The Times*. It plays around with spelling and punctuation both to inform and to amuse the reader.

Read it carefully and then do the following:

1 Rewrite it in Standard English, using correct spelling and punctuation. There are also some examples of grammatical errors. 'Correct' these, too.

2 Identify within it examples of good practice in spelling and punctuation.

THE TIMES

Letters Pray

Why can't spelling bee easier?

Aoccdrnig to rscheearch at Cmabrigde Uinervtisy, it deosn't mttaer in waht oredr the ltteers in a wrod are, the olny iprmoatnt tihng is taht the frist and lsat ltteer be at the rghit pclae.

But that doesn't make it right. It doesn't make it big and it doesn't make it clever. If you're going to rite it at all you might as well right it write, wright? Otherwise you end up making stupid mistakes like the pamphlet that began by welcoming Nelson Mandela back to freedom after 27 years in goal.

And don't think your new-fangled computer will help you out. It can't spell to save it's life. Or punctuate. Four example; a paragraph could have floors and miss steaks but wood bee past by the spell chequer. An it will not fined words witch are miss used butt spelled rite.

It's a pain to learn. English wud bee a lot better if it were fernnetic. But it isn't. And it's irregular. The plural of leaf is leaves and the plural of chief is chiefs. Why? Just is.

There's more bad news. To become a decent speller you need to learn about 200,000 words. There are, at least, 29 spelling rules that can help. Here's one. The silent final e helps to distinguish between homophones. Clear? Try this one. The letter i can have lots of different sounds as you can see in the following sentence: 'in silent police onions gym my baby yo-yos'. Helpful? Thought not. I before e except after c? Better draw a veil over that one.

But there is a better way: 1,354 schools entered *The Times* Spelling Bee, the first national spelling championship for schools. The finals are today, in Lester Skware in Lundun. Or something like that anyway.

Check your answer

How many of the following did you 'correct':

- 45 spellings
- 9 items of punctuation
- 2 items of grammar?

As you now know, there are alternative ways of rendering some details into Standard English so these numbers are approximate!

My learning

This lesson will help you to:
- identify different sentence structures
- use a range of sentence structures for effect.

Use a range of sentence structures

Types of sentences

Here are the main types of sentence structures:

- A **simple sentence** has a subject and a main verb. For example:

- A **compound sentence** is a series of simple sentences joined together (usually with 'and' or 'but'). For example:

I feel happy and I am enjoying preparing for my GCSEs.

- A **complex sentence** is often longer, with one part dependent on another (using words like 'because', 'although', 'until'). For example:

subordinating conjunction

I feel happy because I am enjoying preparing for my GCSEs.

- A **minor sentence** isn't a sentence at all because it doesn't have a main verb, for example:

Gutted!

Variety of sentence structure is one of the ways to sustain the interest of your reader. Make sure that you vary the length and construction of your sentences in order to keep your reader's attention. This is particularly important in the exam where you have to sustain the interest of your examiner reader – someone who has to mark a large number of exam papers in a short space of time.

Activity 1

Decide which kind of sentence (simple, compound, complex or minor) each of the 11 sentences in the passage opposite is. Each sentence is numbered to help you identify them.

One of the most shameful records at this year's French Open was for the grunt with the loudest decibels. (1) That honour went to Maria Sharapova who emitted the loudest guttural noises, in a match which she eventually won, since records began. (2) Ms Sharapova may be one of the prettiest tennis players and may have graced the cover of many fashion magazines but she utters the ugliest noises. (3) She may be cute, she may be sexy but she's loud. (4) Some fashion icon. (5) Some role model for young women of the world. (6) Monica Seles was one of the first high decibel grunters. (7) Before Seles came along, grunting was thought to be vulgar and unsporting. (8) Now, however, in these times when celebrities manage to make their individual mark in whatever way they wish, anything, as they say, goes. (9) To grunt is cool. (10) Long live warmth. (11)

QUIET PLEASE...
THE PLAYERS ARE
ABOUT TO BEGIN
GRUNTING

Check your answer

Did you find:

- 4 simple sentences
- 2 compound sentences
- 3 complex sentences
- 2 minor sentences?

Activity 2

Now write your own text. It could be in a similar style to the text in Activity 1 or completely different. It could be about something you like or particularly dislike, or a strange or amusing experience you have had recently.

Make sure you include:

- a simple sentence
- a compound sentence
- a complex sentence
- a minor sentence.

When you have finished, annotate your text to show which sentence structures you have used and for what effect.

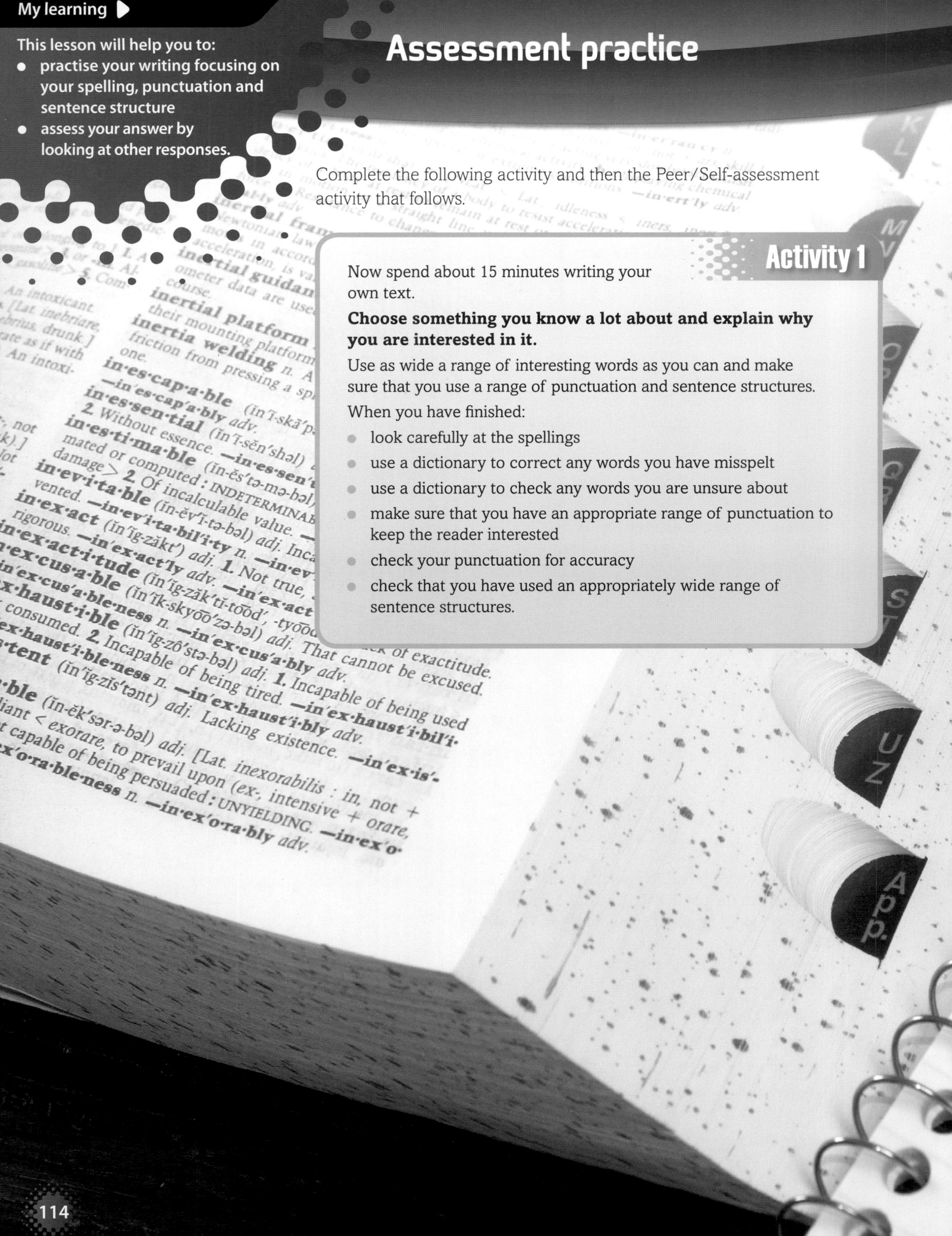

My learning

This lesson will help you to:
- practise your writing focusing on your spelling, punctuation and sentence structure
- assess your answer by looking at other responses.

Assessment practice

Complete the following activity and then the Peer/Self-assessment activity that follows.

Activity 1

Now spend about 15 minutes writing your own text.

Choose something you know a lot about and explain why you are interested in it.

Use as wide a range of interesting words as you can and make sure that you use a range of punctuation and sentence structures.

When you have finished:

- look carefully at the spellings
- use a dictionary to correct any words you have misspelt
- use a dictionary to check any words you are unsure about
- make sure that you have an appropriate range of punctuation to keep the reader interested
- check your punctuation for accuracy
- check that you have used an appropriately wide range of sentence structures.

Peer/Self-assessment activity

1 Check your answer to Activity 1. Did you:
- find your spelling errors
- add any words to your spelling notebook
- check your punctuation
- check your grammar and sentence structures?

2 Now assess the spelling in your answer to Activity 1 using the criteria below. You will need to be careful and precise in your marking. Before you do this you might like to read some sample answers on this activity on pages 116 and 117.

Good

- generally accurate spelling of commonly used words and of more complex words
- generally accurate punctuation
- uses a range of sentence forms for effect.

Very strong

- high level of technical accuracy in spelling of commonly used and complex words (with occasional lapses)
- high level of technical accuracy in use of a range of punctuation marks (with occasional lapses)
- uses a full range of sentence structures accurately.

Excellent

- near perfect technical accuracy in spelling of wide range of complex words
- near perfect technical accuracy in punctuation
- uses a full range of sentence structures accurately and effectively.

GradeStudio

Here are two student answers to the activity on page 114:
Choose something you know a lot about and explain why you are interested in it.
Read the answers together with the comments. Then check what you have learnt and try putting it into practice.

Extract from an answer rated 'Good'

Extract from Student A

Cooking is fun. Unregenerated mysoginists think that cooking is women's work but the majority of famous cooks are male. Take 'Masterchef', for example. The winners are nearly always men. Lets ignore the fact that almost all the judges are men, too. You can make almost anything you want and most dishes are quick to make. Organic ingrediants are easy to find in the supermarkets nowadays and the dishes you can make from them are far better for you than supermarket ready meals, with all their E's to add colour and allow the meal to stay edible for far too long. There's nothing nicer than homemade ratatouille or some soup made with stock from chicken bones. Making good holesome food in the kitchen is the recipe for heathy living.

Complex word misspelt

Missing apostrophe

Spelling error

Spelling error

Redundant apostrophe

Careless spelling error

Teacher comment

This candidate is unclear about the apostrophe, making two errors of different kinds. Three words are misspelt which should have been caught by checking. The fourth error is understandable (misogynists). Spelling and punctuation are generally accurate. Technical accuracy could have been higher with careful checking. There is a range of sentence structures here, some of them used for effect.

Extract from an answer rated 'Excellent'

Extract from Student B

Allotments are all the rage now. Now the recession is biting, people want high quality food without spending oodles of money; growing your own is how to achieve it. I'm afraid that the windowsills in my mum's house have been invaded by seedlings and shelves have sprouted over the radiators. Baby triffids are taking over, all destined for the table in a few months' time. She's got designs on the bathroom, too, though I'm still running a campaign to keep it as a seedling-free zone. When I complain, she warns me that without these accretions I can say goodbye to homemade soup, ratatouille, spring asparagus and healthy salads. We shall see.

Although this phrase can sometimes be seen in print without an apostrophe, it is correct because it is the time belonging to a few months

Teacher comment

The spelling and punctuation here are entirely accurate. There is a range of complex words spelt correctly and a range of accurately used punctuation. There is a range of sentence structures, each used to contribute to effect, variety and reader interest.

Spelling, punctuation and sentence structure

To improve your answer, you need to be able to:

- read what you have just written very carefully
- find and correct any errors
- use a wide range of words, punctuation marks and sentence structures accurately.

What have I learnt?

Discuss or jot down what you now know about:

- finding spelling errors
- finding punctuation errors
- varying your sentence structures
- checking your work.

Putting it into practice

- You can practise this skill with anything you write.
- Keep adding words to your spelling notebook.
- Use a range of punctuation appropriately in whatever you write.
- Use a range of sentence structures, thinking about the effect of your choices on the reader.

Section C

Studying spoken language

If you are taking GCSE English Language, you will study spoken language. Spoken language is the basis for so much of our communication – rarely in your whole life will a day pass without you actually speaking to someone. How you and others use speech, and how speech varies according to different circumstances, can help you to think about what you want to say to people, and what they are saying to you.

How will I be assessed?

Your work will be assessed through one written assignment of between 800–1000 words, which must be written under controlled conditions. You do not necessarily have to write a traditional essay in this assignment, although you are certainly allowed to do so. Instead, though, you could possibly write in forms such as:

- a report (similar perhaps to the way you write in science)
- a piece of journalism
- a review
- any other form, so long as it suits the purpose of your assignment.

What will I be assessed on?

This piece of work will count for 10% of your overall marks for GCSE English Language. Your work will be assessed on the following two Assessment Objectives.

- Understand variations in spoken language, explaining why language changes in relation to contexts.
- Evaluate the impact of spoken language choices in your own and others' use.

This Assessment Objective is asking you to look at how and why peoples' spoken language might alter in relation to various factors – for example, who they are speaking to, where, and for what purpose.

This Assessment Objective is asking you to look at the potential responses people can make to the way you and others talk in any given situation.

What do spoken language tasks look like?

There are three broad areas of Spoken Language Study which you could write about. These are outlined below. For your assignment you have to choose – with the help of your teacher – one of the three areas to investigate and write about. However, you could study all three before you decide which one to focus on.

Social attitudes to spoken language

In this area you should consider the ways in which your own and others' talk is used and judged. For example, these are just some of the things you could look at:

- your own language use now and how it varies depending on different situations – for example, how your language changes when speaking to different people (such as your friends as opposed to your parents)
- how speech can give you the sense of belonging to a group – for example a regional group, an age group, an interest group, or an ethnic group (note that this unit is not just about spoken English, it is about spoken language in general. This means that you can talk about speaking other languages too)
- how speech is an area of public interest – for example how local speech can sometimes be ridiculed and sometimes celebrated.

Spoken genres

By genres we mean types of speech such as interviews, news reports, school assemblies and so on. So in this area you could investigate genres such as:

- genres you might come across in everyday life, such as school assemblies, lessons, workplace briefings
- media genres such as interviews, news reports, weather forecasts
- TV drama genres where spoken language is 'represented' – such as in soap operas, hospital dramas, crime shows, 'reality' shows and so on.

Multi-modal talk

You might think that talk is talk and writing is writing, but in recent years new genres have emerged which have elements of both. Many of these genres come from new technology, but lots of communication these days has a conversational feel to it. In this area you might look at things like:

- text messaging and some of its methods and rules
- instant messaging
- the use of social networking sites
- news stories about the use of such new technology.

My learning

This lesson will help you to:
- gather your own data
- analyse and evaluate data on spoken language.

Investigating data

What is data?

Data is a word used in science as much as in English. It is information and evidence that is collected so that it can be examined, and then conclusions drawn from it. For the Spoken Language Study you will need to be able to gather and analyse data. There are many types of data you could collect and many ways to collect it. Here are some ideas:

- make a recording of people talking
- make a recording and then transcribe part of it
- conduct a questionnaire and/or survey
- collect newspaper or magazine articles
- use digital data from your phone, such as a text message conversation
- print out a chatlog or a screenshot from your computer.

Top tip

- Ideally you will use original data for your spoken language assignment – data that you have collected yourself. Collecting good original data will improve your chances of gaining a higher mark.

Making your own recordings

Recording live conversation can open up all sorts of interesting options for your assignment. It is best to record a conversation that has some shape and purpose to it, and which has a clear context. For example, a family discussion round a table, a seated conversation about a current debate, an interview and a classroom-based discussion should all provide useful data if recorded.

You can also simply record a television or radio programme, and then choose a specific part to focus on.

Top tips

If making your own recording of live conversation:
- Don't try to involve too many people in the conversation.
- Check that all equipment is working before you start.
- Get permission from the people taking part – you cannot secretly record people as it is against the law!
- This so-called 'informed consent' raises an interesting question though, as people who know they are being recorded will not behave normally. This is sometimes called the observer's paradox. One strategy, then, is to ask for permission and then get people used to being recorded before you record your actual data.
- Once you have collected a good piece of data, make sure that you copy it, and keep the copy in a safe place.

Activity 1

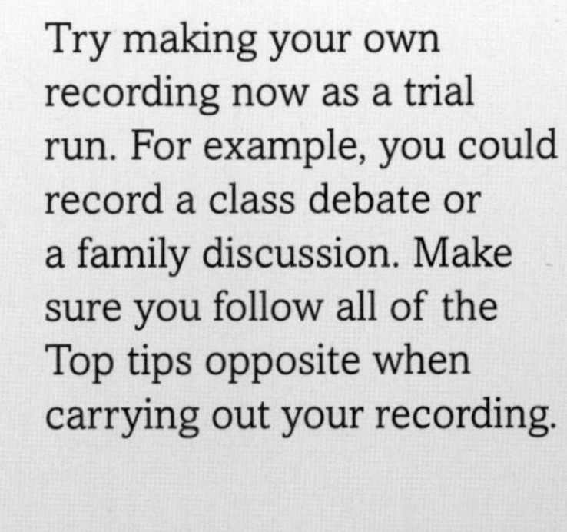

Try making your own recording now as a trial run. For example, you could record a class debate or a family discussion. Make sure you follow all of the Top tips opposite when carrying out your recording.

Making a transcript

A transcript is a written down version of the talk you have recorded. Once you have made a recording, you need to be able to use it to analyse the talk involved. For this reason, it can be very useful to have transcribed the talk.

Transcriptions often include keys or symbols just like a map does. These help the reader understand what happened in the conversation – for example, any pauses in the speech or overlaps (when people speak at the same time). There are no strict rules to these keys – the main thing is to make your key clear and easy to use by another person.

Activity 2

Below is an extract from an interview with the England football manager Fabio Capello after England had lost 1–0 in a friendly against Brazil. This was how the interview was reported in a written account of the game.

> England manager Fabio Capello said 'We played the best team in the world. Still, I learned some things. I understand the value of some players against this sort of team better now – but I will not single out players.'

1 Now look at the transcript opposite which shows what was actually said in the interview. What are the main differences between the two versions? Before you answer this, consider the following:

a Try reading both versions aloud. What do you notice about the difference in how the two flow?

b Do you think English is Fabio Capello's first language?

c Why do you think Capello uses pauses and other fillers (words or sounds to fill some time), such as 'I::::::' and 'erm'?

Key: (1) = pause in number of seconds
(.) = pause in less than one second
: : = a sound that is stretched out

Interviewer: Fabio you'll be disappointed with the scoreline (.) what about the performance

Capello: yes (1) i::: we played against Brazil erm they was the best eleven for Brazil (2) the players that played the first alf was good enough

Interviewer: because you were missing so many players (1) so many senior players this evening (.) what were you actually expecting from the team that you played

(Italian translation of question heard in background)

Capello: no no no yes yes (1) for me for me it is it was interesting to er see the value of er:: to check the performance of some players (.) and I happy because some players play erm:: very well and for the future will be good for me

Interviewer: who caught your eye

(Italian translation of question heard in background)

Capello: no (1) no no I no er I not speak about one single player

Activity 3

Read the paragraph below, which provides you with some further context about Fabio Capello.

Fabio Capello is a highly successful football manager, who managed the England team from 2008 to 2012. An Italian, he spoke virtually no English until taking over the team. In addition to speaking English, here he is under the added pressure of responding to a defeat, and of not wanting to identify players who played poorly.

Now look in more detail at the transcript on page 121 and write an analysis of it. Consider the following questions when writing your analysis.

1 Look at what the interviewer says. What do you notice about the questions he asks and how he asks them?

2 What are the main features of the way in which Capello speaks?

3 Thinking of the overall context you have been given here, how does Capello show a lot of skill in this interview? Think about whether he actually answers the questions being asked.

To help you answer these questions, here is a response to question 1 that might give you some ideas. The Check your answer box below should help with questions 2 and 3.

The interviewer does two things before he even asks a question. First he addresses Capello by his first name, Fabio, and then he makes a statement rather than asking a question. He assumes, probably fairly, that Capello will be disappointed to lose when he says 'you'll be disappointed with the scoreline'. This helps the interviewer to establish his own presence in the conversation and to be seen as an equal, even though Capello is actually far more important.

His second question is carefully and clearly worded, but again contains an assumption, perhaps this time that Capello expected to lose.

The final question is frequently asked of managers, trying to get them to name individual players who played well or badly, but the metaphor 'caught your eye' is much more difficult for a second language speaker than the plain language used in the second question.

Check your answer

Look at your answer to question 2.

- Did you notice Capello's use of fillers such as 'erm' and repetition?
- Did you notice the use of some non-standard expressions, such as 'I happy' and 'They was'?
- Did you pick up on Capello's Italian accent from reading the transcript, even though there is no sound recording?

Look at your answer to question 3.

- Did you notice how Capello manages to make defeat sound quite positive?
- Did you pick up on how Capello does not really answer the questions?
- Did you think about how, perhaps because of his 'performance' of being a second language speaker, he is not given a hard time by the interviewer in the way many managers are?

Here is an extract from one student's answer to the activity on page 122. Read the answers together with the comments.

Extract from an answer rated 'Excellent'

Extract from Student A

Not surprisingly, Capello sometimes needs help when he is asked a complex question, such as 'who caught your eye', a phrase that may not be the same in Italian. He has several methods of keeping his turn while thinking his way into English. For example stretching words (i:::), rapidly repeating 'yes' and 'no' and using fillers like 'erm' and 'er'- which native speakers use too. These techniques all buy him the time he needs in which to think about how to articulate his response.

When you hear the interview, as well as read the transcript, it is clear that he is using his English to say as much or as little as he wants to. He is being quite skilful here and it is not impossible to imagine that he uses his status as a non-native speaker as a benefit rather than a hindrance, allowing him to say as little as he needs to when under pressure in this way.

Teacher comment

This is very good! Here the student really looks closely at the data and comes up with an interesting interpretation, based on the context and what is actually said. Referring to hearing the interview, as well as seeing it written down, is also a good idea.

When analysing transcripts like this, to get the most marks you need to go beyond describing what is happening and actually interpret and evaluate the transcript, referring to specific details. This student does this very effectively, pulling out specific details and interpreting why language is used in the way it is.

My learning

This lesson will help you to:

- explore social attitudes to language
- think about ways of collecting and sorting some data.

Social attitudes to spoken language

Social attitudes are views and opinions that are held by groups of people rather than just individuals. Although it may seem wrong to judge people by the way they speak, it does seem to happen.

Dialect and accent

The terms dialect and accent often crop up when looking at social attitudes to language. **Dialect** refers to the actual words and vocabulary that a particular group use. **Accent** refers to the way in which a particular group speaks – the particular sounds.

Top tips

As well as dialect and accent, it is useful to know what the following terms mean:

Standard English A formal variety of spoken English which is generally taken to be free of regional characteristics in its words and grammar.

Received Pronunciation (RP) A regionally neutral accent, often associated with the educated, the upper classes and so-called important institutions such as the universities of Cambridge and Oxford.

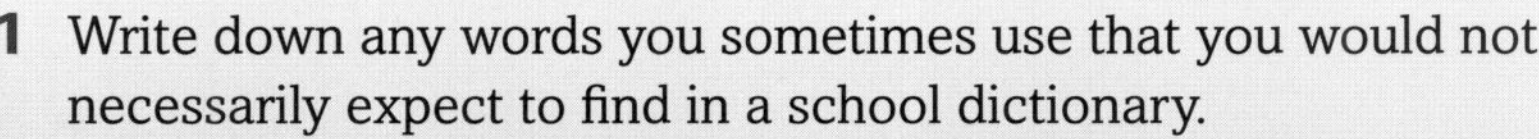

Activity 1

Think about your own dialect and accent.

1 Write down any words you sometimes use that you would not necessarily expect to find in a school dictionary.

2 Do you pronounce any words or sounds in a particular way that is different from how others might say it?

3 What about accents and dialects other than yours? Can you think of regions that have particularly strong dialects and/or accents? Make a list. Then think what your immediate reaction is when you hear this accent or dialect.

Activity 2

Read the article opposite about how different people respond to different accents.

1 Identify the three different types of groups whose accents are mentioned here.

2 Who did the survey and why did they do it? What do we not know about the survey?

3 Think back to the work you did in Activity 1. Do you feel strongly about different accents?

GradeStudio

Here is an extract from one student's answer to the activity on page 122. Read the answers together with the comments.

Extract from an answer rated 'Excellent'

Extract from Student A

Not surprisingly, Capello sometimes needs help when he is asked a complex question, such as 'who caught your eye', a phrase that may not be the same in Italian. He has several methods of keeping his turn while thinking his way into English. For example stretching words (i:::), rapidly repeating 'yes' and 'no' and using fillers like 'erm' and 'er'- which native speakers use too. These techniques all buy him the time he needs in which to think about how to articulate his response.

When you hear the interview, as well as read the transcript, it is clear that he is using his English to say as much or as little as he wants to. He is being quite skilful here and it is not impossible to imagine that he uses his status as a non-native speaker as a benefit rather than a hindrance, allowing him to say as little as he needs to when under pressure in this way.

Teacher comment

This is very good! Here the student really looks closely at the data and comes up with an interesting interpretation, based on the context and what is actually said. Referring to hearing the interview, as well as seeing it written down, is also a good idea.

When analysing transcripts like this, to get the most marks you need to go beyond describing what is happening and actually interpret and evaluate the transcript, referring to specific details. This student does this very effectively, pulling out specific details and interpreting why language is used in the way it is.

My learning

This lesson will help you to:
- explore social attitudes to language
- think about ways of collecting and sorting some data.

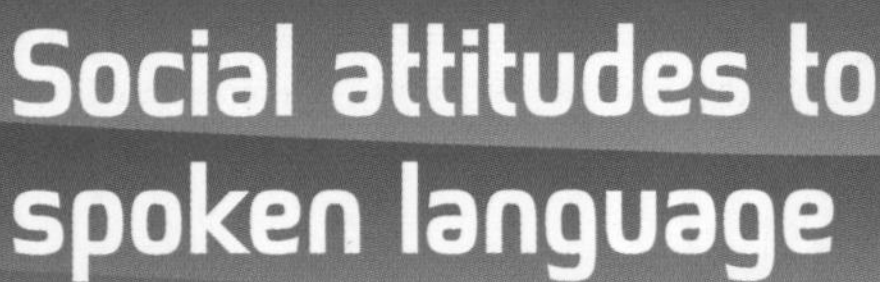

Social attitudes to spoken language

Social attitudes are views and opinions that are held by groups of people rather than just individuals. Although it may seem wrong to judge people by the way they speak, it does seem to happen.

Dialect and accent

The terms dialect and accent often crop up when looking at social attitudes to language. **Dialect** refers to the actual words and vocabulary that a particular group use. **Accent** refers to the way in which a particular group speaks – the particular sounds.

Top tips

As well as dialect and accent, it is useful to know what the following terms mean:

Standard English A formal variety of spoken English which is generally taken to be free of regional characteristics in its words and grammar.

Received Pronunciation (RP) A regionally neutral accent, often associated with the educated, the upper classes and so-called important institutions such as the universities of Cambridge and Oxford.

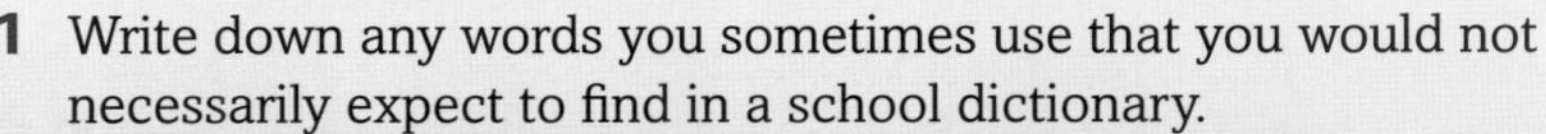

Activity 1

Think about your own dialect and accent.

1 Write down any words you sometimes use that you would not necessarily expect to find in a school dictionary.

2 Do you pronounce any words or sounds in a particular way that is different from how others might say it?

3 What about accents and dialects other than yours? Can you think of regions that have particularly strong dialects and/or accents? Make a list. Then think what your immediate reaction is when you hear this accent or dialect.

Activity 2

Read the article opposite about how different people respond to different accents.

1 Identify the three different types of groups whose accents are mentioned here.

2 Who did the survey and why did they do it? What do we not know about the survey?

3 Think back to the work you did in Activity 1. Do you feel strongly about different accents?

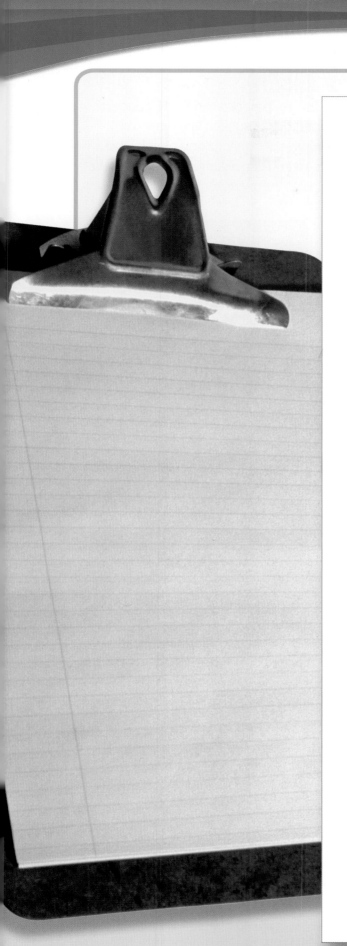

The Guardian

Not all regions like to hear their own accents in ads, survey finds

Many people claim to hate the sound of their own voice, but a new government survey suggests the sensation is more unpleasant for some of us than it is for others.

The study, commissioned by the Central Office of Information (COI), reveals that, while Geordies and Mancunians enjoy listening to their own regional accents in government advertisements, Brummies and Bristolians would rather not be subjected to their own distinctive burr.

The COI found that attitudes to accents vary widely across the generations.

Older people tend to be more accepting of ad campaigns featuring received pronunciation, perhaps because they grew up listening to the "cut-glass" English accents that featured on public information films of the past.

Younger people were more engaged by local accents, it found, but sometimes a more authoritative voice is more appropriate, according to the research.

Advertisements which encourage the public to comply with deadlines, including filling in tax returns, "need to impart trust and authority" the COI said, and are more effective when a Home Counties accent is used.

Local accents proved more persuasive in campaigns which include "credible real-life experiences" to try to change people's behaviour, perhaps to prevent drink driving or encourage homeowners to fix faulty smoke alarms.

Check your answer

- Did you identify the three different kinds of groups mentioned?
- Did you identify who carried out the survey and what the purpose was?
- Did you work out that the article does not tell the reader what the research methods were – who they asked, what questions and so on?

Doing a survey

One way to produce an assignment for this part of Unit 3 is to conduct a survey to find out about peoples' attitudes to spoken language. We have already seen from the article on page 125 that asking people about regional talk can bring interesting results. So can asking people about the ways in which different age groups speak. Here are some possible topics that you could do surveys on.

What annoys adults about teenage speakers?

How do people respond to different regional accents?

What annoys teenagers about adult criticisms of their speech?

What changes in speech have old people noticed over time?

Once you have come up with a good topic, you then need to think of a method that will give you enough data to work on when you are in the Controlled Assessment situation.

Survey methods

When thinking about carrying out a survey, there are certain things you need to be clear about from the start.

- **Who are you going to ask?** – for example, people from a particular age group, gender or social background.
- **What are you going to ask them? -** you need to ask questions which people can answer in detail. For example, just asking someone if they like the Geordie accent might not get much of a response beyond 'yes' or 'no'. Playing them a brief recording of Ant and Dec in the jungle, on the other hand, and then asking about them as presenters could get much more.
- **How will you record what they say?** - there are various ways to record responses, including making notes at the time, making sound recordings, or even asking your respondents to write things down for you.

Top tip

- Be realistic about how many people you can ask, in what is a small study. Choosing three or four people could be enough, especially if they have plenty to say.

Activity 3

Take one of the examples of possible survey topics from the speech bubbles above and imagine you were going to carry out an actual survey. For that topic, answer the three key questions above – the who, what and how.

Using a questionnaire

Another way of gathering data is by doing a questionnaire. Questionnaires are similar to surveys but usually require brief answers. There can be real advantages in using them.

- They can be sent and returned by post, so allowing for a wider range of responses.
- They can lead to statistical data which can then be presented in tables and graphs.

Activity 4

Devise a questionnaire to find out what dialect words are used by your extended family.

Remember, dialect words are words used by groups of people with something in common such as:

- their region (which can also include other countries)
- their age
- their gender
- their social background.

An example would be that some Geordies use the word 'neb' for 'nose' and some people from Yorkshire say 'spice' for sweets.

To get you started, here are some common words, in their standard form, which tend to have other varieties. An example is given for each.

Standard form	Example of a dialect version
Mother	Mom
Father	Daddy
Baby	Bairn
Clever	Smarty
Superb	Mint
To tell tales	Grass
Beautiful	Lush

Top tips

There are various ways to ask questions. In this questionnaire you could:

- give people the dialect word and ask them to say what it means
- give people the standard word and ask for a dialect version
- ask people if they actually use dialect versions as well as know them.

Writing up

Under Controlled Assessment you will need to get all your data together, ready to complete your assignment.

Let's assume you have had ten replies to your questionnaire from Activity 4. First you need to decide which bits of data you find most interesting. Then you can pull that information out and present it in an easy-to-understand format. For example, you could show the number of variations on certain words (as shown in the graph on the left), or the number of old people who use a dialect term set against young people (the graph on the right).

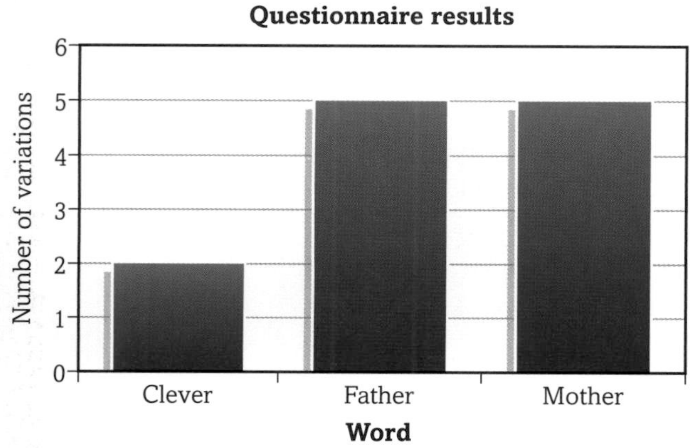

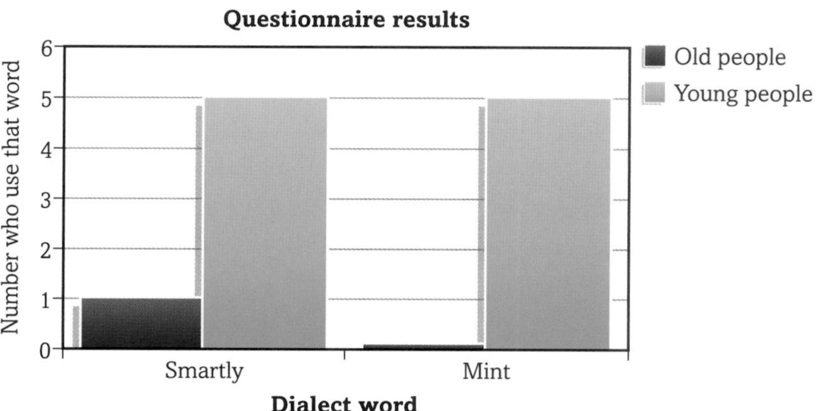

Analysing data

You will certainly gain some marks for the way you present your data, but to really impress you need to attempt to give possible analysis too. Nobody wants you to make outrageous claims from your evidence, but you do need to consider some possibilities. For example, if all old people used a dialect word, but only some younger people, why might this be so? Because the younger people have moved around the country more? Because dialects, like all language, change over time?

Activity 5

Look at the data you gathered from your questionnaire in Activity 4. Focus in on one particular part of that data and write a paragraph explaining and analysing what it shows you about language use.

Think about:

- what your data shows you
- how to interpret the data
- whether your data may possibly show something about spoken language in a wider sense.

The Grade Studio answer on page 129 will help you understand how you could structure your response.

GradeStudio

Here is an extract from one student's answer to the activity on page 128. Read the answers together with the comments.

Extract from an answer rated 'Very strong'

Extract from Student A

This particular piece of data suggests some interesting things but needs to be considered carefully. Clearly in this particular example it is the younger group who are more common users of the dialect words 'mint' and 'smarty'. From this one might conclude that dialect usage is much stronger amongst younger generations than the old. However this does not seem true if you look at other parts of my results. With other words, such as 'bairn' for 'baby', usage was strongest among older participants. Closer investigation of the data shows that both groups use dialect words, but that younger people tend to adopt newer dialect words – such as 'mint' – which may even be used nationally rather than just regionally. Certainly a friend of mine in Kent uses this word too.

Teacher comment

This student uses the collected data, and also introduces at the end an extra piece of relevant information. The student does not just look at one piece of evidence but ranges widely over the set of data. The student also begins to interpret the data, suggesting what it might show and how it might also mislead if taken at face value.

To improve your answer when analysing data like this you need to take account of the data's limitations as well as what it shows. The study of language does not often lead to definite answers and conclusions, so there is no point in trying to make bold assertions based on small amounts of data. You need to think about, evaluate and interpret your data, and make suggestions about what it might show you.

My learning

This lesson will help you to:

- think about the vast range and features of spoken genres
- consider some ways of analysing spoken genres.

Spoken genres

What is meant by 'spoken genres'?

There are many different genres of spoken language that you could write about for your assignment. In this case, 'genre' means the type of speech or text. For example, the following are all examples of spoken genres:

- school assembly
- school lesson
- public speech
- news report
- workplace meeting
- weather forecast
- interview
- TV shows where spoken language is 'represented'.

The list could go on and on, and within each genre it is possible to identify sub-genres.

Top tips

- If you choose to do your assignment on a spoken genre, try to think of a really specific sub-genre. This will give your assignment real focus and purpose. Sub-genres can arise, for example, out of a combination of the topic (football) the circumstances (post-match), the main person involved (the manager) and the structure of the talk (interview).

Activity 1

Think about the interview genre. Make a list of as many different types of interview as you can think of.

We have already seen one example with the Fabio Capello interview on page 121, so your list could begin with 'post-match interview with manager', which then might lead to 'post-match interview with player' and so on.

Check your answer

There are many possible answers here. Yours might include some of the following:

- job interview
- an interview to get into a university
- formal teacher/pupil interview
- informal teacher/pupil interview
- teacher/parent interview
- political interview on TV
- political interview on the radio
- celebrity interview on TV
- celebrity interview for a newspaper
- police interview of witness
- police interview of criminal
- voice in the street interview
- public opinion survey interview.

Features of spoken genres

If a text belongs to a particular spoken genre, this usually means it has certain rules and features. For example, in the interview genre you would always expect to see the following two features:

- one or more person(s) asking the questions (the interviewer)
- one or more person(s) replying to those questions (the interviewee).

Activity 2

1 Look at the list of spoken genres in the table below. What features would you always expect to see in each genre? Copy and complete the table. When doing this, think about:

- particular people or groups of people who must always be present in this genre
- where the spoken genre takes place
- a typical language feature that might appear in this spoken genre.

Spoken genre	Features
Weather forecasts	
School assembly	
School lesson	
Public speech	
News report	
Workplace meetings	
Celebrity interview on TV	

Contexts

The main features of a spoken genre often remain the same. For example, an interview will always consist of someone who asks questions and someone who answers them. Where there might be variations within a spoken genre is when you start to consider the different contexts. For example, look at the different contexts for an interview below

Context	Effect
A celebrity interview on TV	Because this is a celebrity interview on TV, the main purpose for both the interviewer and interviewee is to entertain and interest the viewer. It's likely that the approach would be quite informal and the questions very friendly.
A job interview	In this context, there is a job at stake. The interviewer's main purpose is to find out information and judge personality – whether the candidate is suitable for the job. The interviewee's main purpose is to impress the interviewer. It's likely that the atmosphere will be formal and the questions quite searching.

Check your answer

- For each spoken genre did you identify which people or groups of people must always be present?
- Did you identify where each spoken genre takes place?
- Did you identify typical language features of each spoken genre?

Activity 3

Take any two of the different interview sub-genres mentioned on page 130 and think about how they are different from each other. You could start with, for example, a TV interview with a politician and a police interview with a criminal. Think about how they might differ in terms of:

- their purpose
- the people involved
- the level of formality
- the potential audience for the interview.

If you choose to do your assignment on spoken genres, you could look at a transcript of something such as an interview and explore areas such as:

- the level of formality
- how questions are asked
- how questions are answered.

Activity 4

Opposite is a transcript of an interview between an adult researcher (R) and a student (S). The student attends a school in York. The researcher is making a short documentary film about some of the features of the York accent.

Read the interview, using the key to try and recreate how it might have actually sounded. Then answer the following questions.

1. Is this a formal or informal interview? How can you tell?
2. What do you notice about the questions being asked? How does the researcher's style of questioning change as the interview goes on?
3. Interviews are often written down as records of what was said, for later reference. Write an official record of this interview. What do you notice? What kind of text does it remind you of?

Check your answer

- Did you identify whether this was a formal or informal interview and explain your reasons using evidence from the transcript?
- Did you notice how the interviewer's questioning style became more direct?
- Did you comment on the difference between the transcript of the conversation and your written record of it?

Key
R = researcher
S= student
(1) = length of pause in seconds
| = when two people speak at the same time
o::: = the long vowel sound made by natives of York
? = the rising intonation that signals a question being asked

R: ccan you tell me then what some of the er distinctive features of your York accent are (1) is is it possible for you to describe them to an outsider

(2)

S: erm (1) er (1) it's it's like really strong and you can tell I'm from York and it's it's the way I say things like I'll say Yo::rk and others like I'll obviously emphasise the O in that and other people will say it differently but I can't really say that

(1)

R: so would you spot an outsider|
S: yes|

R: like me|
S: yes|

R: saying York

S: yes

R: instantly??

S: yes

R: would you?

S: yes

R: and you can tell if someone is a native of Yo::rk|
S: (laughs)|

R: is that right|
S: (laughs)|

R: by the way by the way they would say it

S: yes

Represented conversation

Another area you could explore in your assignment is scripted or 'represented' conversation. These are found in TV and radio dramas, as well as novels, short stories and other texts. It is called 'represented conversation', because it imitates the ways people speak to each other, rather than being an example of natural or real conversation.

Talk that is written to be performed is, on the page, much neater and tidier than actual talk. There are a number of reasons for this, not least the fact that scripts are written for audiences to understand.

The audience

When we watch drama, or read a novel, the conversation takes place for us – the audience – not for those who are in the drama. Sometimes the audience might know more than the characters – for example, that one character is secretly in love with another. Sometimes the audience knows less than a character – for example, a detective might typically know more than he or she let's on.

For your Controlled Assessment, you could look at an example of scripted conversation and explore some if its features. The activity below helps you get started on this area.

Activity 5

Look at this brief clip from a soap opera and answer the following questions.

1. What does the audience know that the character(s) do not?
2. How do you think pictures and actions in this script contribute to the overall drama? What effect do they have?
3. How do you react to this scene? Is it funny, sad or something else? Explain your reasons.
4. What similarities and differences does it have with real-life talk? You could compare it to the transcripts you've seen earlier in this section.

Story so far: the audience knows that Glen is keen to ask out Shelley, and that Shelley does not want to go out with him, but does not want to hurt him either.

Scene 12: Long shot of school canteen. Cut to Glen opposite Shelley at long table. Long pause with other conversation in background.

Glen: um um don't suppose you'd like to go to town Saturday (pause)
Shelley: oh oh sorry can't
Glen: Why not?
Shelley: I'm going away with my parents
Glen: Where to?
(pause – close up of Shelley thinking hard. Cut to food being eaten next to her – a pizza)
Shelley: um Italy
Glen: Italy? Just for a week-end? What are you doing there?
(through Shelley's eyes we see a female chef dolling out food)
Shelley: um my Mum's doing a cookery course for two days.
Glen: (puzzled) Ooh

Check your answer

- Did you comment on what the audience knows about Glen and Shelley?
- Did you comment on how the pictures and actions heighten the drama?
- Did you explain your reaction to this scene?
- Did you compare this scripted conversation with real-life talk and notice some of the similarities ('um um') and differences (the overall flow of the conversation)?

Speeches

Another area that could provide good data to study for your assignment is the political speech. While there is no spoken interaction between people, as there is in an interview, when the speech is delivered it is important for the speaker to get some sort of response from the audience. More often than not, the main purpose of a political speech is to persuade the audience.

Activity 6

In the speech below, Prime Minister Gordon Brown talked about liberty and freedom.

1 What persuasive methods does Mr Brown use here?

2 How can you tell this is a written version of speech, rather than an actual transcript of what he said? Think of the differences between this text and the transcript on page 132.

I want to talk today about liberty – what it means for Britain, for our British identity and in particular what it means in the 21st century for the relationship between the private individual and the public realm.

I want to explore how together we can write a new chapter in our country's story of liberty - and do so in a world where, as in each generation, traditional questions about the freedoms and responsibilities of the individual re-emerge but also where new issues of terrorism and security, the internet and modern technology are opening new frontiers in both our lives and our liberties.

Addressing these issues is a challenge for all who believe in liberty, regardless of political party. Men and women are Conservative or Labour, Liberal Democrat or of some other party - or of no political allegiance. But we are first of all citizens of our country with a shared history and a common destiny.

And I believe that together we can chart a better way forward. In particular, I believe that by applying our enduring ideals to new challenges we can start immediately to make changes in our constitution and laws to safeguard and extend the liberties of our citizens:

- *respecting and extending freedom of assembly, new rights for the public expression of dissent;*
- *respecting freedom to organise and petition, new freedoms that guarantee the independence of non-governmental organisations;*
- *respecting freedoms for our press, the removal of barriers to investigative journalism;*
- *respecting the public right to know, new rights to access public information where previously it has been withheld;*
- *respecting privacy in the home, new rights against arbitrary intrusion;*
- *in a world of new technology, new rights to protect your private information;*
- *and respecting the need for freedom from arbitrary treatment, new provision for independent judicial scrutiny and open parliamentary oversight.*

Renewing for our time our commitment to freedom and contributing to a new British constitutional settlement for our generation.

Check your answer

- Did you identify features of persuasive language used in the speech?
- Did you comment on how the speech lacked any of the features of actual spoken text that come across in transcripts? Or that it includes features of written language that would not appear in actual spoken language?

GradeStudio

Here is an extract from one student's answer to the activity on page 134. Read the answers together with the comments.

Extract from an answer rated 'Very strong'

Extract from Student A

Gordon Brown's speech is a clear attempt to persuade his audience – essentially the whole country – that although our liberty has to be controlled because of things like terrorism, we still have lots of freedom. He does this by using pronouns like 'I' referring to himself and 'we' for the country as whole. The latter is an inclusive pronoun that makes the listener feel involved and addressed.

Although the speech is written down, and on the page looks like a piece of writing rather than speaking, it is possible to imagine that the list of ideas, each beginning with the word 'respecting' would receive applause or acknowledgement form his audience, especially in the way one idea quickly follows another.

The speech also uses other features of written language that you don't see in spoken language. For example, the list of bullet points would not be found in a transcript of spoken language – they are structural devices that belong to written language.

Teacher comment

This has the makings of a very good answer. This student is aware of the context surrounding the speech he is studying and links some analysis of language with the purpose of the speech. He also shows that he understands that although written down, this text has been written to be spoken.

When writing about formal speeches, it is best to start by providing the context of the speech, such as who is talking to whom, and why, where and when. Then it helps if you can imagine hearing the speech and consider what it would sound like. Remember too that many web sites let you hear the speech as well as read it.

This lesson will help you to:
- understand what is meant by multi-modal talk
- consider some of the ways in which people use texting to 'talk' to each other.

Multi-modal talk

What is multi-modal talk?

Traditionally language has been separated into speech and writing. New technologies mean this distinction is becoming more blurred. For example, when people 'chat' online, it could be said they are writing a form of talk. This kind of communication is an example of multi-modal talk – communication which has many of the qualities of talk, but is not actually spoken.

This section will focus on texting as a form of multi-modal talk, but there are of course many other examples that you could look at, such as instant messaging, social networking sites, emails and so on.

Activity 1

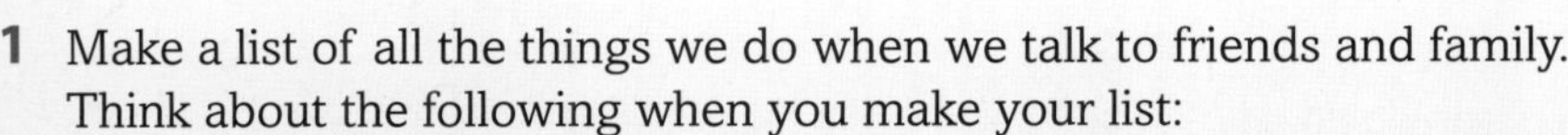

1 Make a list of all the things we do when we talk to friends and family. Think about the following when you make your list:
- The purpose of the talk – why is the conversation taking place and for what reason?
- How we sound – what we say and how we say it.
- Non-verbal communication – how do we use sounds and body language as a speaker or listener?

2 Compare your list with the one below. Are there any you missed out? Are there any you came up with not included below?

Possible purposes of talk
- to entertain – e.g. tell stories, jokes, gossip
- to make social plans
- to argue with someone
- to persuade someone

How we sound
- using informal language and slang
- at different tempos – quickly or slowly
- at different volumes – loudly or quietly
- placing emphasis on particular words

Non-verbal communication
- making expressive noises to show agreement/disagreement and other emotions
- nodding to show agreement
- smiling or laughing to show you find something funny
- using other hand and face expressions to add effect to your talk

Texting shares many of the same purposes and features of talk that you identified in Activity 1. For example, people often text to share gossip or to arrange a meet-up. Likewise, people often text using the same informal language that they would actually speak in. People also show emotion and even body language through creative use of the text system.

Activity 2

1 Below are some text messages sent by students in one class. Read the messages. For each one, see if you can say:

a Whether it is the opening to a series of messages or a reply to a message already sent.

b What the purpose(s) of the message is.

2 Now look at the work you did in Activity 1. Look at your own answers as well as the list provided. What do you notice about the similarities between texting and spoken language? Think about:

- the purposes of both
- the level of formality of both
- what features texting uses in order to imitate some of the non-verbal features of spoken language.

Erm problies about 8 what time use going? X

U nearly ready darl? lol. x ☺

Hi hope u r ok. Hannah is off poorly. Did u sort out paying trip? See you soon, hair appt thurs 3 dec, love u, mum xxxx

hey hun u'll nvr guess who I saw in twn 2day!

Game Time! Describe me in ONE word using the third letter of YOUR name. Answer me, then forward on and see what crazy responses you get.

just wonderin if u wanted 2 come play 4 an hr. 👍

Haha consider it dun then :) awww gorge i do love you! Ur the perfect girlfriend! :) ♥ xxxxxxxxx

Whos radioheads lead singer?

Just trying to sort out someone to do it for me... I wasn't told exactly if it was swine flu or not and don't want to run the risk of passing it on...!

Check your answer

Look at your answer to Activity 2.

- Did you notice the shared purposes of spoken language and texting – for example, to make social plans, to request information, to gossip and so on?
- Did you notice how the language in texting is on the whole very informal – much like the language we use when we actually speak to someone?
- Did you notice how some of the text messages use emoticons and other methods to indicate non-verbal sounds and gestures?

Collecting and analysing text data

There are many ways to analyse text message data. Conveniently, all the data you might need could be on your own mobile phone – looking at a string of sent and received messages can work especially well! You could look at:

- texts that are similar in purpose, such as informational texts
- how one person uses texts – their texting 'idiolect' (the speech habits of a particular person)
- length of texts and whether predictive texts are longer than non-predictive
- methods people use to be brief when texting
- spelling and the use of symbolism in texts.

Activity 3

In this activity you will look at spelling and symbolism in texts. Text messaging is often criticised for its poor spelling. Another way of looking at this is to say that texters know precisely what they are doing and are in fact being creative with language – in the way poets are.

1 Look again at the text messages on page 137. Can you find any patterns to the way texters spell? Think about the following when answering this question:
   - How many words are spelt correctly and how many are not?
   - How are symbols used by texters to create words?

Check your answer

Look at your answer to question 1.

- Did you comment on whether you thought words were spelt incorrectly on purpose?
- In doing so, did you think about the informal nature of text messaging and the need to type messages quickly?

Sounds and emotions in texting

We saw earlier that texting is a form of talk, so it needs to express sounds and emotions as well as actual words. This is all part of the multi-modal nature of text messaging.

Activity 4

Look at the four text messages below. What techniques do they use to suggest how words might be said and how the sender is feeling?

Text message
It woz AMAZING.

Text message
Erm I dunt know wot his problem is??? Do u?????

Text message
That's great!!!!
C u soon

Text message
Ha ha ha so funy its untrue

Texting controversy

Texting, and other forms of new communication, are often the subject of news stories. Many of these are negative, ranging from damage done to people's health and intelligence, to people being sacked or dumped by text. Sometimes there are good news stories involving multi-modal talk, such as miraculous surgery done by a complete novice under texted instructions from a surgeon.

Activity 5

1 Search the internet for news stories involving multi-modal talk and make a collection of headlines. Make a list of advantages and disadvantages of texting mentioned in these articles.

2 Now read the 'How predictive texting takes its toll on the brain' article on page 140 and answer the following questions.
  - a What statements are made about texting and its effects?
  - b What evidence is used?
  - c What people are named and quoted as further evidence?
  - d Does the article say anything positive about texting?
  - e What do you think about the claims the article makes?

  You could look at the sample answer on page 141 to see how one student approached this question.

Top tip

- As well as using your own data for an assignment it is also possible to look at articles such as that on page 140. If you do this, you would need to read the article closely, look carefully at its arguments and then put forward your own ideas.

Daily Mail

How predictive texting takes its toll on a child's brain

By Caroline Grant

Predictive text messaging changes the way childrens' brains work and makes them more likely to make mistakes generally, a study has found.

Scientists say the system, which involves pressing one key per letter before the phone works out what word the user wants to type, trains young people to be fast but inaccurate.

They claim this makes them prone to impulsive and thoughtless behaviour in everyday life. Modern mobile phones come with a built-in dictionary which enables them to predict what word a user wants from only a few key presses.

Each key represents three letters. It differs from an older system in which users had to hit keys several times per letter, for example pressing the 5 key three times for the letter L.

But it can lead to embarrassing miscommunications because some words use the same keys. For example, it is easy to end up asking a friend out for a quick riot (pint) or telling them about being stuck in a Steve (queue).

The study compared the mobile phone use of children aged between 11 and 14 with the results of IQ-style tests they took on computers. A quarter of the children made more than 15 calls a week and a quarter wrote more than 20 text messages a week.

Professor Michael Abramson, an epidemiologist who carried out the research, said: 'The children who used their phones a lot were faster on some of the tests but were less accurate. We suspect that using mobile phones a lot, particularly tools like predictive text, is behind this.

'Their brains are still developing so if there are effects then potentially they could impact down the line, especially given that the exposure is now almost universal. The use of mobile phones is changing the way children learn and pushing them to become more impulsive in the way they behave.' He added that the effects could have dangerous repercussions for a whole generation.

Experts concerned about the possible impact of mobile phone radiation on developing brains say that parents should be wary of allowing their children to use mobile phones too much.

But the researchers said the amount of radiation transmitted when texting is a mere 0.03 per cent of that transmitted during voice calls, suggesting radiation is not to blame for the brain effects.

Instead, Professor Abramson, from Monash University, Melbourne, believes functions such as predictive texting pose more of a risk for those whose brains are still developing.

'We don't think mobile phones are frying their brains,' he said. 'If you're used to operating in that environment and entering a couple of letters and getting the word you want, you expect everything to be like that.'

The study, which is published in the journal Bioelectromagnetics, will now be extended to look at the impact of mobile phone use on primary school children. Previous research has shown that predictive texting makes people sloppy when it comes to spelling, with many flummoxed by words such as questionnaire, accommodate and definitely.

But it is so popular that some of the mistakes that regularly crop up due to words sharing the same keys have been turned into a slang language by teenagers. They can be heard describing something as 'book' when they mean it is ' cool', for example. If a mobile phone predicts the wrong word, the user can scroll through a list of alternatives.

In 2007, a total of 57 billion text messages were sent in the UK, with 6 billion of these sent in December alone.

Check your answer

- Did you list the statements about the effects of texting?
- Did you quote the evidence used in the article?
- Did you find anything positive about texting in the article?
- Did you express what you thought about the article and explain your reasons?

Here is an extract from one student's answer to Activity 5 on page 139. Read the answers together with the comments.

Extract from an answer rated 'Very strong'

Extract from Student A

WHERE'S THE PROOF?
Caroline Grant's article seems to make vast assumptions based on very limited evidence. The research of one man, who conducted a vague experiment with IQ tests, is used to support some very strong claims about the effects of texting. For example the professor 'suspects' that texting is to blame for children making mistakes but he has no real proof. This is pure opinion rather than fact. The suggestion that you would ask someone out for a quick riot sounds made up, especially as 11–14 year olds are unlikely to be going for pints anyway!

Teacher comment

This is a very good start! Here the student assumes the examiner has read the original article, so gets on with writing in a critical way, showing lots of response to the original ideas, and a clear personal voice in the writing.

When criticising articles like this, to write a good response, you need to think carefully about the evidence that is put before you, and criticise it if it seems flimsy.

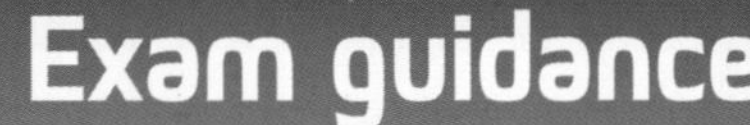

Exam guidance

Revision

Many students say that you can't revise for English because you don't know what the passages are that you are going to be answering on. How wrong can they be?

You need to go into the exam room with a clear sense of what you are going to have to do.

For the **Reading** section of the exam:

Make sure that you go over what features to write about if you are asked about:

- language
- presentational devices
- structure
- purpose
- audience.

Pick up a book, magazine or newspaper and practise looking for:

- the effects of language choices
- how the piece is structured
- how it is arranged on the page
- the effects of pictures
- the effects of colour
- the effects of other presentational devices.

Practise looking for:

- the main points in an argument
- different points the writer is making
- what facts there are and how the writer uses them
- what opinions there are and how the writer uses them
- any other ways that the writer supports the points being made.

For the **Writing** section of the exam:

Keep saying to yourself over and over again:

- plan
- write
- check.

Make sure that you do all three in the exam room.

Go over common mistakes that you make:

- in spelling
- in grammar
- in punctuation
- in sentence structure.

When you get into the exam room:

- don't be in too much of a hurry
- read the question several times
- underline the key words of the task
- do exactly what you are asked to do
- spend your time wisely and stick to your time allocations.

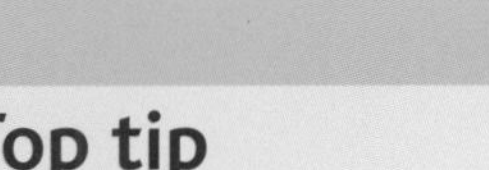

Top tip

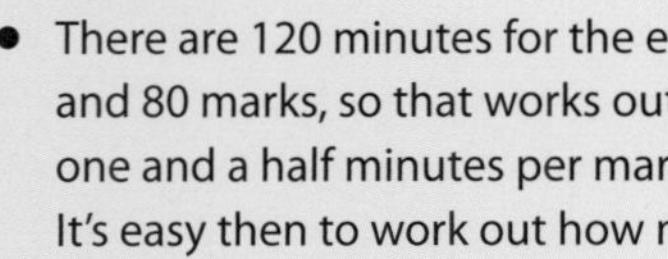

- There are 120 minutes for the exam and 80 marks, so that works out at one and a half minutes per mark. It's easy then to work out how many minutes you should spend on each question. For example:
  4 marks = 6 minutes
  6 marks = 9 minutes
  8 marks = 12 minutes
  16 marks = 24 minutes
  24 marks = 36 minutes.

  If you do this, then you will give yourself the best chance.

Do well!

Sample Higher tier exam paper

English/English Language

(Specification A)
HIGHER

Unit 1 Understanding and producing non-fiction texts

Time allowed
- 2 hours

Answer **all** questions

Section A: Reading

Answer **all** questions

You are advised to spend about one hour on this section.

Read Item 1, *Bring back the beaver – he will save money and clean our rivers*, and answer the question below.

1 What, according to the article, are the advantages and disadvantages of beavers? (*8 marks*)

Now read Item 2, *Seasonal stray-dog crisis*, and answer the question below.

2 How do the picture, the headline and other presentational devices contribute to the effectiveness of this text? (*8 marks*)

Now read Item 3, an extract from a prose work by the poet Gillian Clarke, and answer the question below.

3 How does Gillian Clarke reveal her attitudes and feelings in this passage? (*8 marks*)

Now look at **all three** items.

4 Look at Item 3 and **either** of the other items.

Compare the ways language is used for effect in the two texts. (*16 marks*)

Section B: Writing

Answer **both** questions in this section.

You are advised to spend about one hour on this section.

5 You have been asked to contribute to a collection of pieces of writing where the writers choose a moment from their past which was really important to them.

Write about such a moment and explain its importance to you. (*16 marks*)

6 Your local newspaper has been running a campaign recently about your local council wasting public money on causes that some people think are trivial.

Choose a cause which you care about and write an article justifying spending public money on it. (*24 marks*)

Item 1

THE TIMES

Bring back the beaver – he will save money and clean our rivers

Valerie Elliott Countryside Editor

The return of beavers to England after being hunted to near-extinction in the country 400 years ago could help hard-pressed households by bringing down water bills.

According to an independent scientific study, beavers are natural engineers and help to clean rivers and prevent flooding. Their presence would save spending on expensive treatment works and other flood defences as well as the benefit of lower charges, researchers say.

The study for Natural England, the Government's wildlife advisers, and the People's Trust for Endangered Species, raises the prospect of an eventual return of this shy, nocturnal creature to almost any English river, even the western reaches of the Thames in London.

Resistance comes from landowners and farmers concerned about damage to trees and culverts, the spread of disease, a rise in sightseers traipsing over private land and hefty costs for fencing.

Online

Read our dedicated environment blog

timesonline.co.uk/greencentral

Beavers: 'No threat to human health'.

But despite the opposition, South West Water is keen to use beavers to help to purify drinking water. Researchers point to their role in creating upstream ponds that capture sediment and other organic matter. Other benefits are identified in terms of biodiversity, with cleaner waters providing improved conditions for fish spawning.

John Gurnell, a wildlife biologist at Queen Mary, University of London, who led the research, described beavers as 'ecosystem engineers'. He said: 'The potential for them to give benefits to the country at large is quite enormous.' Water quality, the effects of flooding and river levels during drought would all be helped, with the added hope of lower bills, he added.

He wanted the study to demolish the myth about beavers. 'Most negative effects are probably more minor than major,' he said. He denied that beavers were a threat to human health.

'We don't recommend hugging beavers even though they are mild-mannered, gentle and docile, but they have teeth,' he said.

Even though beavers largely died out in England in the 16th century, a few natives survived until the 1900s and about 40 are in captivity at five locations. They live in the wild in most of Europe, however, and in Vienna they live on river banks near the city.

The most likely scenario for a comeback in England is to introduce three of four families – about twenty beavers – on a single site. Costs could top £1 million. Best-suited areas for a colony are along river banks in the Weald of Kent, the New Forest, Bodmin Moor, the Peak District and Forest of Bowland.

• Freedom may be short-lived for a beaver that escaped from a farm in Devon in October and set up home on the banks of the River Tamar. Derek Gow, a conservationist, says he plans to lure the beaver into a trap with scent from an imported female and return him to his enclosure.

Item 2

The Dogs Trust has offered advice to pet owners: feed dry food instead of tinned, insure your pet – and avoid costly accessories such as sparkly collars.

Seasonal stray-dog crisis comes early as families abandon pets to save cash

Fiona Hamilton
London Correspondent

Luxuries were the first things to go: foreign holidays, expensive Christmas presents, office parties. Now Rufus, Spot and Max, along with many of their furry brethren, are the latest victims of the financial crisis.

Dog charities have reported an unprecedented number of stray animals after the credit crunch, with families forsaking their pets to save money.

Battersea Dogs & Cats Home announced yesterday that it had almost reached capacity – for the first time – because of the high number of strays and lost animals being brought in. The Dogs Trust, the country's largest dog welfare charity, told *The Times* that it was experiencing a similar trend.

Animal charities are used to coping with spikes in demand after Christmas, when new pets turn from a novelty into an unwanted gift, but the deluge this year has come a month early.

The Battersea home, in southwest London, has taken in 6,430 stray dogs this year, compared with 5,335 by the same time in 2007. Strays account for more than 80 per cent of its dogs.

The charity attributed the high number of strays to the credit crunch, as well as the impact of new legislation that has led to fewer owners being reunited with their lost dogs.

Jan Barlow, chief executive of the home, said it appeared that many owners whose animals had strayed were not actively looking for them, because of financial pressures.

She added: '[The increase] could be because people can't afford to keep their dogs any more, so are dumping them on the streets.

'For those who cannot look after their dog or cat because they cannot afford to keep them, we urge them to contact Battersea, or their local rescue centre, rather than dumping them or allowing them to stray.'

People are also more reluctant to take on the cost of adopting a pet, with the Dogs Trust experiencing greater difficulties than usual in rehoming strays. At the charity's centre in West London, it is taking as long as six months to rehome dogs, whereas under usual circumstances they would be found homes within three months.

The trust offered advice to dog owners wishing to cut costs, suggesting that they feed their pets dry food instead of tinned, and buy dog food in bulk rather than as part of the weekly shop. It also suggests taking out pet insurance so that vet bills are not overwhelming, and avoiding over-the-top pet accessories such as sparkly collars.

Ms Barlow expressed concern that, after the implementation of legislation in April, many owners did not know where to find their lost dogs.

Under the Clean Neighbourhoods and Environment Act, stray dogs were made the responsibility of local authorities, whereas previously they were taken to the police.

Ms Barlow said: 'If you've lost your dog, you could be reunited with it in time for Christmas by contacting your local authority.'

Hounded by costs

- £13,000 – the average cost of keeping a dog over its lifetime; 24 per cent higher than in 2000
- The annual cost of between £710 and £810 includes:
- £150 on dog food
- £100 on grooming
- £120 on insurance
- £30 for deworming
- £20 for defleaing
- £140 for two weeks at a kennel
- The one-off cost of neutering is between £150 and £250

Source: Intune pet insurance provider

Item 3

I try to ignore Christmas. It all starts too soon. I hate the bling, the cheap glitter, the unremitting materialism, the waste, the flashing lights, the destruction of rural darkness by the spreading disease of giant illuminated nodding Santas and snowmen and, God help us, flashing inflatable cribs. I want an airgun for Christmas so that I can shoot Santa Claus and watch him deflate with a hiss. Lights fidget on houses all the way from Ceredigion to Cardiff, eating the ozone layer and melting the Greenland glaciers. Where is the romance of the one lit tree in the window we used to count on winter walks with the kids? Bah! Humbug!

I have a theme for the Cardiff poem, but they won't like it. The winter solstice. The darkest night. The year's midnight. We brazen out the narrowing days with light. Out there in the temperate city an ice rink glitters on a civic lawn as if we dreamed Victorian glitter when lakes were dancing floors, the rivers froze for goose fairs and all was marble winter. For now, the city puts on party clothes. We say, dress every tree with electricity. Switch on the lights. Let streets and houses glow. When the party's over, and we step into the night and feel the Ice Queen's wand of cold, an imagined hush of snow will touch the heart, and we'll know that for the pleasures of here and now we are borrowing bling from the glacier, slipping Greenland's shoulder from its wrap of snow.

Oh, ice-makers, who can make a frozen floor
in the maritime air of our mild city,
bring your alchemy to the melting permafrost.

Chain the glacier. Put the wilderness under locks.
Rebuild the gates of ice. Hold back the melt-water
for footfall of polar bear and Arctic fox.[1]

Fast forward again to the now of a cold, dry December. Frost glitters on the sandstone terrace, and on the hedge banks frost stays white all day. The slate table is laid with glitter. I put a red enamel plate of crumbs on its cloth-of-silver for the robins, who do not like the bird feeder. The birds are getting through all the seed, nuts, crumbs, bacon fat, cheese rind I can give them – sacks of it. There are treecreepers in the plum trees, a greater spotted woodpecker on the nut holder. The white-collared female blackbird sees off two male competitors for food – or is she displaying her spirit and resourcefulness, ready for spring mating?

We walk hard-frozen ground to check and count the sheep. One year, before Christmas we lost a yearling ram. Accurately counting sheep can be difficult. The little ram may have got under a gate. By the time we found him he had been alone for weeks. He was thin and weak, found wandering at the far end of the wood where no sheep ought to have been. We brought him home, fed him, gave him shelter for a few days, and he improved. We kept him in the field closest to the house, and watched him grazing there, thinking he'd make it. But sheep are strange animals. They don't thrive on their own. They are flock creatures and seem to lose the will to live when away from their kind. One day we could not see him grazing in the field. He had found a corner to die in. The wool torn from his fleece by the crows lay scattered on the grass for months. It was later taken by nesting birds. Nothing goes to waste in nature. That winter our Christmas cards used his story, and a photograph of our midsummer hayfield. The poem expected him to live. The words celebrate his response to us, the slow improvement in his strength, and the good sight of him pulling clean hay from the manger. By Christmas he had changed his mind and lost heart, and one night he lay down in the field to die. Such failures always hurt. As children we learn the pain of the loss of animals: guinea pigs, hamsters, birds saved from the jaws of a cat. But it still hurts.

[1] 'Solstice' (unpublished).